THE MAN WHO "FRAMED" THE BEATLES

THE MAN WHO "FRAMED" THE BEATLES

A Biography of
RICHARD LESTER

BY ANDREW YULE

Introduction by Paul McCartney

DONALD I. FINE, INC.
New York

Library of Congress Catalogue Card Number: 93-072582

ISBN: 1-55611-390-0

Manufactured in the United States of America

10   9   8   7   6   5   4   3   2   1

Designed by Irving Perkins Associates

for
RICHARD LESTER
who not only "framed" the Beatles, "but won the war" with John Lennon, "rode" with the Musketeers, took a chance on the "Phantom" and "flew" with Superman.

ACKNOWLEDGMENTS

My thanks to interviewees James Garrett, Gerry Humphreys, Robert Littman, Paul McCartney, Rick Nicita, Nicolas Roeg, Judy Scott-Fox, John Victor Smith, Pierre Spengler, Rita Tushingham, David Watkin, Charles Wood—and Richard and Deirdre Lester.

Thanks also to Russell Galen of Scovil, Chichak, Galen; Cecilia Shields and Rajashekar Reddy.

Special thanks to Walter Shenson for his kind permission to include the Beatles pictures from *A Hard Day's Night* and *Help!*

CONTENTS

Introduction by
PAUL McCARTNEY

Not a lot of people know this, but about a year before *A Hard Day's Night* came along, Brian Epstein told us we'd been offered a film called *The Yellow Teddy Bears*. We were anxious to do a movie, but there was one major snag—the director insisted on writing all the songs himself. So that was out. And eager as we were, there was no question of doing a cheapo rip-off like the typical pop musicals of the time (although we'd been to every one of them, since they provided our only chances to see black legends like Clyde McPhatter, Little Richard and Chuck Berry in action). We were determined to hold out for something better for ourselves and our fans.

We liked producer Walter Shenson, although we did take the mickey out of him from time to time (producers, we reckoned, were fair game). When he came up with the idea of Dick Lester to direct what became *A Hard Day's Night*, we were excited, for as far as we were concerned anyone connected with *The Goon Show* and *The Running, Jumping and Standing Still Film* had to be the goods. We hit it off right away. He was urbane and witty and had a nice personality and sense of humor. He was also a bit of a clever git who played a mean jazz piano (even if he did play "My Funny Valentine" in C). When Alun Owen entered the equation as a writer, we felt we were home and dry.

xi

" Paul, what you've got to realize is that acting isn't easy . . ."
(COURTESY OF RICHARD LESTER)

"Directing is, though."

We were still nervous initially when filming began, although Dick put us at ease fairly quickly. My solo scene was an encounter with a girl in eighteenth-century costume, filmed in a dance studio above a pub in Shepherd's Bush. I had hoped that my great acting moment would be preserved for all time, but alas, it was not to be. It ended up on the cutting-room floor after Dick expressed the feeling that it held up the pace of the finished movie. Just as well, really, because I think the scene was a bit suspect, a little po-faced, with the camera swirling round and round. I'm sure Dick was right to ditch it—but I still point out that pub to my kids every time we go through Shepherd's Bush.*

The reception that greeted the movie was gratifying, although the comparisons many critics made with the Marx Brothers set us thinking. Who was who? Well, we decided that Ringo was a natural for Harpo, John simply had to be Groucho, George was the definitive Chico—which left me, I suppose, as Zeppo. Oh, well.

Filming *Help!* was another terrific experience and stretched us a bit, giving us more than one line at a time to say. As the years rolled by, however, I kept waiting for Dick to make up for that lost scene in *A Hard Day's Night* and transform me into a big-screen megastar. I thought I was in with a shout for D'Artagnan in *The Three Musketeers*, but no luck. Robin in *Robin and Marian*? For some inexplicable reason, he chose Sean Connery instead. Finally, when I heard he was involved in the *Superman* series, I awaited his call with confidence. The Man of Steel? Just up my street! Oddly enough, the call never came. Some mate!

Finally, at my behest, we got together again—twenty-five years after *A Hard Day's Night*—for the documentary of my

---

*Editor's note: For the original script of this scene, see pages 367–374

world tour in 1990 that ended up as "Paul McCartney's *Get Back*, Un Film de Richard Lester." Top billing at last! During the shooting of this, I discovered that nothing much else had changed—Richard was still playing "My Funny Valentine" in C.

Apart from our own undoubted natural genius (!) we were lucky as a group to have had Brian, George Martin and Dick back then to manage, record and put us through our paces. Dick Lester isn't just one of the most skillful and versatile directors in the world, he's also someone I regard as a great guy and a good mate.

THE MAN WHO "FRAMED" THE BEATLES

CHAPTER ONE

"We knew it was better than other rock movies."

—JOHN LENNON ON
A Hard Day's Night

When "Love Me Do," the Beatles' first single, languished in the lower reaches of the British charts late in 1962, it was merely the lull before the storm. A few months later, in February 1963, they enjoyed their first number-one single, "Please, Please Me," while supporting a chart phenomenon of yesteryear, Helen Shapiro, on a nationwide UK tour. Their debut album remained in the charts for six months and yielded a second number one, "She Loves You." Beatlemania had well and truly arrived.

Although the genesis of the group's first movie, *A Hard Day's Night*, had begun in the London music department of United Artists, it clicked into gear when film producer Walter Shenson, with *The Mouse That Roared* and *Mouse on the Moon* already to his credit, was approached by George H. "Bud" Ornstein, European head of production for UA: "Would you produce a film that United Artists wants done? It's a pop musical, real low-budget, and you do these things so well . . ."

"What's the subject?"

"The Beatles."

"The Beatles? Who are they?"

"Four boys with a guitar."

"Oh, *those* Beatles, their records are driving my children crazy. I don't think I'm interested."

"Look, will you do this as a favor to me? Our record division wants to get the soundtrack album to distribute in the States and what we lose on the film we'll get back on the disc. Just say yes so I can get to New York and tell them we're proceeding."

There were a couple of stipulations, apart from the soundtrack going to UA (EMI and Capitol, the Beatles' labels in Britain and the U.S., had little say, since the standard contract they had with the group neglected to cover film soundtracks. When, after all, had this clause ever been necessary before?): first, the movie must cost no more than £150,000; second, it had to be in cinemas by July 1964, before the group ran out of steam and the screaming stopped as everyone was certain it would.

After opening negotiations with Beatles manager Brian Epstein back in London, Shenson took a call from his *Mouse on the Moon* director, Richard Lester, inviting him to lunch. A thirty-one-year-old native of Philadelphia—never better described than by George Melly as "an amiable space creature, very thin, with a great domed bald head, tiny childlike features and large kind eyes"—Lester had been resident in the UK since the mid-fifties and was gradually making his mark in movies after early television and commercial experience. As soon as Shenson mentioned the Beatles movie in the Hilton's coffee shop, he jumped excitedly to his feet: "Can I direct it?"

"I'd love you to direct it, Dick," Shenson replied. "I think you'd be perfect for it. Leave it up to me. Let me see what I can do. Let's get them signed—let's get this thing going."

Modern jazz, rather than pop music, was Lester's consuming musical interest. His fortuitous awareness of the Beatles was thanks to a group who had appeared in his first full-length movie, *It's Trad, Dad*, starring none other than Helen Shapiro. One of the Temperance Seven was an art director working at ABC-TV in Manchester who often visited the Cavern Club in nearby Liverpool and had brought their early records down to London. The Beatles were also familiar with Lester's work, and their interest quickened at the mere mention of *The Running, Jumping and Standing Still Film*, as well as his earlier *Goon Show* associations. Among the tentative titles chosen for the project were *Beatles No. 1* and *Beatlemania*.

Desperate to secure the group, and prepared to concede 25 percent of net revenues, Shenson's negotiations with Epstein produced an unexpected windfall. "I should warn you now. I'm not prepared to settle for less than 7½ percent," was Epstein's opening gambit. With this agreed at the speed of light, plus a flat £20,000 and an option for three more movies with escalating scales of pay and percentages, Shenson left the meeting walking on air. Ignoring the "Quick, before it melts" aspect of the Beatles' popularity, he had also stipulated that all rights to the films would revert to him after fifteen years. The same clause was easily agreed with UA, who, like everyone else—except the canny Shenson—were certain that the group's popularity would never endure. The producer's introduction to the Beatles themselves took place during a frantic taxi ride across London that helped to set the tone of the movie they were about to make.

As the months passed and the group rapidly moved from

3

being a British phenomenon to achieving international status, Ornstein voluntarily increased Epstein's share from 7½ percent to 20 percent and their flat fee to £25,000. This magnanimous gesture reflected not only the burgeoning popularity of the Beatles, which reinforced what a tremendous bargain Shenson had struck in the first place, but sensibly pre-empted any accusation of shortchanging. Ornstein also reduced options on further movies to only two more.

On the afternoon of Wednesday, October 15, 1963, Lester, accompanied by Shenson, went to his first meeting with the Fab Four at the BBC Playhouse on London's Northumberland Avenue, where they were rehearsing a radio broadcast. His interview, if such it was, was short, amiable, inconsequential and larky. What you saw, he reflected, was very much what you got. While the Beatles were already teasing the tall, jovial Shenson—what they considered his ducklike walk particularly cracked them up—he, being an affable fellow, simply laughed along with them. "I think I can do something with these four boys I've just met," Lester enthused to his wife Deirdre when he arrived home that evening.

He had one particular domestic matter very much on his mind that acted as a counterbalance to his concern with the Beatles and their movie. Together with a neighboring couple, he and Deirdre had pooled resources to buy a manor house at Petersham, on the river at Richmond, planning to sell off the house itself and build themselves a home each in the orchard behind.

Lester drew up his plans exactly as he had always envisaged an ideal English house—an atrium open to the sky in the center, its two-story steel-and-glass construction requiring no supporting walls. The edifice was loosely based on

Philip Johnson's model in New Canaan, Connecticut, re-garded as being at the cutting edge of late fifties' building design. It could also be traced back to a working encounter Lester had had with Frank Lloyd Wright a decade earlier that had sparked a fascination with modern architecture.

He decided to ignore rumors that although these homes looked terrific when photographed, they could be hell to live in, and set about interviewing a series of architects. "Very interesting indeed," one of them declared after perusing Lester's carefully detailed plans, "but you've forgotten one fairly important item. There's no staircase connecting the floors." In the instant sulk that followed, Lester decided that an individual with that kind of nit-picking attitude was not for him.

The man eventually appointed was Leonard Manasseh, head of the Architects' Association, who suitably impressed the Lesters when he appeared in an artist's smock and beard in front of a peat fire (in Hampstead!). This was more like it, they felt. With the staircase duly added, there was an unex-pected four-year wait before the couple were to move into their dream house. By that time their five-year-old son, Dominic, had acquired a sister in Claudia, born in October 1966.

■

Lester's first thoughts on a writer for the Beatles' movie settled on Johnny Speight. When this failed to work out, he remembered his days of working with Alun Owen in the mid-fifties on a misbegotten early television special, *The Dick Lester Show*. Brian Epstein and Paul McCartney were also keen on Owen, by now best known for scripting a gritty television play they had liked, *No Trams to Lime Street*, as well as co-writing *The Criminal*, a movie directed by a friend of

Lester's, Joseph Losey. And Owen was a free-range Celt and a Liverpudlian to boot—who better to capture the wayward sensibilities of the group?

When Owen asked Shenson what he had in mind, the producer, remembering his hectic taxi ride, answered, "An exaggerated day in the life of the Beatles." Packed off to Dublin for the weekend to see the group and judge what this might be like, Owen returned with his answer: "I've got it—they're prisoners of their success. They go from the airport to the hotel to the theater or stadium or concert hall, back to the hotel, back to the airport. In any city it's always the same. They travel in a cocoon of Liverpool. There's the manager, the road manager, a publicity man, the car driver, the guy who carries the equipment. That's all they see, because they'd be mobbed if they got out of the car or the hotel room or away from the concert hall." Shenson felt satisfied that the script was in safe hands. (The way John Lennon later told it, there never was much of a romance with Owen: "They came up with this guy and we knew his work and we said all right, but then he had to come round with us to see what we were like. But he was a bit phony. He was like a professional Liverpool man. He stayed with us two days and wrote the whole thing based on our characters as we were then . . . We were a bit infuriated by the glibness of it and the shittyness of the dialogue.")

With the movie set for filming in March 1964, the Beatles' success continued unabated, with "I Want to Hold Your Hand" delivering a third number-one single. On January 25, Lester, Shenson and Owen flew to Paris, where the group was appearing at the Olympia on a bill with Trini ("If I Had a Hammer") Lopez and local chanteuse Sylvie Vartan. By the end of the weekend spent with them at the Georges Cinq Hotel, they had seen the four in a variety of situations—in cars, on telephones, with waiters in their rooms, giving their minders the runaround. Backstage they watched them neatly shift whiskey and Coke (whiskey was deemed chic; Coke was to disguise their drinking from the press) and chain-smoke cigarettes.

Just watching them in action brought home to Lester how exciting the project might be and how far removed from a run-of-the-mill pop musical; since the last thing he wanted was a retrograde Cliff Richard *Summer Holiday* "Let's have fun on a bus," approach, he was happier with the idea of a fictionalized documentary, a style he would later refer to as "film journalism." Owen's notions were reinforced for Lester by the reply John gave to a reporter who asked, "Did you like Stockholm?"—"It was a plane and a room and a car and a cheese sandwich."

Far from being kids with stars in their eyes, the Beatles had a combination of maturity and healthy cynicism that was both disarming and refreshing. None of them displayed any great sign of nerves before he went on stage, with Paul in particular happily chatting to guests until the last possible moment. As for the sound that greeted their entrance and was kept up throughout their entire performance, Lester had heard nothing like it since the early Sinatra broadcasts before the war—and that had at least settled down during the actual singing. In the background, looking on just like a fan, there was always the discreet, gentlemanly but slightly melancholy figure of Brian Epstein.

"There's one thing I'm putting into this script if I die for it," Owen declared. "Ever noticed how much celebrities are pushed around in public? *Really* pushed around? Managers guiding them, fans pulling at them, compères patting them. You get to feel like so much movable property. What it *feels* like to be a Beatle: that's the first priority." To establish an

7

element of conflict within the group's claustrophobic isolation, Owen dreamt up an extra character who would act as a catalyst, Paul's meddlesome, grumpy grandfather. For this role Lester first considered Irish actor Dermot Kelly, who had enjoyed considerable success as Arthur Haynes's stooge. In the end it went to Wilfrid Brambell, who had shot to fame in Galton and Simpson's *Steptoe and Son*.

■

Any doubts that Beatlemania was here to stay were squashed during the group's U.S. tour in February, the hysteria that followed them everywhere unknown since Elvis Presley's heyday. They appeared twice on *The Ed Sullivan Show* and enjoyed a brief holiday in Miami before their return to England and what became *A Hard Day's Night*.

The group recorded the songs for the movie between February 25 and 27 at EMI's Abbey Road studios, laying down nine tunes from which the final numbers would be chosen. The first day's shooting, on March 2, was on a train hired for six days that would shuttle between Paddington and the west country. "The plan was to shoot it for real, which was crazy, but we wanted it to look like a real train," Lester recalls. "I decided to do the whole thing hand-held, mainly because there wasn't much else to look at, and it needed a documentary flexibility. Unfortunately, in those days you didn't work with a little hidden lapel microphone, you had a boom man using the same instrument originally invented in the nineteen-twenties and christened on *The Jazz Singer*. In that sense not much had changed between the era of Al Jolson and the Beatles, so three cars down there was half a wagon full of Westrex recording equipment, massive stuff. Clumsy and awful though it was, everyone watching the movie would know it was a real train."

With a crowd of onlookers screaming and fighting their way forward at Paddington, even filming the Beatles boarding the train posed problems. Lester grabbed a camera, focused and shot the group attempting to break through the melée. They did not fully appreciate the immediacy he wanted to capture, and furiously regarded the whole event as a security cock-up, a shaken George even waving his fist at Lester on camera. The shot was captured so quickly that several of the crew blinked and missed it. The continuity girl wrote in her notes that morning: "First shot, Beatles wearing their own clothes. I was in the toilet. Director was the operator. If this is the way the film is to go on, I'm resigning now."

At the end of the day's work, the Beatles were dropped off at a prearranged spot out of town, decanted into their own transport and driven off. When the train returned to Paddington the last person to leave was clapper loader Peter Ewens, a small, dark-haired individual sporting a Beatle-style haircut. Carrying the cans of the first day's rushes to get them to the laboratory for night processing, Ewens ran into lingering fans as he stepped off the train. His haircut proved his undoing—the crowd thought he was a Beatle. Since he was loaded down with cans of film, running was out of the question. There was only one thing for it. Throwing the precious reels up in the air, he bolted for his life. Unfortunately, light penetrated the cans, wasting the entire first day's shooting.

There was a general feeling of tension on the set whenever scenes involving the group in dialogue were imminent. When they could simply run, jump, fall and let loose, on the other hand, that was something they really looked forward to, and did with great abandon and relish, as in the "Can't Buy Me Love" sequence in a field.

9

From the beginning, by avoiding the casting of anyone too high-powered against them, Lester had tried to create an area of comfort for the group, to diminish any sense that they would end up either intimidated or objects of ridicule. As it worked out, the biggest of the names besides Brambell appeared for only a day or so and left when their scenes had been completed. If there remained any sense of ribbing from the technicians—not a completely unheard-of eventuality— the fact that there were four of them in the same boat left them feeling fairly well protected.

Lester had plenty of time to observe the differences among the group: "Historically, if you had to say who had the most impact at the beginning for me, it would be John. Paul had the fans because he was the cute one and the most profes- sional, handling the press best, most interested in film and theater. He went out with an actress, he understood the public relations of the job from the beginning. John could be very caustic, very brittle, very wounding. You'd approach Paul if the group was required to hand over the likes of Variety Club awards, whereas John's reaction would be, 'Why don't you line up the cripples here?' George very much kept his head down and could be just as cutting as John in his own way. Ringo was cozy and lost at the back."

Part of John's "sarky bastard" image emerged purely be- cause of his nearsightedness; he was captured on film laugh- ing three times after running in the wrong direction, with Lester deciding to leave the scenes in the finished movie. When the group performed their songs to playback, Lester found they were able to synchronize the lip movements to the prerecorded sound with amazing accuracy, with Paul in particular emerging as a master mime. (In the mid-eighties MTV presented Lester with a scroll acknowledging him as the founding father of the modern music video, singling out the scene in the baggage car and the transition from the Beatles playing cards to performing "I Should Have Known Better.")

Notwithstanding the primitive filming techniques of the time, Lester, in a bout of youthful enthusiasm, rashly attempted to create a sequence involving stop-frame animation. The aim was to team each of the Beatles with a chorus girl, moving their bodies but not their feet in Busby Berkeley patterns, with the film frames being hand-cranked two at a time. In the end he was forced to throw in the towel, a full half-day of his precious schedule blown and nothing to show for it.

Following a decision to give each of them a scene of their own, John's encounter with Anna Quayle was organized, as was George's with Kenneth Haigh and Ringo's with the kid on the towpath. A scene with Paul chatting to a girl in eighteenth-century costume was subsequently cut; it was the longest sequence and Lester decided that it slowed down the pace of the movie. Once this was explained to Paul he offered no objection.*

Lester concedes that the choreographed look of the crowd scenes was largely a matter of luck, as well as judicious editing:

> Their fans tracked them all over the place. Every time we got to a new location there would be these mobs of girls trying to get their hands on them. One day, after we finished shooting, the boys headed for their car to be chauffeured home. I told the cameraman to keep turning, record whatever happened. Just then a drove of screaming fans cut loose and began converging on the car. When I saw the rushes I took one look at the expression on the boys' faces and decided to put the

---

*For the script of this scene, see pages 367–374.

scene in the picture. The rest was pacing and rhythm worked out in the editing. If you look closely at the scene with the Beatles in the train station, you will see that they are wearing one set of clothes on the train and an entirely different set in the car. As far as I know, nobody spotted the discrepancy.

Lester knew that he was freezing in time the catalytic nature of the Beatles' contribution, for better or worse, to the contemporary social revolution in sixties' Britain:

> I think they were the first to give a confidence to the youth of the country, which led to the disappearance of the Angry Young Man with a defensive mien. The Beatles sent the class thing sky-high; they laughed it out of existence and, I think, introduced a tone of equality more successfully than any other single factor that I know. Eventually it became taken for granted that they were singlehandedly breaking Britain's class system without the benefit of an education or family background. They were, of course, much more middle class than most people admitted.

Although Lester saw few signs of it—his hands were never less than full—the Beatles, used to hyperkinetic activity, soon became bored with the endless hours they were obliged to sit around waiting in their trailers while scenes were set up. To help keep them quiet, an 8 mm projector was obtained, together with a selection of porno films. Soon afterwards, the young girls acting as extras on the set found themselves being quietly propositioned and steered towards the trailer for a series of "quickies." If *A Hard Day's Night* had true-to-life pretensions, John later admitted, it should have closely resembled Fellini's *Satyricon*. One extra who resisted the lure of the trailer was young Patti Boyd, whom Lester had previously employed in a Smith's Crisps commercial and whom George spotted on the first day of filming.

12

Eventually, he succeeded in asking her out—and, later, marrying her.

When John, reportedly hung over, failed to turn up at the appointed hour one day during the fifth week of shooting, Lester began his camera shots focusing on four pairs of feet, one of which was his own. He then carefully panned up to the other Beatles, creating the illusion that there were four of them, all present and accounted for.

One scene had to be canceled following police protests that a disturbance was being caused. Lester hastily improvised the press conference episode, calling up several actors who lived close by to act as reporters—it was either that or he would have had nothing to shoot that day. Many of the funniest ad libs, which most people swore were typically John, were in fact contributed by George ("What do you call your haircut?"—"Arthur"; "How do you find America?"—"Turn left at Greenland"). It was similar, Lester reflected, to the common yet fallacious notion at the time that Paul always wrote the music and John always wrote the words.

The movie gained its final title during a lunch break at Twickenham Studios, with Paul reminiscing to Bud Ornstein and Shenson on Ringo's distinctive phraseology. After one late gig Ringo had remarked, "That was a hard day's night." "We just got our title," Ornstein declared, while Shenson nodded approvingly. Surprisingly, UA received the title with bland politeness, not to say downright indifference. "Look, we're never going to improve on it," Shenson told them. "It's very provocative. It means nothing, has nothing to do with the film. But it *sounds* like a Beatles title." Convinced that he was on a winner all the way, Ornstein even authorized a modest budget increase; eventually the film came in at £175,000.

Towards the end of filming it dawned on Shenson that

they needed a song to go with their new title. John's reply was, "We've already recorded all the music. And where would you fit it in?" "Over the title, obviously," said Shenson. When John asked if the song's lyrics should reflect the movie's "story," Shenson said no, since none of the others did. The one thing he did specify was that it should be up-tempo, in the "Twist and Shout" mold.

Around 8:30 next morning, Shenson took a call on the set saying that John wanted to see him in his dressing room. When he got there he found John and Paul holding their guitars. John proceeded to take out a matchbook cover, which he opened and propped up on the dressing room table. The duo then treated Shenson to his first hearing of "A Hard Day's Night," reading off the lyrics John had scribbled down the night before.

All of the Beatles' final show in the movie was filmed at the old red plush and gilt 1,200–seat La Scala Theater in Soho, converted to a television rehearsal studio for the occasion. Seventeen minutes of footage were captured in one single day, using six cameras. Since up until then Lester had shot with two or three cameras, this involved bringing in several additional crews, with three cameras on stage and three in the audience under cinematographer Gilbert Taylor. One out of the six ended up contributing not a single usable frame of film. Although some operators had a flair for holding a shot until a certain moment was captured, this individual had the uncanny knack of panning away just as something interesting was about to happen. With each of the cameras unspooling around five thousand feet of film, one unusable batch represented a lot of wasted stock.

The final scene of *A Hard Day's Night* was shot at Ealing Studios on April 24, with Ringo gallantly laying down his coat for the lady to walk over. The end-of-picture party was held in the Turk's Head pub near Twickenham Studios, Lester's home base, where he ceremonially had red wine poured over him by the group after being presented with a greeting card inscribed, "To Walt Disney: Thanks for directing us, sir, from your favorite actors—John, Paul, Ringo—and Garry!" Ringo, the only one of the group at a loose end, came around for dinner that night with the Lesters.

In post-production Lester deliberately slowed the pace down in terms of cutting and editing the Beatles' musical contributions: "I wanted their music to speak for itself. The Beatles were musicians first, actors second. Musically they were fantastic perfectionists. I'd seen them record a passage twenty, thirty times and still not be satisfied. They felt they had a obligation to their public. Fans like to think the sounds come from God, not from hard work, and the Beatles were very conscious that being free and easy was part of their image. What fan wants to be told that her idols *work* ten hours a day?"

Having rushed the movie through post-production—Lester produced a fine cut in just two and a half weeks—Shenson and his director arranged a preview on May 7 in a preview cinema in Aubrey Street, inviting David Picker of UA, together with his uncle and boss Arnold Picker and his wife, and Bud Ornstein. All seemed to go well until two-thirds of the way through the train sequence in the first reel, when Lester heard Mrs. Picker mutter, "Tch, tch." "Oh, God, she's bored stiff," flashed through his mind. Every five or six minutes thereafter another rendition of "Tch, tch" was unfailingly delivered, reducing Lester by the end credits to a nervous wreck. As soon as the lights went up the lady turned to him, beaming, and said, "Oh, Mr. Lester, the *film* . . . *tch, tch!*" She had, it seemed, loved it, and this was her way of expressing her enjoyment.

As the party shuffled out, another UA executive asked if there was still time to revoice the movie for America, since they would never understand "those Liverpool accents." "Forget it!" Shenson and Lester chorused. For once the moguls were wise enough to listen.

There was still work to be done, and it had to be carried out at lightning speed. Following post-synching on May 13 and 14, Beatles A&R man George Martin began to dream up forty-seven seconds of original linking music, together with an orchestral pastiche of old Beatles numbers. After grading runs the movie was shown to Paul and Ringo on May 28; a new number was recorded on June 1; Martin's contribution was recorded on June 8; an end-of-crew party was held on June 26; the movie opened on Monday, July 6.

UA's juggernaut, already rolling with Tony Richardson's *Tom Jones*, as well as the James Bond series, continued on its apparently unstoppable path as *A Hard Day's Night* followed *Tom Jones* into the London Pavilion, the company's West End showcase, after a run of over a year. At the royal premiere, attended by Princess Margaret and the Earl of Snowdon, thousands of fans did their best to bring Piccadilly Circus to a halt as they thronged the theater.

The reviews on both sides of the Atlantic were ecstatic, reflecting not only what this author saw as the visual wit and exuberance with which Lester had packed the movie, but the sheer unexpectedness of the venture. (Having seen Lester's earlier *It's Trad, Dad*, I was less surprised. Despite its threadbare budget, the movie had possessed a manic energy that overcame purely fiscal limitations.) "Fresh and engaging," Time magazine raved. "Fresh and lively," Newsweek agreed. Bosley Crowther in the New York *Times* found it "surprisingly good, a whale of a comedy," while John Coleman in New Statesman pronounced it "Splendidly engaging." To Vogue magazine it was "fast, energetic and hip," while Arthur Knight in Saturday Review found it "almost good enough to be taken for a French New Wave work."

To Andrew Sarris in the *Village Voice*, the movie was "the *Citizen Kane* of jukebox musicals, a brilliant crystallization of such diverse cultural particles as the pop movie, rock 'n' roll, cinema verité, the nouvelle vague, free cinema, the affectedly hand-held camera, frenzied cutting, the cult of the sexless subadolescent, the semidocumentary, and studied spontaneity." To Arthur Schlesinger, Jr., it was nothing less than "The astonishment of the month," although he found it hard to decide who should be granted the lion's share of the credit—Lester, Owen or the Beatles themselves.

The group, according to the Monthly Film Bulletin, was "too inexperienced" to make the most of the "frantically paced script." "Beatles are fine," countered the London *Times*; "Beatles are engaging," Time magazine concurred. In the Illustrated London News, a fairly isolated Alan Dent summed up the group as having "little talent, but some charm, little of which is revealed." Ray Hagen, in Films in Review, differed: "The Beatles themselves as personalities make the film succeed." Arthur Knight found their mystique "puzzling," although the movie revealed them as "natural comedians." Richard Mallett in Punch felt "the personalities and natural talents of the Beatles help make the movie." "Film confirms all the discussions of the Beatles' charm," Isabel Quigley commented in the Spectator. "Beatles show great comedic promise," Variety reported. "The movie fits the Beatles' natural talents," wrote Stuart Walker in Report, "and plays down their shortcomings by letting them interact rather than act."

With reviewers waxing particularly lyrical in their praise of Lester's scene featuring the group romping in a field,

Shenson decided that credit should be equally shared. "That's a classic scene in our movie," he agreed, "and it's true that Dick did a brilliant job of interpreting the scene and adding music to it and all that. But that scene was in essence written by Alun Owen."

Although Lester is the first to admit that moviemaking is a collaborative process, he also felt obliged to have his say:

> What it said in the script was, "With a whoop boys run down fire escape into field. Thereupon a fierce game of soccer is played," and that was it. It didn't say there was going to be a musical number and it didn't say what they were going to be doing. I wanted to contrast the claustrophobic feeling you get in all these trains, hotel, studios, cars. We taught the boys three games, then told them to go ahead and play them anyway they liked. Then we shot the scene from different angles, from a helicopter one day, from various distances the next.
>
> I hated the very first version of the script; the only part that finally remained was the train sequence. Alun is an enormously creative but nonvisual writer. I think his dialogue is excellent, but the structure is mine and all the visuals were mine. I think his dialogue was perfect for that, and therefore I think he was a very good choice. He was fiercely protective of his work and whenever I complained would throw the script on the floor and sulk, "You tell me what you want and I'll do it. I'm paid as a *cheap writer!*" It was very difficult for him on those terms because he had always worked for television where he had complete control.

Even before its release *A Hard Day's Night* made close to 200 percent profit on advance album sales alone. Once the film was let loose in cinemas, the return zoomed to astronomical proportions; in the U.S. and Canada net rentals of over $5 million were recorded, worldwide receipts at least doubling that figure. With a U.S. network paying $2.5 million for just four television airings, Lester and Shenson had turned out one of the most profitable movies ever. It also garnered two Academy Award nominations, one for Alun Owen's screenplay, the other to George Martin for Best Original Score (at forty-seven seconds surely the shortest ever nominated).

John was relatively generous when discussing the finished movie, but he had distinct reservations about apportioning credit. "Well, I think it wasn't bad," he conceded. "You see, there's another illusion that we were just puppets and that the great people like Brian Epstein and Dick Lester created the situation and made this whole fuckin' thing. But it was really precisely because we were what we were, and realistic. We didn't want to make a fuckin' shitty pop movie . . . We were always trying to make it more realistic, even with Dick and all that, but they wouldn't have it."

Several critical comparisons with the Marx Brothers would prove unfortunate, as Lester discovered when he was hired to make a cigar commercial with the living legend, Groucho himself, shortly after *A Hard Day's Night* was released. Egged on by his friends, Groucho had gone to see the movie and had hated absolutely everything about it—the music, the Beatles, the works. Resentment bubbled over at the first meeting with Lester at the Dorchester Hotel. "At least you could tell us apart," Groucho barked. "What you've got there is four heads and one person." (The Beatles, for their part, had never seen the Marx Brothers in action until *Duck Soup* was shown on television just before they began filming *Help!* After that they asked Shenson to organize screenings of the entire Marx Brothers oeuvre.)

Having had firsthand experience of how cantankerous Groucho could be, Lester faced the prospect of filming the commercial with some trepidation. The set was a bedroom door in a hotel corridor, the set-up itself straightforward enough. Groucho was to chase a big-busted girl (Margaret Nolan) down the corridor before she runs into the bedroom and slams the door in his face. He was to turn around, speak one line of dialogue, get out his cigar, say another line, light the cigar, give the third line of dialogue, then slope off down the corridor.

Asked if he wanted to rehearse, Groucho declared he would do it in a single take. With a larger crew than he was used to, just in case anything went wrong, Lester shouted, "Action!" Down the corridor came Maggie Nolan, followed by Groucho, mistiming it so that he was miles behind. By the time he caught up she had long since slammed the door. Then he fluffed his first line, reached into the wrong pocket for the cigar, fumbled around until he found it, got his second line wrong ("But fixable," an increasingly fretful Lester reassured himself), had the same trouble finding the lighter (which didn't light the first time, despite having been endlessly checked by the props department), eventually lit the cigar, got the last line of dialogue completely wrong— and then, to cap it all, sloped off in the wrong direction.

During the stunned silence that followed Lester's "Cut," Groucho shuffled along to the director, walking his famous walk, trademark cigar in hand, and cracked, "Well, kid, I suppose you're going to tamper with perfection?"

Another legendary comedian, W. C. Fields, reportedly wanted the inscription "On the whole I'd rather be in Philadelphia" carved on his tombstone. For Lester, a native of the city, there had been little choice during his formative years.

CHAPTER TWO

I find the actual shooting of movies agony from beginning to end. I think it's something to do with turning the lights off as a child, and I still eat the outside of the celery first; by the time I get to the inside it's limp. I have an absolute paranoic compulsion to do the day's numbers. If it says on the call sheet this is what we have to shoot, I'm almost physically ill if I don't shoot it."

—RICHARD LESTER

William Young, Richard Lester's maternal grandfather, emigrated to Philadelphia from Ballymena, County Antrim, a few years before the turn of the century. Lester's mother, Ella, was born in Ireland in 1891 and was five years old when the family moved. Starting with a barrow selling vegetables, William prospered and became an importer of Chinese luxury goods. The house he built as a result was crammed with a variety of chinoiserie, including cloisonné, jade, ivory and soapstone figures and seals, all of them strategically placed on dark, heavy Chinese teak furniture. William died in 1936, when his grandson was four years old.

Richard's mother was a small, sturdy lady, just five feet tall, with brown hair and an extremely upright posture. He invariably pictures her in a long white dress, mainly because that is what she wears in the few photographs he still has of her. Her first husband's family had been devotedly church-going; she had met him, ironically, it turns out, singing in the church choir. Her subsequent atheism, following her abandonment in 1915 during her pregnancy with Richard's half-sister Dorothy, can be seen as a reaction both to the circumstances of their introduction as well as to the church's attitude towards a single mother trying to earn a living. Exercising a fiercely independent streak that served her well, given the parsimony forced upon her, she worked as a theater nurse and brought up her daughter on her own before meeting Elliott Lester.

A teacher of English literature in a preparatory school who moonlighted as a playwright, Elliott was five foot six, with a round face and full head of hair and bustling manner. The couple's first son, Robert, died in 1930, less than a month after he was born. Ella was forty-one when she gave birth to Richard in 1932.

In 1928 Elliott undertook a side trip to Hollywood to compose titles for silent movies. Thanks to the advent of Vitaphone sound, he was back in Philadelphia within a few months. Shortly afterwards, although he managed to have a play successfully staged on Broadway, his timing again proved erratic. In the year before the stock market crash he invested every penny that was left after building a large house in suburban Wyncote, only to lose it within a year. When his son looks back, which is seldom, he sees that the crash was the single event that affected all of their lives. The country had been led to believe that banks, shares and the stock market were wonderful, then suddenly—bang! And there was no recovery at all during the thirties, right up to World War II. Elliott continued to write plays, his son recalling many occasions when he would hobble downstairs, cramped from long sessions at the typewriter where he obsessionally tried for another crack at Broadway. His first tantalizing encounter with success proved to be his last; Elliott remained a teacher, with an extremely modest income, for the rest of his life.

As a result the family was obliged to be stringently money-conscious; to Ella it was a return to the parsimony with which she was all too familiar. No room was vacated without all the lights being switched off first; an open fire in the living room was lit only on holidays. In the mid-thirties Ella returned to nursing to help supplement their finances.

In Dickensian terms the young Lester turned out to be an Infant Phenomenon. By the time he was two and a half years old he could spell 250 words; a few months later an IQ test threw up a figure of 186, top of the genius range. The figure should be taken with a grain of salt, as he is the first to point out, since his parents had concentrated on coaching him in the questions that would appear on a test. Even so, they decided that severely restricted funds notwithstanding, their prodigy should be privately tutored, learn everything in two languages, and begin intensive schooling straightaway instead of waiting until he was six.

As a result he was three years younger, less aware and less socially adept than his contemporaries throughout his time at school. It was a singular burden to carry, in terms of everything from sports to clothes and, eventually, dates. The age gap left him feeling isolated at the William Penn Charter Boys' School, a Quaker establishment where he was extremely well educated despite his parents' example of dedicated atheism. The equivalent of Bible class was a forty-five-minute period each day where the class was expected to sit quietly and think ecclesiastical thoughts—this on rock-hard benches, uncomfortable for small children. He admits that the unhappiness of his school years has led him to close most of the memories off.

Further alienation came from being stranded on the outskirts of town, surrounded by several acres of land, over a mile from the bus one way and the same distance from the train station in the opposite direction. In 1935 Elliott finally decided it was sensible to get a car and bought a Model A Ford. Mobility at last, the family thought. Wrong! On his way home from the car showroom, never having driven a car before in his life—in those days no license was required—Elliott went straight into a lamppost. Nursing his bruises, he decided that driving was not for him. Leaving the vehicle where it lay, he called the garage and told them to take it back—and never drove again.

Unlike the Lesters' finances, their three-story house was solid and stone-built. There was a garage (now empty) and a maid's room commissioned in the heady pre-Crash era. An attic had been converted and fitted out with a desk and typewriter for Elliott's use, and there were three bedrooms on the first floor. Since his sister was never there—Dorothy, sixteen years older than her half-brother, had long since flown the coop—Richard was able to switch rooms as often as he fancied. In the rarely used living room, towering over a splendid gold-and-blue Chinese rug, a legacy from William's import years, was a heavy built-in bookcase groaning under the weight of complete sets of Thackeray, Dickens and Scott, together with anthologies of poetry and short stories, as well as a full set of the *Encyclopedia Britannica*, exactly what a conscientious schoolteacher would spend his money on. His son came to regard books as sternly educational rather than entertaining. As for comic books, they were banned completely.

There were no drapes in the house; what they had instead were linen roller blinds, which were never used because the springs had long since stuck. In any case, the family went to bed when it got dark. Richard recalls the feelings, wandering about in his shorts when he got older, that anyone could walk in. Despite their isolation, this was America, and every house was an open house, with doors never locked. Until he left the country Richard had never possessed a keyring— there was no need, since he had no keys. When he eventually landed in England the sense of privacy brought such an overwhelming feeling of relief that he suddenly felt at home, more so than he ever had back in the States.

The Lesters grew their own vegetables, fruit and flowers, and had planted apple trees, dogwoods and conifers, together with a huge larch and plane tree in which Richard played on his own, or with the family's Samoyed dog for company, until he was twelve. The family ate in the kitchen most of the time unless they had guests, which was rare. Elliott and Ella eschewed all forms of alcohol and were completely uninterested in food; it was "body fuel" and nothing more. Ella raised dreadful cooking to the level of an art form, stewing their fresh garden vegetables to mush, carbonizing their regular meat loaves, liquifying their fruit desserts and heaping white sugar on less palatable items like canned tomatoes. She would invariably stop eating at some point in the meal, quietly lay down her knife and fork and remark that she didn't "need any more." Richard recalls a variation on their normal diet when a friend of the family cooked a formal Polish meal, featuring twelve courses for the twelve apostles, with Matthew turning out to be something like mushrooms on toast. Much hilarity was enjoyed by the

Lesters at the dedication with which their friend undertook the elaborate process.

Ella was one of life's charming eccentrics, in her element in the cellar creating her own perfumes from essences she bought and mixed. Then she branched into wax flowers, into which she injected her concocted scents. She never kept presents she was given, choosing instead to rewrap them and give them away to other people. Her son had a theory that a present someone had given Ella would be eventually returned.

Richard felt no lack of parental affection, although his father had a tendency to sulk, leading to days on end when not a word was spoken in the house. Not knowing any different, since he had nothing with which to compare his own situation, Richard regarded this as perfectly normal behavior, and in any case spent much of his time lost in study. The question of whether he had a happy or an unhappy childhood hardly arises, since arguably he had no early childhood at all. The move of a large half-Irish, half-Italian family next door produced an overnight transformation, furnishing him with the first friend of his own age. There were eleven children altogether, nine girls and two boys.

All of a sudden, with the onset of war, the Lester household became a hive of activity as America prepared for invasion. Once a week first-aid classes were held in their cellar, with Richard invariably assuming the role of the patient awaiting the attack that was bound to come from the Germans. His father became involved with the Cooperative food movement. Although a worthy project on paper, Elliott's branch amounted in the end to a bunch of intellectual amateurs playing grocers. Following the eventual dissolution of the cooperative, the cellar was filled with canned food of appalling quality. When the war ended Richard wished he could have said the same for the canned peas that were served up at every meal for months afterwards.

Aware that he had a good ear and relative pitch, he decided to teach himself piano, having earlier turned down endless offers from his parents to be taught properly. Although there had always been classical music on the radio and gramophone throughout his childhood, he had also been listening for years to the popular music of the day—the orchestras of Glenn Miller, Tommy and Jimmy Dorsey, Benny Goodman, Tex Beneke and Charlie Ventura, the Gene Krupa Trio, the vocals of Buddy Clark, Bob Eberly and Frank Sinatra; later he graduated to the Artie Shaw band and Mel Torme and the Meltones. A poor sight reader, it took him a year of heartache to master "Body and Soul," an unfortunate choice to start with due to its extraordinarily difficult modulation. Then he moved on to "Tenderly" before setting out to teach himself the clarinet. Every summer he would rent another instrument, trombone followed by alto saxophone, teaching himself the basics of jazz improvisation.

Towards the end of his time at William Penn, Richard's attention was increasingly taken up with the activities of the all-girl Quaker school across the way. A pupil a year ahead of him, Jack Kelly, four years his senior at eighteen, had two sisters there. One of them, Liz, was extremely well developed, while the other was an uninteresting, sticklike creature. A double blind date with the desirable Liz left him the envy of his class and thankful that he had managed to avoid being stuck with the other one, the skinny kid sister who grew up to be Grace Kelly.

At fifteen his entrance to the university of Pennsylvania provided a further release. At the start of the second year, after a summer job packing men's suits, he joined a fraternity house, an arrangement that lasted precisely three months. He did not enjoy the "frat house" atmosphere, regarding the concept as a fairly nasty invention. After three months he decamped for an apartment of his own on the campus.

His parents seemed to have understood their son's need to leave home, with his mother particularly willing to subjugate her own feelings towards what she felt was best for him. The couple were left behind in a house that must have seemed immeasurably larger with only the two of them occupying it. On campus Richard began to spend much of his time playing piano and making friends with people on the musical side, going on to form a vocal group along the lines of the Meltones and the Judd Conlon Rhythmaires. His awareness of a budding sense of humor began with the realization that one of the other members of the group—Ian Freebairn Smith, now a West Coast composer in films and television—shared the same quirky, offbeat amusement at the vagaries of life. Until they met it had never occurred to Richard that what amused him would appeal to anyone else. He even became a bit of a social animal, learning how to mix martinis, considered the very essence of sophistication. Time was also found for a fling along the way with James Thurber's daughter, Rosie.

Meantime, he was supposed to be studying clinical psychology, a degree course chosen because it seemed less demanding than the alternatives. During his last year he did field work assessing and testing mentally retarded children in a clinic. Having the power to separate these children from their parents and institutionalize them made him absolutely determined never to have anything more to do with psychology, a profession he regards to this day with the gravest suspicion and cynicism.

Although still far from a cineaste, he finally began to watch films at college. Purely by accident they were all foreign movies, a specialty of the most convenient cinema, and included several early Ealing comedies. On the musical side his personal triumph was to be able to play piano in a bar and earn some pin money. Here he decided to disguise his formidable lack of technique by investing in a white tie and tails. Unfortunately, his sartorial elegance did not manage to stun his audience into an appreciative silence. He began writing music, and found to his relief that he was a better composer than a player. He also wrote for the University Dramatic Society and the Mask and Wig Club, Penn's version of Harvard's Hasty Pudding Club.

Following a massive heart attack in 1949, Elliott became an invalid. A lifetime of abstinence ended when he was ordered by his doctor to have a medicinal glass of wine or spirits: he literally had to have his nose held to get it down. After a year of inactivity, and fully aware of the consequences, he decided to return to the classroom and within two weeks suffered a second attack, this time fatal. He was a man whose life had disappointed him, but who had done his level best by his family. With Ella too distraught to make the arrangements, her son was left to organize the cremation. In keeping with the family tradition, no funeral was held. Public displays of grief, then as now, were utterly foreign to the Lesters. They grieved, but strictly in private.

While still at college Richard's vocal group was taken on by WCAU, the local CBS-TV station in downtown Philadelphia, as backing group to their lead singer, Ginny Stevens. With brilliant originality they called themselves Vocal Group and doo-waa'd on a couple of her locally released records. After three shows they were fired for incompetence, which helped to persuade young Lester that his future might lie with the incompetents on the *other* side of the camera. He

Richard Lester conducting his WCAU-TV "glee club" in Philadelphia. (COURTESY OF WCAU-TV)

applied for a job at CBS after graduating in 1951, and was
taken on as a stagehand. That the company was like a
pyramid, with people climbing on each other's shoulders,
prompted the discovery of an aggressive streak in his nature
that surprised him. With everyone aware that three of their
group of four would be fired, Richard made up his mind that
it wasn't going to be him. He was kept on, and promoted

first to floor manager, then assistant to the directors. The first of these was a fat, jolly lad known as Skippy, another (and much better) piano player. His real name was Alan Bergman; together with his wife Marilyn, he is a top songwriter today.

Within a year of joining WCAU, Lester was directing programs, thrown in at the deep end one day when his boss deliberately failed to turn up. Back then a director did five shows a day, all of them live, covering the weather, sports, an advertising/entertainment feature involving music, a science/educational segment (providing his introduction to Frank Lloyd Wright), even a daily western. He plugged his headset in, talked to the various cameras and edited the shows live, using two sets of buttons that enabled him to cut from one camera to the other. As a mere assistant he had always felt, despite his brash front, that it was the others who had the talent; in his eyes he was an imposter. As a full-fledged director, he began to develop distinct confidence in his own emerging abilities. Working at the pace he had—often for 100 hours a week—and constantly improvising as he switched programs, Lester developed the skills for his future profession.

After two years it became clear that he could settle down, make a lot of money, buy a house in the suburbs and live comfortably (and boringly) ever after. Deciding this was not for him, he talked a local newspaper syndicate into paying him ten dollars a week as a roving correspondent. Then he handed in his resignation to the somewhat less-than-stunned executives at CBS Television City, and embarked for Europe on the old *Queen Elizabeth*.

31

CHAPTER THREE

*I try to keep a sense of excitement going in all
my films, the feeling that none of us quite
knows what's going to happen next. I'm
pretty good at this, because I never know
what's going to happen next. As long as
people watch they know that a shambles is
imminent.*

—Richard Lester

Following his boat journey to Cherbourg, Lester hopped a
train to Paris. His sojourn in the city was spent in a remark-
ably cheap pension full of young working girls that turned
out to be the living quarters of the local brothel. The scales
of innocence having been well and truly removed, he hitch-
hiked to the south of France, then to Rome and through the
Russian-occupied corridor in Austria. His "grand tour" continued through Vienna, Saltzburg and Munich, where, for a
couple of dollars or a meal, he tuned pianos at a U.S. army
base. (For this purpose he carried a musical spanner contraption, two strips of felt to dampen down the strings on either
side of the one being worked on, and a tuning fork; with
moderately good pitch it was possible to do basic tuning.
Besides, by the time anyone found his work wanting, he

would be long gone.) It was a question of anything for a meal, and, with a return ticket tucked safely away, he had the security of knowing he could always get back.

Besides tuning pianos and dispatching communiqués, Lester found other ways of surviving as he traveled, first back to Paris (and a fractionally higher class of accommodation), then on to Lisbon, Seville and Barcelona. While in Spain he made the bringing of coals to Newcastle seem a first-class business proposition by playing guitar in a small café in the evenings, a plate by his side in which he deposited a starter of a few pesetas in change. At the end of many a stint he disconcertingly found less on the plate than when he had begun. Carrying currency from Torremolinos to Tangiers (bus to Algericas, ferry across), where the exchange rate was considerably better than in Spain, proved a better bet. He balked at putting his share of the profits into marijuana for the return journey and more modestly invested in lighter flints, easily smuggled and in great demand in Spain, where the government had a monopoly on matches and had banned cigarette lighters and their component parts.

In Spain, where fresh fruit was plucked from a tree, lettuces pulled from the soil and newly caught sardines roasted over an open fire on the beach, Lester's palette began to recover from the years of overcooked sludge back in Philadelphia. When a liking for wine was added to his newfound craving for good food, he began to assume the emergent aspects of a bon vivant.

In April 1955, he returned to Paris for a second time and took stock of his situation. Although his first car in America had been an Austin A40, and despite his predilection for English film comedy, he had never felt emotionally drawn to England. Yet having lived on his wits on the continent for a year, he could now see how limited the opportunities were for him, unable to speak any language fluently except English, and lacking any of the social skills that would land him a decent job. What he had discovered in his travels was an ability to survive, to come up with something that would at least keep him alive. It was a good lesson to learn, and one that afforded some hope for the future. He decided to make for London, hoping to raise interest in *Curtains for Harry*, a musical he had written.

Soon he had managed to coax a singer who had achieved some popularity—Dick "Robin Hood" James, later to make two separate fortunes, first as the Beatles' publisher, then as Elton John's—into making a demo record of his songs with simple piano accompaniment. While peddling this around during May (mercifully, he swears, it *was* curtains for *Curtains for Harry*), he heard that commercial TV was about to start up that August. Offering his services, he was interviewed by Associated Rediffusion's Captain Brownrigg. Details of his considerable experience in television, particularly the magic words CBS-TV, did the rest and led to his obtaining a position. A lawyer named Clive Nicholas, who would later become Lester's business manager and a lifelong friend, was thus able to obtain a recurring thirteen-week work permit for his client.

The salty gleam in Brownrigg's eye indicated that he had not only found someone who could turn out his own programs for ARTV, but who could instruct and tutor the batch of inexperienced trainees the station was lining up. Two early young hopefuls were Douglas Hearn, later to work in entertainment shows for the BBC, and Philip Saville, who went on to direct *Boys from the Blackstuff*, the TV version of *Life and Loves of a She-Devil* and *Fellow Traveller*, among others. With skills in a craft that was about to experience an explosion, Lester had landed in exactly the right place at the right time—in more ways than one, as it turned out. Informed that the office he had been allocated was being turned into a men's toilet, he was asked to share and was thus flung together on a daily basis, romance blossoming over tea breaks, with the woman who would become his wife and the mother of his children. Deirdre Vivian Smith was a tall, striking blonde with, Lester notes fondly, a dancer's turned-out feet, perpetually in the "ten to two" position.

Following her training as a classical dancer at the Cone-Ripman School, Deirdre had gone on to teach before landing a part in the chorus of *Oklahoma!* Later she was lead dancer and assistant choreographer in *Finian's Rainbow*, then in *Kiss Me, Kate*, *Kismet* and *Guys and Dolls*. She had also worked in movies, with Gene Kelly in MGM's *Invitation to the Dance*, with the legendary American dancer and choreographer Jack Cole on *Gentlemen Marry Brunettes*, and with director Joseph Losey. When she met Lester she was choreographing the London production of Cole Porter's *Can-Can* as well as acting as one of Associated Rediffusion's two choreographers for their resident troupe of dancers.

Lester came over to her as one of the brashest people she had ever met, "A Mr. Knowall who thought he could do everything and play the Trumpet Voluntary at the same time." It was her roommate and principal dancer in *Can-Can*, Gillian Lynne, who made her take a second look by suggesting, "He's really quite dishy." After further inspection, Deirdre agreed.

She had never seen anyone work so fast, both on the set and off. "He'd draw the scenes, write the music and dialogue for sketches and rush into production," she recalls. "He was the first person to give me the whole studio to stage what he called a 'suicide ballet,' *Slaughter on Tenth Avenue*. Coming from the theater, I had a slightly snobbish attitude

35

towards him and the whole set-up to begin with. That soon melted away." Lester's early training at WCAU stood him in excellent stead. One show a week instead of five? A relative snap.

The very first program Lester put together for ARTV was a showcase for American singer Marti Stephen. He went on to direct commercial TV's first jazz show, *Downbeat*, which featured the Johnny Dankworth Quartet, the Tommy Whittle Band and the Eric Delaney Orchestra, as well as staging Deirdre's "suicide ballet."

Almost totally convinced that Deirdre was the girl for him, Lester decided to submit her to the ultimate test, a visit to Philadelphia. To his delight Ella immediately adopted her as one of the family, while her future mother-in-law impressed Deirdre as a "total eccentric, slightly nuts but lovely."

Within hours of their meeting Ella took her to one side: "Deirdre, don't *ever* buy perfume. There's no need. I'll make all you'll ever need. I went to the factory years ago and got the ingredients out of them and they're all downstairs in the basement." Deirdre remembers the smell to this day *("awful")* but also recalls the generous waves of affection that followed her everywhere. That Ella utterly adored her son brought it home to her how hard it must have been not to have him around. She could also see the tremendous influence Ella had exercised, delving into the background of whatever he took up.

Back at the ARTV grindstone, and stuck for inspiration one day, Lester began to compile a half-hour program with Philip Saville in which he planned to showcase his manifold talents—he would play piano, guitar and bass, sing and ad-lib. As Deirdre had discovered, his parents had always addressed their son as "Richard," while the British had immediately awarded him the diminutive "Dick" or

"Dickie." He tacitly approved at the time, to the extent of allowing his maiden TV outing to be dubbed *The Dick Lester Show*.

Early in December 1955, when a hole in the scheduling developed, a live version of the show appeared, with his solo turn augmented by a young Liverpool actor, Alun Owen, as well as the Reg Owen Orchestra. The show's "gimmick" was to give the impression of being under-rehearsed, taking place an hour before originally scheduled, with tables and cameras visible and complete informality the order of the day. Sandwiched between *Dragnet* and the first Independent Television Christmas pantomime, in the prime-time 8:30–9:00 P.M. slot, the show had the fourth highest rating in the country. It was also an unmitigated disaster. Everything that should have clicked serendipitously misfired instead, with no discernible trace of wit or comic timing during the ad-lib sequences, and a puppet segment that was a total embarrassment. Next morning the reviews were lethal, one of the critics offering the fervent hope that Lester's effort remain strictly a one night stand.

Later that day, while Lester was wallowing in despondency, the phone rang. "I watched your program last night," he was informed. "And it was either one of the worst shows I've ever seen, or you are on to something. If it was the latter, would you like to meet for lunch?" "Fine," said a startled Lester as the caller revealed his name. It was Peter Sellers.

Over the meal the comedian revealed that he was thinking about a TV version of the enormously popular BBC radio series, *The Goon Show*, and suggested they visit Spike Milligan for further discussions that afternoon. Discovered prone on the floor with his head resting on a huge coil of rope, Milligan remained in that position never so much as glancing in Lester's direction, while Sellers held forth. "TV," he finally intoned, "will never work with comedy. If I want to write about Eskimos who disappear into their igloos and come up in the Houses of Parliament, I can do it on the radio. You can't do that on TV. First of all, it would cost too much, and then I couldn't physically do it. It's a visual medium and it won't work." (Milligan's views may have been colored by the less-than-ecstatic reception to *Down Among the Z-Men* and *The Case of the Mukkinese Battlehorn*, two movie shorts the Goons had already released or allowed to escape.)

Sellers and Lester left, with Lester feeling more than a trifle deflated. Despite the fact that Harry Secombe was

Humor is a serious business!
Spike Milligan (left) and Peter Sellers (seated) recording *Idiot Weekly*.   (COURTESY OF RICHARD LESTER)

Deadly serious!
Spike Milligan (in goggles) and Peter Sellers (in kilt) recording *Idiot Weekly*.
(COURTESY OF RICHARD LESTER)

unavailable due to panto commitments and that they would be unable to use the word "Goon" itself, since this was BBC-copyrighted, Sellers was undeterred. Hired as gag writers for the enterprise under script editor Eric Sykes were such future luminaries as Frank Muir and Denis Norden, Johnny Speight, John Junkin, Terry Nation, Lew Schwartz and Dave Freeman. The stage was set for Sellers's and Lester's first TV series, entitled *Idiot Weekly, Price 2d*. Sellers appeared on the first show, which also featured the BBC's "Man in Black," Valentine Dyall, and harmonica ace Max Geldray (both *Goon Show* regulars), together with comedians Kenneth Connor and Graham Stark, and Canadian singer Patti Lewis.

The morning after the airing, on February 24, 1956, Lester was in his office, savoring the rave reviews, when Milligan called and announced that he was bringing over the schedule for the following week's show. Without a word of explanation, let alone apology, he marched into Lester's office twenty minutes later and commandeered his secretary: "Can you take shorthand? Fine, off we go." He had brought a 16mm film with him, which he proceeded to feed into the telecine machine used at the time. Lester watched as a short, silent cartoon film unfolded that had been put together by animator Bob Godfrey. Milligan accompanied this with the most extraordinarily funny ad-libbing, which the flustered secretary frantically tried to capture. Lester has never seen anyone, before or since, who can match Milligan in full flow. He had, in his own unique way, joined *Idiot Weekly*—and fully expected to contribute an extra tuppence worth.

Milligan taught Lester the art of casting traditional, "safe" establishment figures to counterpoint and augment the comedy. The *Goon Shows* had always employed stiff, formal British announcers like the tall, cadaverous Dyall, whom Lester found a delightful character. A declared bankrupt, he would turn up regularly at rehearsals caked in dried blood ("Just a minor altercation with the bank manager—I say, you couldn't see your way clear to allow me to have ten shillings, could you?"). At the end of the week he would always pay it back and was perpetually "skint." Casting these figures became a regular habit of Lester's, all the way from Frank Thornton in *It's Trad, Dad* to John Le Mesurier in *Mouse on the Moon*, Richard Vernon in *A Hard Day's Night* Patrick Cargill in *Help!* and the incomparable Michael Hordern in *A Funny Thing Happened on the Way to the Forum, How I Won the War, The Bed Sitting Room* and *Royal Flash*.

While preparing the third show in the series, Sellers had an anxiety attack and, although not normally a drinker, sent out for a bottle of brandy. Despite having consumed half of it before the live transmission that night, he was word perfect. Unfortunately, his reactions had slowed down to the point where the sketches ended up eight minutes longer than they should have been. By chopping the last sketch, Lester managed to squeak home without anyone noticing. As on many similar occasions, he recalls just hanging on for dear life.

A later sketch had Sellers, dressed in bowler and city gent outfit and reading the *Times* next to Graham Stark, in pilgrim costume, on a park bench. "The prices these days are shocking," says Sellers, eyes fixed on his paper. "Do you know how much I paid for a flat?" "A flat what?" asks Stark. Slowly the two men gaze at each other and realize that they are in a dream—but whose dream is it? The camera then pans to the large St. Bernard dog lying asleep under the park bench, revealing that it is the dog's dream.

All through rehearsals everything went smoothly, with the backdrop of the park in place and the dog fast asleep on a leash under the bench. As soon as transmission began it awoke, perhaps sensing the nervousness in the air. Deciding to go home, it got up, pulling the bench and scenery over in the process, and knocking Sellers and Stark to the floor. It then proceeded to drag the bench to the nearest exit, growling balefully.

Since this was the last sketch and there were still five minutes to go to the end of the program, Lester pleaded from his control box, "Take us off!" "We can't," he was informed. "Tell them to keep going, tell them to ad-lib." Sellers and Stark did as they were told, and so brilliantly that very few noticed. With no record kept of these transmissions, everyone involved was obliged to go home to their wives or family and ask how it had come across, then await the verdict of the TV critics in the morning. The response was encouraging, with Wolf Mankowitz describing the show as "intelligent, pointed, skillful, professionally conducted, and very, very funny," while Herbert Kretzmer found it "crazy, offbeat, and the most original program since Independent Television took the air." The team's antics, way in advance of Monty Python, included an underwater violin recital, an advertisement for Footo, the Patent Boot Exploder, and a surreal interview between one Fred Nurk and his son's school headmaster, which terminated when they glided into each other's arms and waltzed off into the distance.

Occasionally the show ventured out on location for filmed inserts. One jaunt took them to London Zoo where the sketch was to portray out-of-work actors standing in for the animals. Graham Stark entered into the spirit of things by plunging into the sea lions' pool and splashing around briefly—until one of the creatures began to display an unconscionable interest in his nether regions, prompting an extremely hasty exit. Valentine Dyall, dressed in a dark green velvet cape, was perched uneasily on the branch of a tree beside a vulture. "Don't worry, Val," Lester reassured the nervous actor. "We wouldn't put you up there unless it was absolutely safe." Then he turned to his cameraman: "Right, are they both in shot? Turn over." Just then the vulture took one look at Dyall and vomited in terror. Milligan insisted on filming his contribution in the monkey cage, while Kenneth Connor, in city gent outfit and rolled-up umbrella, stood on one leg beside the storks. The finale was set up by a plummy BBC-type voice-over announcing, "And now we present Professor Hugh Jampton reading his latest paper on the

"Why don't you do it Lester?"
Lester with Peter Sellers about to board the camel in *Idiot Weekly*.

" 'Cause I'm the director, that's why!"

Bactrian Camel." The camera cut to a massively bearded Peter Sellers, sat astride a bactrian camel perusing not the expected scholarly thesis, but a copy of the *Daily Sketch*.

In the midst of the chaos Lester continued to pursue the musical side of his career. Reg Owen, his *Dick Lester Show* musical collaborator, had been a tenor saxophonist with the Ted Heath Orchestra before leading his own band on ARTV. A rally driver enthusiast, his partial paralysis following a headlong crash into a wall opened up a new career. As an arranger he enjoyed a top-twenty hit in Britain with Manhattan Spiritual. He and Lester worked together on the British equivalent of Richard Rodgers's *Victory at Sea*, using Ministry of Defense and naval material for what became *Sea War*. With Lester dreaming up the themes and Owen orchestrating, their work proceeded on a threadbare financial basis that precluded even a glimpse of the ultimate footage before their backing themes were composed. Instead, a written summary describing the scene in essence would be forwarded, along the lines of "Two bomb disposal units defuse a limpet mine, 2 minutes, 25 seconds."

From this the two men attempted to perform dramatic miracles, conjuring up a mental picture of sweaty close-ups as the device ominously ticked away, with tension screwed up to crisis point. When they finally got to see the footage, it would probably consist of antlike bomb teams, photographed in one long shot from a distance of several hundred yards. As a result their music invariably had a hothouse element that seldom squared with the images on the screen.

Since Lester's compositions ended up in the copyright catalogues, the musical mills of God, they still yield him a steady income in performance royalties every six months, along the order of £30 and always accompanied by a precisely detailed computer printout indicating which benighted radio station played which tune in which remote hinterland. The sight of these neatly stacked sheets, Lester says ruefully, always seems to promise so much more, especially since it includes playlist details of a piece he composed for *How I Won the War* as well a twelfth-century pastiche he knocked off for *Robin and Marian*. Whenever the printout arrives, he imagines the eighteen-wheeler that must be drawing up outside Paul McCartney's premises, with an entire squadron of fork-lift trucks unloading several tons of computer printouts.

Following seven editions of *Idiot Weekly*, the team embarked upon an even more *Goon*ish series entitled *A Show Called Fred*. First, Lester decided to take advantage of the three-day break between shows. Although he had felt that getting married on Deirdre's birthday would be a good idea, something that would prevent forgetfulness in years to come, he failed to obtain seats on an economy package night flight to their honeymoon destination, Oslo. Instead, they married the day after her birthday, the flight they eventually caught landing them in Oslo at 3 A.M. Unfortunately, their rented car failed to turn up, and with all the taxis long gone they were faced with the distinctly humiliating prospect of spending their wedding night on a bench in the airport lounge.

With the lights about to be switched off, a janitor listened to their tale of woe and called his brother, who came out and gave the couple a lift to their hotel. By the time it was found and they were checked in, dawn had long since broken. Utterly exhausted, they fell fast asleep on top of the bed, to be rudely awakened a couple of hours later at 9:00 A.M. It seemed that their car had arrived, could Lester come down and sign for it?

By the time this was done, an unrequested breakfast had

been delivered. With a maid endlessly tidying their room, Lester's thoughts turned to jumping into the car and driving Deirdre to the nearest deserted field. The rental firm had left their vehicle facing the front of the hotel, directly below the restaurant. With his beloved sitting beside him, Lester struggled in vain to find a particularly elusive reverse gear, in his efforts repeatedly achieving first and butting the hotel wall, with highly amused guests observing the debacle from the restaurant window.

Back in London, with their first home established in a rented basement flat in Belgravia, the shenanigans of *A Show Called Fred* proved just as popular as *Idiot Weekly*. "You mustn't hit your mother like that," one character scolded. "You must hit her *like this!*" Bernard Levin joined the team's fan club with a series of articles in the Listener and Spectator that made them feel they must be doing something right. "This marvelous program is not merely funny," Levin raved. "It acts as a purgative to the congested soul, sweeping away under its healing touch all the tensions, all the frustrations, tions, all the impossibilities that life involves. It's by far the funniest thing I have yet seen on television, and indeed one of the most magnificently sustained examples of humor I can recall in any medium."

By the beginning of the third series, *Son of Fred*, Milligan had decided he was bored doing the same old thing and was going to shake things up a bit. This meant abandoning all scenery, simply having a backdrop with numbers attached, with a prop's significance changing from one sketch to the next. He was laying down, without realizing it, the blueprint for much of what the Python team would eagerly go on to develop. Halfway through the series, fed up with this avant-garde minimalism, the audience became so alienated that

ITV pulled the plug, deeming that the boundaries had been pushed unacceptably beyond the limit.

"To its eternal credit," says Graham Stark, "commercial television, not too well known for its vision in the world of entertainment, had given Peter and Spike carte blanche. It had also given us a young director, Dick Lester, who had the good sense to realize that he had to tread the fine line between lunatic invention and coherence." Stark had hit the nail on the head. While the team had been achieving its wonders, Lester had contributed a necessary element of control even as he was reveling in and fully contributing to the madcap proceedings.

Although the three series also afforded him a unique opportunity to observe the different lifestyles of the chief participants, few hints emerged of how they would change in the future. Sellers was the sober family man with a wife and two kids living in a semidetached house in Mill Hill. It was Milligan who had to be sedated in order to survive, swallowing tranquilizers strong enough to knock out a horse. He would often turn up for dinner with Lester, depressed over some governmental stupidity, intransigence or injustice to the point of not talking or eating. Several glasses of white wine would be required to draw him out. While Lester was directing the madhouse of the three series, juggling jazz bands with out-of-control comedians, Deirdre had her hands full in the studio next door with Tony Hancock, a manic depressive who, when he wasn't performing, would spend the whole time silently facing the wall in utter torment.

Lester watched in alarm as Sellers began to change, first turning simply "odd," then getting crazier and crazier, the major turning point arriving with his conviction, after co-starring with Sophia Loren in *The Millionairess*, that he was a ladies' man—or could be if he took off just a few pounds. Within weeks he had transformed his image, via a strict yogurt diet, from a fairly jolly, roly-poly Jewish boy to a thin, high-strung individual living on his nerves.

In their art Lester saw Milligan as the great creator, Sellers as the great adapter, with a wonderful mastery of mimicry that enabled him to do anybody. For a send-up of Richard III he tackled the voice of every leading character using Olivier's makeup girl and costumer. Lester showed the stills he had taken to Olivier's agent, who couldn't tell them from Olivier himself. For the end of the sketch, Milligan had wanted the camera to zoom to the sentinel on the battlements overlooking Sellers's impersonation. Lifting his visor, he would be revealed as Olivier himself, shaking his head in mock sorrow. Unfortunately, their courage failed and they decided against approaching Olivier, convinced he would disdain such antics. When he later heard of the plan, Olivier murmured, "If only they had asked me!"

The termination of *Son of Fred* also produced a terminal dust-up with Captain Brownrigg. "*Lester*, how old are you?" the interview began. "Twenty-three, *Brownrigg*," said Lester, a reply whose nuances of mockery went down like a lead balloon. "Harrumph. And you're earning £65 a week?" (Sellers had started at £100 weekly and was getting £500 by the end of the series.)

"That's right."

"Don't you think you're far too young to be earning that amount of money?"

"No, Brownrigg, I don't."

Following the fairly heated argument that followed, Lester found himself "at liberty"—and with a wife and basement flat to support.

CHAPTER FOUR

It was all mates in a field.

—RICHARD LESTER on
*The Running, Jumping and
Standing Still Film*

Partly due to the unscheduled departure from Associated
Rediffusion, and partly due to his reaction to the Suez crisis,
Lester decided, early in 1957, that it was time to hit the road
again and leave Britain for a spell to escape the distinct
feeling of something nasty in the air. Stories had been put
about that all Egyptians were drug addicts, that they couldn't
run the canal on their own, that Britain had to protect its
own interests—while the rest of the world looked on, convinced that the British and French had lied and cheated,
conned by the Israelis into an indefensible misadventure.
Lester was a member of the Studio Club, a small jazz haunt
on Swallow Street, where one of the staff was a naval reserve
who found himself called up. *What the hell for?* was the
question on everyone's lips. Deirdre, still earning decent
money at ARTV, took a fair bit of convincing. "He felt
strongly," she recalls. "I felt less strongly."

Off they nevertheless went, stopping only to join the
queue of similarly disgruntled emigrants at Canada House,
where the necessary forms were completed that would en-

able them to seek employment. With one small suitcase each, they traveled first to Cherbourg, then onward to Caracas, Martinique and all through the Caribbean, intent on seeing the world together before trying their luck in God's country.

Several passengers on the Cherbourg-to-Venezuela journey were Hungarian refugees. One of their number was a classical guitarist who intended to try his luck in South America. Speaking mainly Hungarian, with just a few words of French, he appeared diffident when asked to play for some of his fellow passengers, but was finally coaxed into giving a recital. The Lesters were about to witness a scene that might have been dreamt up for *Idiot Weekly*. Armed with a microphone, a straight-backed chair and a little footstool, the guitarist positioned himself at the center of the ship's highly polished ballroom, and tuned up endlessly. When he finally seemed to have it all together, a hush fell over the assembly. His countenance was grave, his voice tremulous with emotion as he announced, "Je vous joué un chanson de Sebastian Bach." Just then the ship gave an almighty roll, causing the microphone, footstool and chair—complete with startled musician—to slide clear across the dance floor and straight out the open door on to the deck. He then disappeared from view, never to be seen again by his intended audience. The couple often wonder whether it was disgust, embarrassment, loss of nerve—or whether he had taken the ship's roll as a message from God.

Their Caribbean cruise led them to Miami, then home to Philadelphia for a brief visit to Ella, still resolutely puttering about in the basement, before a move across the border to Canada in April. With the aid of a few references from his ARTV contacts, Lester landed an assignment writing gags for a Canadian Broadcasting program called *The Barris Beat*, directed by Norman Jewison. With Deirdre choreographing a band show for $300 a week and Lester chipping in $200 for his two nights' work, four months were spent before boredom and wanderlust set in.

With the considerable amount of money they had been able to save they were off again, stopping only at Australia House, where the necessary forms were again completed that would enable them to obtain work while having a look around. Then it was back through America to San Francisco, and on to Los Angeles, where they boarded a luxury cruise to Tahiti. With its heavily scented flowers, tropical fruit and exotic black sand beaches, it was still possible to imagine the island as it was in the era of Gaugain. As the couple bicycled, swam and relaxed, Deirdre's only complaint was that the men were singularly unattractive, while all the girls seemed to be stunningly beautiful. After an all-too-brief stopover it was on to New Zealand and finally their new mecca of Australia.

After initially lodging in Melbourne with an ex-dancer friend of Deirdre's, Lester undertook a trip to Sydney to check out the available jobs. There he was asked to appear on an ABC-TV game show, *I've Got a Secret*, a cross between *What's my Line?* and *Twenty Questions* in which contestants challenged the panel to guess their secret, with a voice-over at the beginning to give viewers the answer in advance. Lester felt that the experience would be a useful test to gauge the state of the infant Australian television network.

The first woman who came on carried specimen bottles, which turned out to contain waters of the famous rivers and lakes of the world. Lester's "secret," as the next guest, was that he had directed *Idiot Weekly*, *A Show Called Fred* and *Son of Fred*. This was guessed in fairly short order, the shows having been extremely popular in Australia; a minor scandal had arisen over some of the language used, with questions raised in the Australian Parliament.

With his spot out of the way, Lester stayed to watch the rest of the show from the sidelines. Primitive as the facilities were, all had gone smoothly enough up until then. The show's host had two bits of wire with cards that he flipped over, with numbers 1 to 20 indicating how many questions the panel had left. The wire snapped when he got to question four, scattering the cards all over the studio floor. "I told you that was bloody well going to happen!" he yelled in the direction of the control box. Bending over, with the camera faithfully focused on his upturned rear end, he began picking up the cards and replacing them, all out of sequence, on the wire loops.

When the next guest arrived, the voice that was supposed to tell viewers the secret echoed all over the studio, giving the game away completely. Although he was clearly exerting enormous self-control, the host's grin was agony to watch as he desperately tried to ad-lib his way out of trouble. "Have you got *another* secret, love?" he asked the contestant. As she whispered to him Lester saw his grin becoming, if it were possible, even more fixed. "Okay, love, that's your *other* secret," he declared, more than a hint of desperation in his voice. "Off we go!" With the panel stumped, the panelist's second "secret" was out—she had once accompanied Albert Blair! "Albert *who*?" the panel chorused. "Well, he's not very well known here, but he's very big in Northern Ireland," she explained.

While in Australia the Lesters discovered the delights of what the inhabitants jauntily referred to as "the six o'clock swill." Bars opened for precisely sixty minutes at 5:30 P.M., and after an hour of steady drinking everyone was totally out of their minds. They visited a pub up country, where the front of the bar was corrugated iron, with a trough at the strategic height so patrons could relieve themselves where they stood. While in the sticks the only restaurant the couple could find one day had a menu, in true Monty Python style, consisting of nothing but Spam. When this arrived it was stuck to the plate, curling like a British Rail sandwich. "Excuse me," said Lester politely to the gentleman who had banged down their plates, "do you have any pickles or relish?" They found themselves being stared at menacingly before the kitchen hatch was slammed open and the individual yelled, "Send up some Pan Yam, bloody bastard here thinks its Christmas!"

Taking it all in all, the couple decided that Australia was not quite ready for them. Lester smilingly resists the suggestion that he and Deirdre had overcompensated for Oslo and had a delayed year-long honeymoon in their circumnavigation of the globe. "It's a great way to get to know somebody," he suggests. "Deirdre and I were together practically every minute of the day. We didn't have much money for most of the time, but it was wonderful. It's just the sort of thing you *should* do when you are young. Why wait until you retire?" On their return to Blighty, on Christmas Eve, 1957, and with £9 left in their pockets, they found their basement flat in Belgravia still available and moved back in.

In the New Year Lester began working with Michael Bentine on two shows, one for BBC radio, *Don't Shoot, We're English*, and another for ABC-TV, *After Hours*. Deirdre had a harder time resuming her career, having given her job at ARTV to her best friend, Pamela Devis. It took nine months before she was re-established, at Rodgers and Hammerstein's London office, and working successively on *Flower Drum Song*, *The Sound of Music* and *Once Upon a Mattress* (one of her favorite musicals, although it failed to click). With the regular money Lester got from the Bentine series, the couple was emboldened to move from their basement and, in March 1958, took a long lease on a two-bedroom apartment in Chelsea's Tedworth Square, where Daniel Massey lived just across the hall.

Lester's work on film had been restricted, up until then, to the occasional excerpts—the Shortest Distance race, the Zoo visit and the Backwards Slow Hurdles—he had shot for the *Goon Shows*. These he had often found more rewarding than the actual programs themselves; he was able to fine-tune them, and they made him acutely aware of the impernence of the medium in which he was working. Tape-recording of TV had not yet been invented, and the only process available was tele-recording, simply placing a 16mm camera in front of a tube in the telecine room and filming the resulting image. Since the process cost £75 to film a half-hour show, only key programs were preserved in this way. Of Lester's entire television output, only fragments of three shows survive.

Never having even remotely been a film buff, Lester took to regularly visiting the National Film Theater. Now it was continental films he favored, especially the works of Truffaut (*The Four Hundred Blows*) and Renoir (*Vanishing Corporal, The Rules of the Game*). Then there was the early Fellini and Bergman's *Wild Strawberries* and *The Seventh Seal*. The only American moviemaker whose work he never failed to catch was Buster Keaton, whom he saw as the master of comedy. With these as his heroes he was about to go from the sublime to the ridiculous—in fine company.

The American Danziger brothers, Harry Lee and Edward J., had their own tiny studio near Elstree (not to be confused with Associated British's Elstree Studios), which they grandly (considering it was a converted dairy) dubbed New

Elstree Studios. Isolated highlights of the dozens of B-pictures they had produced include the transcendentally awful *Babes in Baghdad*, starring stripper Gypsy Rose Lee and shot in the wonder of "exotic color" in 1952, and the abysmal *Devil Girl from Mars* ("Earth menaced by Fantastic Powers!") shot without color of any kind in 1954. Of their planned series of thirteen half-hour films for television, Lester was to direct six, American blacklist victim Joseph Losey another six, and actor Kieron Moore the thirteenth. Each of them was allocated just two and a half days to film his episode, Monday morning to Wednesday lunchtime, then Wednesday afternoon to Friday night. The series starred one-armed Donald Gray as one-armed private detective Mark Sabre. Just like his character, Gray always wore a hat whether on set or off, drove a Porsche, and invariably joked to the continuity girl at the beginning of a take, "Now, which hand did I have my hat in?" Among the actors used—with striking redhead Diana Dekker on hand as Sabre's girl Friday—was Colin Tapley (the Chief Inspector) who Lester reckoned must have been Marlon Brando's role model in that he made a religion out of never bothering to learn his lines. As a result individuals wandered all over the set with huge cue cards for Tapley to read off.

One of the main sets for Mark Sabre was a nightclub, staffed by a pretty receptionist, Jennifer Jayne, and the craggy club owner, played by Michael Balfour. If time ran out and an episode was a few minutes short when pieced together, the drill was for Lester and Losey to fill in with a stock shot in which Sabre drove up to the nightclub in his Porsche, rushed past Balfour at the entrance and looked left, jaw firmly clenched. At this point there would be a cut to the stage and a paper-tearing act, or jugglers, or whatever else had been shot in advance, which would go on for as long as it was required. Then it was cut back to Sabre, rushing outside, jaw still clenched, muttering, "He's not here!" as he brushed Balfour aside.

Lester found the entire process hysterical, although he was less amused by the antics of the Danzigers, who played good cop–bad cop with him whenever money was mentioned. One was kindness itself, the other a study in viciousness. The brothers were both short, in their early forties, and seemed to Lester like little white mice. At least he was given the opportunity, on top of his £40-a-week salary, of meeting some extraordinary people. The focus puller on several episodes was Nicolas Roeg, of whom both he and Losey said, "We'll be working for him one day." Then there was Losey himself, who adopted an old Hollywood technique in his early films after being relocated to Britain. If there was a big crowd scene he would bring in someone else to choreograph the players. Because Deirdre had done so much of this work, Lester was introduced to Losey and, through his good offices, to the delights of toiling for the Danzigers. "I rather fancied Joe before I met Richard and he married Dorothy," Deirdre cheerfully admits. "He was quite dishy, a warm, interesting, lovely man. And he had great faith in me. Apart from my work on the crowd scenes he used to say, 'Just be there.' No wonder I warmed to him."

Lester too found the tall, burly Losey a fascinating character, someone who gave the illusion of having no idea of what he wanted, then turning out work that seemed totally controlled. He overate and drank between movies, then pulled himself into shape when he had to. And he always lived way beyond his means, camped in the most luxurious houses in London, even when he was without a penny to his name. Although there was little comedy in his life or work, both Lester's and Deirdre's memories are filled with shared laughter. For an older man he always seemed aware of the leading trends—the young actor to watch for, the latest directions in jazz, architecture and painting. He had fought to have Peter O'Toole in a movie long before *Lawrence of Arabia* and was turned down. He was the first to back production designer Richard Macdonald, who went on to have an extremely successful career. Although Lester went on to compose a jazz score for eight trombones and a rhythm section for Losey's Aero chocolate commercial, he felt he didn't know enough to attempt the full-length score the director requested for his movie, *The Criminal*. The commission was duly handed to Johnny Dankworth, providing him with his first major film assignment.

In the company of Losey and his actress wife Dorothy Bromiley, Lester and Deirdre attended several social gatherings. One of these was a party thrown by Donald Ogden Stewart, writer of *The Philadelphia Story*. A quiet, retiring man, Stewart was married to Ella, an ex-mistress of Maxim Gorky. Producer Carl Foreman was another in the gathering of communists and fellow travelers, the Lesters excluded, who admired the Stewarts' marvelous art and antique collection, including tomb objects and pre-Colombian artifacts. Foreman, Lester found, had one particularly disconcerting habit: he would nominate a serious subject for conversation, then point to various people to discuss it. Lester refused to go along with this, protesting that he did not attend parties to undergo an examination. Politics aside, Losey's philosophic influence on Lester was considerable.

Lester ventured into the world of the theater in 1958, when, courtesy of an invitation from actor/impresario Sam Wanamaker, he directed George Axelrod's Broadway hit, *Will Success Spoil Rock Hunter?* With a cast headed by Bonar Colleano, Paul Carpenter and June Cunningham, and with

Michael Balfour, Lester's nightclub owner in *Mark Sabre*, also featured, the play opened at Wanamaker's New Shakespeare Theater in Liverpool for a week in early August prior to its London premiere. Although well reviewed, the production seemed ill-fated from the start. On the second night a key supporting actor dislocated his shoulder, while a romantic entanglement left the thirty-four-year-old Colleano despondent and slugging heroic quantities of booze. After the last performance on Saturday night, considerably under the influence, he crashed his car headlong into a wall, killing himself outright and hurtling his passenger, Balfour, through the windshield.

Lester was awakened at three in the morning by a phone call from a distraught London theater manager. As the news of the tragedy sank in, it was suggested that the play simply had to open as scheduled. "With Bonar gone and two others incapacitated?" he protested. *"You* could play Bonar's role, you must know the lines," came the reply. This was one showbiz legend in the making, Lester decided, in which he had no wish to participate. Instead he helped keep body and soul together by taking on a job as straight man to comedian Clive Dunn on BBC-TV's monthly *Children's Corner*, touring seaside resorts at £10-7-6d a time.

He returned briefly to the theater a couple of seasons later, directing "An Exhibition Devised by Michael Bentine" entitled *Don't Shoot, We're English*. Several of the sketches were co-written with Bentine, including "The Stag at Bay," followed by "The Stag at Whitley Bay," "The Black Hole of Calcutta—A Comic Recitation," "The Blood Sausage—A Dramatic Sketch" and "Balaclava—The Story of a Helmet." On this occasion the run was limited to a few weeks in the provinces. In Newcastle-upon-Tyne it was greeted by the distinctly underwhelmed Geordies with a degree of non-attendance that bordered on indifference. Lester began to harbor serious doubts that he had ever been intended to make his way on the boards.

During his spell with Bentine, Sellers recruited Lester to help devise a television commercial for Persil laundry detergent. Together they came up with the idea of a plowed field, where peasants carrying large straw baskets filled with Persil were sowing it like seed; cut to little plants growing, until they reached a reasonable size, with the sun shining on the little Persil packets. Harvested, they are carried off in hoppers and placed in a huge vat where more peasants trample them like grapes; cut to finale, the bung hole being opened and soapy water pouring out, then a white-coated technician, in the tradition of a wine connoisseur, tasting the liquid, rolling it about on his tongue, then pausing thoughtfully before spitting it out and declaring, "It's only fit to wash in." Carried away with the idea, and giggling helplessly in their innocence and naiveté, Sellers's and Lester's notion that they could push this past the powers-that-be proved shortlived, their idea replaced with the long-running "What is a Mum?"

Shortly after this debacle, Sellers bought himself a 16mm Paillard Bolex camera, very much on the technological cutting edge of its time, and planned the making of a short film to break in his new toy. Having already shot a half day in a field with Milligan during the summer of 1958, he asked Lester to join in the fun. Armed with his gags, together with contributions from Sellers himself and Joe McGrath, Lester's graphic designer all through the TV *Goon Shows*, the group ventured out to the same field where Milligan and Sellers had already shot. With Milligan abroad, they filmed for one more day with a cast that included Leo McKern, Graham Stark and his girlfriend Audrey (later his wife), Bruce Lacey,

Johnny Vyvyan, David Lodge and Sellers's driver Mario Fabrizi. With few exceptions it was one take for everything. Lacey, a props master who worked for Granada Television, had "borrowed" a few bits and pieces for a small set, its interior lighting powered by his old prop van's batteries.

What they came up with, purely for their own amusement, was an eccentric version of a typical English Sunday, with a camping enthusiast, an avid jogger, a farsighted violinist studying his score through a telescope, then cycling across to turn a page on the music stand, a photographer developing his film in a pond, a painter (Lester!) carefully following the numbers drawn on his model's face, a gamekeeper in a frogman suit, a music fan racing around his record with a needle plowing through the grooves, and an astronaut attempting lift-off in the world's first space kite.

Taking the clapperboard off, all of the scenes were topped and tailed like french beans and the footage laid end to end and spliced together, using a table-top editing machine perched on Sellers's drum kit. The result was an eleven-minute silent movie they called *The Running, Jumping and Standing Still Film*, with Lester adding some background music he had written and recorded with four of his jazz friends and with Joe McGrath contributing the titles. The whole affair, blown up to 35mm in sepiatone, cost £70.

Sellers ran the movie for Herbert Kretzmer, the *Sunday Express* TV columnist and early *Idiot Weekly* enthusiast (now making ends meet as the writer of the English lyrics for *Les Misérables*). His reaction was immediate: "You've got to show this around." When they did and it was featured at the Edinburgh Film Festival, a representative from the San Francisco Festival took it back to the States with him, where it won first prize. The amazing snowball continued with an Academy Award nomination.

From out of nowhere "Dick" Lester had become a film director. "And I really thought I was," he recalls. "For a year, though, all I got were comments like, 'If we ever want a full-length version of your movie, we'll let you know!' " When the short was released in Britain it was initially billed as a Peter Sellers film, since he was coming off a huge hit with *The Millionairess*. Later, following the advent of *A Hard Day's Night*, it became a Richard Lester movie, and later still, after the success of *Son of Oblomov* on the West End stage, a Spike Milligan film. In the last few years Milligan claims to have directed the film by himself—quite a feat, since he was out of the country when most of the shooting took place.

For Lester it was the last time he would work with Sellers, for the jolly lad he had known was now accelerating his transformation into a deeply troubled individual. "I smoke pot to relax and understand jazz," he informed a group of musicians in Lester's presence. "We smoke pot to understand you, Peter," the leader of the group replied. Sellers turned to clairvoyancy in an effort to contact his recently deceased mother, and soon appointed his own clairvoyant, Maurice Woodruff, who advised him on his every decision. Eventually, Sellers's young second assistant, Bobby Howard, found himself fired from a movie set when he arrived one day wearing the "wrong" color of sweater that spelled bad luck.

Lester met Sellers again several years after the success of *The Running, Jumping and Standing Still Film*. By this time the world had changed for both of them—Sellers was a major movie star and Lester was a top director with the Beatles movies and *The Knack* behind him. "Wasn't it great in the old days?" was the plaintive theme Sellers pushed all through their conversation. Lester had the impression that Sellers was desperately trying to hold on the past, when things had been simpler, before the demands of wives, houses and cars and the awful pain that had entered his life.

Six months before Sellers died, the two men met again on the same Concorde flight from New York to London. There was a marvelous, sentimental reunion, and at dinner together the following evening they fondly recalled a New Year's party Sellers had thrown, where Harry Secombe had convulsed them all as he listed the imaginary activities of burglars he swore were in the house, assiduously removing Sellers's variety of toys and gadgets one by one. (Since Secombe had been the only one of the company who could actually see into the upstairs hall as he spoke, there had been just the edge of possibility that his side-splitting commentary was true.) Although Sellers's note was the same— "What a time we had back then!"—there was a warmer glow than on the previous, distinctly bitter occasion. Lester was glad for the time they had together before saying goodbye for what proved the last time.

CHAPTER FIVE

He brought to pop exactly the right qualifica-
tions—a sophisticated innocence, a brilliant
technique, an encyclopedic knowledge of
twentieth-century avant-garde experiment
and a shameless, magpie-like eclecticism.

—GEORGE MELLY

One of the main problems for James Garrett in running TV Advertising lay in finding enough directors prepared to make his commercials. There was snobbish intellectual and industrial antipathy to overcome, with established directors wanting nothing to do with television, regarded as the enemy of cinema. Although by the late fifties he was able to lure several down from their Olympian heights, using Mammon-like arguments, on the whole he was left to invent his own team of foot soldiers, trained from the ground up. (Joe Losey, as in many other particulars, was an exception to the rule. In an effort to help him control his free-spending ways Garrett doled out a single £5 note to him daily.) The field of documentary, where filmmakers were accustomed to being paid money to deliver a message, proved a fertile recruiting area. It was also a source with which Garrett was familiar, having begun his career as an assistant director at British Transport Films.

Before his ex-boss, Ronnie Dickinson, left to form his own agency, Collet, Dickinson and Pearce, he suggested that Garrett check out Lester's work, up to and including *The Running, Jumping and Standing Still Film*. Garrett liked what he saw and signed Lester up in 1960. Then began the long and lonely business of persuading advertising agencies, from whom all commissions flow, to use him. Gradually, what the tall, erudite Garrett, an individual not given to superlatives, refers to as "a goodish demonstration reel" was assembled, and after a slow start Lester became a mainstay of TVA.

One of the first commercials he produced was for Cadbury's Coaster Biscuits. He set about recruiting a bunch of kids from the local orphanage and showed them a series of drawings that could have several interpretations, encouraging them to make up little adventures of their own. During filming, the kids chattered uninhibitedly, climbed trees in a park and raided biscuit tins, all of which Lester edited into three one-minute commercials in which a totally naturalistic storyline was put across and ending, naturally enough, with a close-up of the product. After initial transmissions the Independent Television Authority began to raise all kinds of objections along the lines of, "Did you have permission to film in the park?" and "We can't have children seen eating biscuits and going straight to bed without brushing their teeth." Although the series was eventually "pulled" on the ITA's authority, it went on to win top prize in its category at the 1961 World Commercial Festival in Cannes, then America's International Broadcasting Award the following year.

Garrett says:

Richard's greatest strength lies in his ability to work out more effectively and pragmatically than anyone I've ever known the correct balance between the use of time and money, for the two are totally intertwined; if you use time well, you use money well. He's the most economical director I've ever worked with, provident to the point of being parsimonious. And he's not a double-standard man. He's careful with his own money and *extraordinarily* careful of other people's money. He will compromise, but last rather than first. He has an intellectual ability to decide on priorities and accept the inescapable.

If a call is for 8:30, he'll be there at 8:00, so crews are always punctual to match him. The camera's invariably set up by 8:30 instead of 9:00, and he's probably filmed something by 9:15, if only to prove that film can go through the gate. It might be a shot he'll later decide not to use, but it gets things going, people see that something is happening and the whole show gets on the road. Another Lester speciality is that he never sits down on any shoot. His theory is that if he does, even if nobody else physically follows, they'll sit down mentally. As for his well-known impatience, it's both a strength and a curse. I once attended a meeting with Peter Walker, Jim Slater and Jimmy Goldsmith, three intellects with laserlike minds who didn't have to conceal from each other the speed at which their minds were working. Seen separately, you know that their minds are still racing ahead, but they acquire a skill that disguises the fact, since they know it frightens and distracts lesser intellects. Richard has that problem.

He decided from the beginning to use commercials to find out about film. I'd watch him at lunchtime toy with the camera, discuss lenses and film stocks. He'd ask to be shown how to operate everything, having decided that he wasn't going to become the captive of technicians. He would visit labs and talk about processing techniques. At the same time I watched others not bother to learn the "grammar" of their trade. It can be done and they can survive perfectly well, thanks to the splendid support system we have in this country. Take that away, however, and they'd be lost. Richard hates to be ignorant of any aspect, and could never bear to be dependent on others. His authority on set as a result is total. He's a disciplinarian, not through fear, but because the crew know that *he* knows.

Lester went on to turn out hundreds of commercials for Garrett, including work for Benson and Hedges, Flower's Beer (featuring the word-mangling "Professor" Stanley Unwin), Grant's Whisky, Smith's Crisps, Hamlet cigars, Birds Eye peas and three series of After Eights. There was also a documentary commissioned by Esso on Jim Clark and Colin Chapman; Chapman's idea of building Lester's camera into his Formula One at Silverstone produced some remarkable footage. During a shoot for Smarties, Nic Roeg on camera was amused to hear Lester raise his voice in exasperation to one of the junior cast. When he impishly asked, "What about your child psychology degree?" he was rewarded with a wan smile. Garrett, on the other hand, was afforded a glimpse of his caring side when Lester returned from one casting session, plunged in gloom. "I've seen at least five children today," he said, "who are deeply emotionally disturbed and could do with clinical help. I don't know what will become of them if something isn't done about it."

Well aware that Lester was using the work as both learning process and stepping stone, Garrett resigned himself to granting him leave of absence if a movie project was offered. It didn't take long.

■

The script for *It's Trad, Dad,* a projected cheapie feature film designed to cash in on the craze for traditional jazz that was briefly flowering in Britain, arrived in mid-1961 out of nowhere, or, to be more precise, from U.S. emigré Milton Subotsky, who together with his partner Max Rosenberg had just established his ultra-low-budget Amicus banner in Britain. Lester looked through the twenty-three pages submitted, which seemed to him totally unstructured, and called Subotsky: "I've read what you sent and could be interested. As soon as you've got a first-draft screenplay, let me know."

"That's *it*," Lester was informed. "You've got my entire shooting script. That's all I've written and that's what we're going with. If it turns out too short, we can always stick another couple of numbers in." (Subotsky was already a past master of the musical quickie, second only to Sam Katzman of *Rock Around the Clock* fame. His first movie had been *Rock! Rock! Rock!* produced in the U.S. in 1956, featuring among its acts Chuck Berry, the Flamingos and Frankie Lymon and the Teenagers. The plot? Tuesday Weld has to find thirty dollars for a strapless dress for the prom.)

Lester found Subotsky an odd but thoroughly engaging character, a "cartoon American innocent abroad" with a grey crewcut, who drank a lot of milk (highly suspect, in Lester's view) was naive to the point of being downright silly, but whose one redeeming feature lay in his living, eating and sleeping movies. And however modest, *It's Trad, Dad* represented Lester's first full-length feature, as well as his first credit as "Richard Lester." (Although he now claimed that he had never liked being addressed as "Dick" or "Dickie," most of his colleagues continued to use the nicknames throughout the sixties.)

With a £2,000 fee for his services, a total budget of £60,000 and a three-week schedule projected at Shepperton studios, Lester set to work, utilizing the multiple camera technique—three, in this case—familiar to him from his work in television and on commercials. With each number filmed three times, he had nine different shots to choose from in the editing process. Between numbers the modular sets were quickly dismantled, then reassembled with variations to provide each act with a slightly different backdrop.

Paraded before the cameras was a line-up of Britain's top "traditionalists"—Acker Bilk, the Chris Barber Seven with Ottilie Patterson, Terry Lightfoot, Kenny Ball, Bob Wallis and the Temperance Seven—interspersed with pop stars Gene Vincent, Del Shannon, John Leyton and the Brooks Brothers. The leads were played by two eager, perky chart residents of the moment, Craig Douglas ("The Singing Milkman") and

Richard Lester at ease behind the camera; relatively speaking, of course.   (COURTESY OF RICHARD LESTER)

Helen ("Don't Treat Me Like a Child") Shapiro. A completely unknown group named the Beatles provided the support act on the subsequent tour Ms. Shapiro headlined.

Also gracing the movie (if that is not a contradiction in terms considering their decidedly robotic performances) were the three top disc jockeys of the era, David Jacobs, Pete Murray and Alan "Fluff" Freeman. To Lester's eternal shame he auditioned jazz and blues singer George Melly and turned him down on the basis that the two songs he recorded for the film convinced Lester that he was incapable of singing in tune for more than a few bars at a time. (If you subscribe to Melly's account, they had a dispute over "differences in material.")

Lester slid in as many *Goon*-ish jokes and surreal touches as he felt he could reasonably get away with, including live musicians stacked on shelves in a TV studio's "Music Department" and greenfly spray being trained on lettuce sandwiches in an espresso bar. In the editing process background film was hastily rearranged, visible sprockets and all, to transport characters from one locale to another, the cast interrupted the narrator, and Derek Nimmo emerged as a waiter on steroids thanks to a deft piece of fast-forward and reverse work.

Meanwhile, the first Chubby Checker Twist hit was zooming up the charts, tolling what ultimately proved the death knell of the traditionalist boom on which *It's Trad, Dad* was perilously based. Lester's prompt suggestion to Subotsky was that they try to recruit Checker; he could fly to New York, hire a cameraman and a studio and, using a simple background of drapes—presto, they would have the first movie featuring the new dance sensation *and* its original artist! Subotsky agreed, with the proviso that Lester pay his own fare to New York. This he did, making the trip even more worthwhile by lining up additional U.S. talent in the shape of Gary "U.S." Bonds and Gene McDaniels (performing "Another Tear Falls," one of the first songs by the new team of Burt Bacharach and Hal David). Checker sang "The Lose-Your-Inhibition Twist," a little ditty composed, like many others in the movie, with a beady, not-so-naive eye firmly fixed on performance rights, by none other than Subotsky himself. On Lester's return to Shepperton the shooting of the movie's final scene was staged, extras having been taught to wiggle their behinds in convincing Twist style to intersperse with Checker's own gyrations.

■

In December 1961, the Lesters moved to a modest terraced house in Ham, between Richmond and Kingston. Their son, Dominic, was born a month later. Early in the new year, with *It's Trad, Dad* awaiting release, Lester was commissioned to spend two weeks on a cruise ship to produce a twenty-five-minute 16mm promotional documentary for an early cheap travel pioneer who had leased the *Empress of Canada* and the *Empress of Britain*, normally used for Liverpool-Montreal North Atlantic runs, and was offering bargain Mediterranean tour packages. Several days after embarkation a nightmare scenario developed as the minimally paid crew began to realize that their passengers, most of whom had never been on a cruise before, had no idea of the tipping etiquette their Atlantic regulars followed. Since this was an essential perk that made their meager wages tolerable, they demanded instant renegotiations with the owner, and turned to Lester and his troupe, who were neither officer nor crew class, to act as go-betweens.

The situation went from bad to worse when passengers disembarked at Valencia and the crew were ordered to stay aboard. In the unrest that followed one of the officers accidentally killed a crew member when he fell, after a struggle, against an iron bulkhead. As Lester, back on board, was lining up his models to illustrate the delights of deck quoits, the corpses began to pile up. After two more deaths had resulted from heart attacks among the passengers, all three bodies ended up ensconced in the all-too-aptly named cold meat store. The finished documentary, designed to help travel agents entice future passenger traffic, had a distinct air of enforced gaiety.

■

Following its release in April 1962, *It's Trad, Dad* emerged, with its £300,000 take, as the second biggest grosser of the year on Britain's third circuit, a rather dubious collection of fleapits outside of the grander auspices of the Odeon and ABC chains. Even so, with the movie's miniscule budget, money poured into the coffers of Columbia Pictures, and undoubtedly filtered back, in one form or another, to the resourceful Subotsky. (Another of his songs, "Ring-a-Ding," was featured no fewer than three times in the movie and gave Columbia the idea for a change of title to *Ring-a-Ding Rhythm* for the American market.)

Of equal importance, from Lester's point of view, was the fact that the movie also received some unexpectedly good reviews. Alexander Walker in London's Evening *Standard* wryly discerned "disproportionate inspiration" in what was ostensibly an unpromising assignment, while Philip French in the *Observer* described the proceedings as "extraordinarily inventive, one of the most imaginative British movies of the decade." In the *Times* David Robinson cavilled at "Lester's immoderate interest in technical tricks—speeded-up action, multiple exposures, eccentric angles and tricky masking," while conceding that it was all done "with such frantic enjoyment and at such a determined pace that criticism is disarmed." The "most interesting aspect of this bright little film," said Variety, was "the direction of Dick Lester." If there was, as another critic pointed out, "not one memorable song performed," perhaps this highlighted Lester's highly effective box of tricks and the skillful cast of British comics he had employed—Arthur Mullard, Frank Thornton (years before *Are You Being Served?*), *Goon Show* stalwart Bruce Lacey, Hugh Lloyd, Ronnie Stevens, Derek Nimmo, Mario Fabrizi and Derek Guyler. Several critics detected echoes of the 1942 Olsen and Johnson comedy, *Hellzapoppin!* Much more to the point, three seasons with the Goons had left an indelible mark.

The element of anarchy that had seldom found a place before in such an ostensibly straightforward undertaking was craftily introduced by Lester. All of the deejays were seen as strictly self-serving charlatans, an aspect of the script that obviously soared way above their heads. Healthy cynicism was loaded into the "plot" of the small-town mayor trying to prevent the kids staging a trad jazz/rock benefit, with Lester's sympathies fairly and squarely on the side of youth. With *It's Trad, Dad* he had shown that he could deliver the goods, not only on schedule and on budget (Garrett would have been astonished had he done less) but with a highly individual touch that was instantly identifiable. Although the movie in its *Ring-a-Ding Rhythm* incarnation failed to find an audience in the U.S., Lester would not have long to wait for a breakthrough in his native land.

■

In 1959 Peter Sellers had appeared in *The Mouse That Roared*, playing three roles, in the style of his idol, Alec

Guinness. These included the lead of *Gloriana*, head of the Duchy of Grand Fenwick, the world's tiniest country, whose answer to bankruptcy is to declare war on the United States, thus qualifying, after swiftly backing down, for Marshall Aid. Based on a novel by Leonard Wibberley, the movie had been adapted by Roger MacDougall and Stanley Mann for the screen, produced by Carl Foreman and Walter Shenson and directed by Jack Arnold.

Despite its success—particularly in the States, where it established Sellers—none of the principals, with the sole exception of Shenson, was keen to contemplate a sequel. The fairly conservative Shenson was yet another expatriate American citizen, like Lester, Subotsky, the Danzigers, Losey and Carl Foreman, either disenchanted with or disenfranchised by their home country. He had served his time as a film publicist at Columbia before settling in Britain to try his luck as a producer. After *The Mouse That Roared* he misfired with *A Matter of Who*, a semi-documentary comedy thriller starring Terry-Thomas that sank without trace.

His answer was to turn to writer Michael Pertwee and commission a sequel to *The Mouse That Roared*. The scenario had Grand Fenwick's economy in a state of collapse when bottles of its "Shampain" wine, the country's sole export, begin to explode inconveniently. Under pressure to replace the Duchy's diabolical indoor plumbing, the Prime Minister applies to the U.S. for a loan, ostensibly to finance a moon shot. The U.S. goes along with the wheeze, cynically content that the space race, hitherto confined to itself and the USSR, is thus "internationalized." When Russia, terrified of being left out, contributes a used rocket, this is the cue for Grand Fenwick's resident genius, Dr. Kokintz, to discover that the exploding wine is—guess what?—the perfect rocket fuel! Hence, thirty pages later, *Mouse on the Moon*.

Adamant that he would not repeat himself, Sellers turned the project down, at the same time recommending to Shenson that he consider Lester to direct the movie. An immediate chord was struck when the two men met, and the tall, amiable Shenson offered Lester his second feature film assignment.

With Sellers's roles allocated to Margaret Rutherford (the Duchess), Ron Moody (the P.M., Count Rupert of Mountjoy) and Bernard Cribbens (the P.M.'s son, Vincent of Mountjoy), the supporting cast of David Kossoff (Dr. Kokintz), Terry-Thomas and June Ritchie fell into place, together with a virtual roll call of the finest character actors and comics in Britain, including fleeting cameos by jazzman George Chisholm and Frankie Howerd.

No stranger to a micro-budget, Lester was required to use the sets left standing from a Cornel Wilde historical epic entitled *Lancelot and Guinevere* that had been shot at Pinewood. And before the film could proceed the entire cast had to undergo a medical examination demanded by the insurance people. When the young doctor prepared to test Rutherford's blood pressure, he made fairly heavy weather of her seventy-odd years. Thoroughly upset, she "confessed" that she would be appearing in the evenings in a West End play throughout *Mouse on the Moon*'s schedule. With her blood pressure soaring in line with her mounting agitation, she failed the examination. Disaster!

Faced with the impossibility of replacing her at the last minute, Lester made a lightning calculation, estimating that he could shoot all of her scenes in two days at a cost of £9,000. If he put up his salary of £4,000 and Shenson matched it, and she either died or became too ill to complete the two days of work, the duo would guarantee the money themselves without involving the insurance company. And with Rutherford's two days in the can, Lester could use a double and long shots to see them through the rest of the film.

With the decision taken to go ahead on this basis, Lester sat the redoubtable Rutherford on a stool on her first day, with a camera running, and told her to go through all her dialogue, scene by scene, looking first to the left, then to the right. Moving swiftly along, he next asked her to turn to scene 83, where she was supposedly seated on a horse. "Look down here," he asked, pointing, "then here." At lunchtime Lester watched as the inimitable grande dame drew herself up to her full height and said to a friend, "I suppose"—a disdainful shudder of the jowls—"this is what they call the *nouvelle vague!*"

Lester knew of cinematographer Wilkie Cooper's reputation for combining speed with artistry, but was unaware of his other role. He took a call one day on the set from someone asking, "Is this Cooper Motors?" it turned out that the call was indeed for Wilkie—the busy veteran wisely kept on his day job between movie assignments, buying and selling secondhand cars. It was not a bad idea, as Lester well knew, to have more than one string to one's bow.

Although reviewers in Time magazine, *Christian Science Monitor* and Variety bemoaned the absence of Sellers, *Mouse on the Moon* fared reasonably well in running the critical gauntlet in mid-1963. Bosley Crowther in the New York *Times* found the movie "delightful," the script "droll," enhanced, if anything, by the "erratic direction." Variety noted the absence of satire and its replacement by farce, which they felt blunted the approach. Time magazine found even the farce on display "sparse" and judged some of the humor "tasteless."

Lester particularly cherished a notice from the *Times* of

London. After describing the gags as "silly but endearing," the reviewer added that the end result was "a strangely likable piece of British rubbish." He had distinctly mixed feelings, however, about the "erratic direction" Bosley Crowther had detected.

I saw *Mouse on the Moon* as having several items going for it, not least Rutherford as the ever-regal if almost totally absent Gloriana XIII commending her bandmasters' truly awful outpourings with a delighted, "Bravo. Splendid. *Such precision!*" while Prime Minister Moody goes through the motions of inspecting all six of his horseguards: "That man needs a haircut! . . . Do up those buttons! . . . *Filthy fingernails!*" Ron Grainer's jaunty music is another plus, while Maurice Binder's excellent title sequence raises expectations not entirely fulfilled. Even if the whole affair is stuck in a decidedly minor key, "delightful dotty" is still the phrase that springs to mind. Apart from a few Goon-ish contributions, like George Chisholm's wine waiter beating hasty retreat before another bottle of the Duchy's finest explodes, Lester seems to have been content simply to have steered the leaky old vessel (HMS *Ealing* Studios?) safely to the nearest port.

By the end of 1962, with the Beatles on the charts with "Love Me Do," James Garrett decided he had had enough of acting as "paid management" to an absentee landlord at TVA, and by February 1963 he had formed his own company, James Garrett and Partners, with Lester and his manager Clive Nicholas as three of the four founding partners. Peter Duffel, Philip Saville and Ken Russell were signed in quick succession (Russell's guaranteed salary of £5,000 was a considerable increase on the £3,500 the BBC had paid); later Joe Losey and Nic Roeg joined.

Lester remained Garrett's most important and prolific director throughout 1963, even while preparing for his next, groundbreaking feature assignment and an association with the most successful musical group of the century.

CHAPTER SIX

Writing for Richard I always had to fight his instinct for a joke. I write comedy, but I'm not naturally a joke writer. So when I'm writing for him I have to be a tart, a screenwriter, and put myself in the Richard Lester writing mode.

—CHARLES WOOD

The Knack began its life as a two-act play on youthful sexual politics by Ann Jellicoe. With two fingers in the pie, first as director of the Royal Court, where it ran for six weeks, then as partner in Woodfall Films, Oscar Lewenstein asked playwright Charles Wood to cook up a film treatment. Wood had two meetings with Lewenstein's first choice of director, Lindsay Anderson, who decided in the end he didn't want to get involved in the project.

After the triumphant opening of *A Hard Day's Night*, and with a further fifty commercials under his and James Garrett's collective belt, Lester and his family were on a holiday in St. Tropez in September 1964 when a telegram arrived from Lewenstein offering *The Knack*. A follow-up Beatles movie had already been discussed with Walter Shenson but was not due to start shooting until the following February, fitted around the group's increasingly hectic schedule. On his return to Britain, Lester met with the small, ascetic, gray-haired Lewenstein and his Woodfall partners, Tony Richardson and John Osborne, and agreed to look at Wood's treatment.

The two men met at Garrett's office and repaired to a nearby steakhouse for a meal. "Urged on by Oscar, I'd gone to see *A Hard Day's Night*," Wood recalls, "and loved it." The same age as Lester, Wood was a cross physically between Hemingway and Colonel Blimp and was still employed as an artist and typographer on a Bristol newspaper while moonlighting in the theater. Three short plays under the generic title of *Cockade*, starring Alfred Lynch and Norman Rossington, had been staged at the Arts Theater in 1963 and had brought Wood to the attention of Lewenstein.

The pair discovered many common interests over dinner—too many, they both admit today, insofar as the perfect working relationship is achieved most often between individuals who complement each other rather than possess similar strengths and weaknesses. In that respect, despite its initial success, the partnership was fundamentally flawed.

Wood had already developed an acute facility for investing his characters with three-dimensional life, as well as the ability to persuade audiences that they were watching characters with pasts, presents and futures beyond their appearances on the boards. But his work had a tendency to sprawl, seldom conforming to a tight, disciplined structure, and Lester is the first to admit that structure is far from his greatest strength: "I don't have that ability David Lean has of pure cinematic storytelling that is beautifully clear for every member of the audience. I'm flattering myself, but in a funny way I should have had Robert Bolt and David should have had Charles."

Before word processors were invented Wood was compulsively neat. If there was a single typing error on the page it was not enough to simply white it out; he had to start again and retype the whole page. The scripts had to look *right*, they had to look *professional*, Wood happily admitting that he found a page that *looked* good extraordinarily satisfying, almost regardless of what it said. Never having written a film script before, he was furnished with some examples by Lewenstein and, once Lester was recruited, set to work on expanding his treatment.

Jellicoe's work was completely overhauled in the collaborative process, with the character of Tom, "the man who doesn't care," jettisoned for a while until what they ended up with was a piece of total fantasy. Then they pulled the whole thing slowly back in the direction of the original piece, with Tom reinstated in different emotional surroundings that were, Lester considered, a lot more fun. Instead of opening up the play, as most films try to do, they had kept it small, inward.

Before Lester's arrival Lewenstein had already set his Woodfall regular Rita Tushingham, who had burst on the scene at the start of the decade in Tony Richardson's *A Taste of Honey*, to repeat the lead role of Nancy she had made her own at the Royal Court. The trick was to find three boys who would work around her convincingly. Lester chose Irish stage actor Donal Donnelly to play Tom, and Michael Crawford, who had appeared in a small role in Carl Foreman's *The Victors* and had received good reviews on stage in *Come Blow Your Horn*, to play the innocent Colin, the man desperate to acquire the knack with women. (Unknown to Lester, the future Phantom had already made another sex comedy, *Two Left Feet*, that lay on the shelf awaiting release.) The toughest role to cast was sex fiend Tolen, who had been

Rita Tushingham and Richard Lester having fun and forming a lasting friendship while filming *The Knack*. (COURTESY OF RICHARD LESTER)

played on stage with distinctly sadistic overtones. Lester wanted a lot more shading, someone who became ultimately pathetic, not what he seemed, someone whose confidence evaporated as his friend became more assertive. He interviewed Peter McEnery, John Hurt and Ian McKellen before finally settling on Ray Brooks, a twenty-five-year-old repertory graduate. What he liked about Brooks was that although he gave a subtle impression of sexiness, nobody in their wildest dreams would mistake him for a box-office sex symbol. He was someone, Lester felt, who could play the part of a man who has more than his fair share of romantic activity, yet retain the element of absurdity he wanted to capture; a more romantic actor would have been too believable and might have upset the balance of the comedy. Casting Tolen's various conquests was much easier work for Lester, with

Jacqueline Bissett, Jane Birkin and Charlotte Rampling handed their first screen roles after much selfless research.

The man to whom Lester entrusted *The Knack*'s cinematography was David Watkin, a commercial stalwart who made indolence seem like frantic activity, yet somehow always got the job done in Lester's demanding time frames. After joining Garrett's old stomping ground of British Transport Films in 1945, Watkin had developed a technique of using reflected light that worked particularly well with children and had been used in a commercial he made with Lester for Shredded Wheat. An experiment using white for white, instead of the standard grey or beige normally employed to avoid too striking a contrast, turned out less happily for the two men. The location was the all-white kitchen in Dun Laoghaire, Port of Dublin, of actress Barbara Mullen; the product Lyons Quick Brew tea.

While the commercial looked wonderful when projected in the studio, on television it caused a rush to tone control dials to reduce the glaring white background. This had the unfortunate effect of turning Mullen's face black. The memo from Garrett to both men was crisp and to the point: "In future bear in mind a chess board, with equal amounts of black and white." Strolling through the West End shortly afterwards, Watkin bumped into John Taylor, Mullen's husband. The couple had met while Taylor was Robert Flaherty's assistant on *Man of Aran*, where Mullen was a native islander. "Barbara's got a black face on the telly," said Taylor. "Yes, I did that," Watkin unashamedly admitted.

Completing the hat trick of key personnel on *The Knack* new to the big screen was a friend of Lester's from television, set designer Assheton Gorton.

On the eve of filming, with a budget set at £100,000 and a six-week schedule, Lester asked Watkin if it were possible to shoot an all-white Edwardian room and still capture the intricate detail of the ceiling moldings, cornices, etc. Assured that it was, he followed up by requesting that all of the movie utilize Watkin's reflected light. Aware that this could have the effect of making every scene look too bland and soft, Watkin was forced into ways of developing his technique. He found, much to his own surprise, that the challenge pushed him down several avenues of exploration he might never have considered. In 1992, his career capped by an Academy Award for his cinematography of *Out of Africa*, Watkin confided: "Richard is the reason I'm here. He put me on the map."

With filming under way, Lester suffered several anxiety attacks over whether the material he was capturing would ever fit into a cohesive whole. What he was attempting to express was his feeling for London and the youth movement, reversing the idea in *A Hard Day's Night* that the Beatles were four people who could communicate without speech; in *The Knack* he was portraying four people who spoke to each other without communicating. And he was mixing scenes having strong verbal patterns with others, such as the iron bedstead being pushed across London, much of it unscripted and made up on the hoof. Could he pull the two strands together? "I'm a born pessimist and will remain so," he joked to one visiting journalist. "Night after night I come home and bury my head in my hands, while my wife pours drinks into me and I keep saying, 'It's the end of the world!' "

Lester began a friendship during *The Knack* that endures to the present day, recognizing in Rita Tushingham a kindred spirit with a similar sense of fun, dedication and cool objectivity. "I always feel that he edits in his mind," says Tushingham. "The marvelous thing is he lets you do it, but

"This is a woman! Right?"

"Let me out of here!"

Ray McNally with Michael Crawford (top) and Michael Crawford
alone (bottom) filming *The Knack*. (COURTESY OF UNITED ARTISTS)

you know he's there and not missing a thing. It makes you feel very secure. And he'll stretch you to do things. The main thing I've learned from Richard is to play it for real, make it believable, and not to push the comedy, to simply react to outrageous things as if they're perfectly normal. A chair hanging on a wall in *The Knack*? Perfectly normal! Then he shoots from all angles, which cuts down the number of takes you have to do, and in comedy, which goes stale with repetition, that's extremely important. Apart from anything else, one is lucky in life to find friends like Richard and Deirdre. Deirdre is like my sister, and Richard is the closest director to me."

Among the rest of the cast Lester found Michael Crawford astonishing in his physical dexterity. About to shoot the waterski sequence, with the actor fully dressed in Fair Isle sweater, tweed jacket and Daks trousers, he took the precaution of hiring the waterski champion of Great Britain to oversee the event. As they stood on the Lido ready to shoot, the expert pronounced that it was impossible for someone who had never waterskied before to start on the pier and leap into the water when the rope went taut; it would be far easier to start in the water and be pulled up. Crawford confounded everyone by managing the feat, jumping from the pier and straight into the water on the second take. The only unfortunate byproduct of his abilities was the way in which they tended to alienate him from the other performers, who felt he was getting all the limelight.

Whenever he was shooting with his twin cameras in the street, and often taking over the principal camera, as is his wont, Lester employed a third, hidden camera to capture onlookers' reactions. In post-production many of these shots were overdubbed, with Lester and Wood sitting in front of a Steenbeck (an updated 'telecine') providing a running Greek chorus that would become a staple of Lester's in the future.

A house on Melrose Terrace, Hammersmith was hired for the shooting, utilizing the stairs and front room as the set, with the back rooms as office space for the production company. In one scene Nancy is shown making coffee and asks Colin if he takes sugar (he says no but she pays no attention and puts in what she thinks he *should* have, the beginning of their transition to a couple and a harbinger that things aren't going to go too well). Since the props department had no spoons for the scene, an assistant was dispatched to a neighboring house to borrow some. Several months later, looking for locations in Harrod's food hall for a scene in *Help!* Lester felt a tap on his shoulder. Turning, he found a little old lady standing there who sweetly asked, "Do you remember me?" When he confessed that he didn't, she explained, "Well, I live at number sixteen Melrose Terrace, next door to where you filmed *The Knack*. Have you finished with my spoons?"

The United Artists' executives ushered into an advance preview of *The Knack* filed out again uttering epithets like "A piece of shit," overheard with some dismay by Twickenham Studios' sound ace Gerry Humphreys. "We'll put out *The Knack* in a double bill with a cowboy feature," was the message from UA, "but only if you let us have *Tom Jones* for reissue." It was fortunate that Woodfall's Tony Richardson was in a position to call the company's bluff; it was not the first time the company had underestimated his mettle. "Don't do me any favors," UA was informed. "*The Knack* is a perfectly good picture and doesn't need a cowboy film that's been gathering dust on your shelf for years. You'll put out *The Knack* on its own. And you're *not* getting your hands on *Tom Jones*." Richardson's faith in the movie was about to be justified in the most unexpected and dramatic manner.

Britain's two official entries for the Cannes Film Festival in 1965 were Sydney Furie's *The Ipcress File*, the first of the Harry Palmer series starring Michael Caine, and Sidney Lumet's *The Hill*, with Sean Connery. That *The Knack* was invited along by the festival committee Lester felt was an honor in itself that would be hard to top. The news was broken to him while he was perched on a crane during the shooting of the scene in *Help!* where Paul is miniaturized. From the corner of his eye Lester saw editor Tony Gibbs climbing the ladder towards him and thought, "What the hell is he coming up here for?" When Gibbs reached the top he said, "Hands up, all those who haven't got a movie selected for Cannes!"

Lester managed a quick visit to the festival, accompanied by John and Cynthia Lennon, a week before the results were announced. Deirdre and Rita came over for the screening, and as they walked down the steps outside the theater afterwards the three of them turned to see who was being applauded—and found, to their confusion and delight, that it was they.

Back in Britain, the news that *The Knack* had captured the main prize, the coveted Palme d'Or, produced a mixture of utter disbelief and unabashed delight. Up until the last moment the favorites had been *The Hill*, *The Ipcress File* and Japan's *Kwaidan*; it had taken the jury, under Rex Harrison, six hours to reach their verdict. It was a tremendous boost for Lester. The Academy Award meant little to him; it was something that had never seriously crossed his consciousness, a joke vaguely connected with *The Running, Jumping and Standing Still Film*. The fact that he had won the top award at Cannes, sandwiched between the great financial success and acclaim accorded *A Hard Day's Night* and the happy shoot *Help!* had proved, was an astounding delight.

The often other-worldly Charles Wood read about the Cannes win in his morning paper and was rather taken aback, unaware that *The Knack* was even in competition. Emboldened by the thousand pounds he had received for writing the script, bolstered by an extra five hundred of "leftover" money Lewenstein had kicked in at the end, he had taken the plunge and thrown in his newspaper job in Bristol, reckoning that he had enough to live on for a year. "The movie was my start in the film world and was Richard flexing his muscles for the first time," he says today. "Before *The Knack* he hadn't done scenes with real people." Garrett, to whom the advent of the movie had come as a deep professional disappointment—he thought he had Lester back for months of commercials between Beatles assignments—saw *The Knack* from a different angle. "It was historically the first feature influenced by techniques of commercials," he maintains. "All the devices for transition and time lapses were there, together with style, lighting and form. Richard had really hit his stride."

Faced with the Cannes triumph, the same UA executives who had trashed *The Knack* now had a swift change of heart. Now there were murmurs of, "I always said it was a good movie!" A telegram was duly dispatched to Lester from the heads of the house: "OUR THANKS TO YOU AND OUR WARMEST CONGRATULATIONS ON THE CANNES AWARD A GREAT TRIBUTE TO A WONDERFUL PIECE OF WORK ARNOLD DAVID AND ALL OF US AT UA." With the cowboy co-feature to prop up the movie now dismissed as a laughable notion, a subtitle was added for general release. It was now *The Knack . . . and How to Get It.*"

Seldom has a movie so conveniently fitted in with media conceptions of the era it purported to encapsulate, especially in America. "It swells with joy," Newsweek trumpeted; the

London *Times* felt that Lester and Wood had "gaily and wisely" omitted all but the bare bones of the play, adding "glittering, extravagant variations." The New Republic compared the movie favorably to the play and described Lester as "one of the new generation of filmmakers whose ideas are purely filmic." (The final straw for Jellicoe, who hated what he had done to her work, was Edith Oliver's summary in the New Yorker: "The adaptation is total; Miss Jellicoe's play has become Richard Lester's movie.")

Time was less enthusiastic and complained that Lester's visual gags often came at the expense of characterization: "The gimmickry becomes annoying." The *Christian Science Monitor* went further, describing the movie as "restless and tasteless." To Playboy however, Lester had made "the old plot line seem like new," while Commonweal found *The Knack* "as funny in its way as the great screwball comedies of the thirties and forties. Praise goes to Lester's expert direction." To Dwight Macdonald in Esquire it was "brilliant and original" but—the sting in the tail—"overdirected and not funny." Tom Milne seemed to agree in Monthly Film Bulletin, describing it as "half awful, half excellent." In the New York *Herald Tribune* Judith Crist was in no doubt where credit for the movie's success should go: "It's Richard Lester's knack for moviemaking that makes the fragile, zany comedy one of the season's delicious delights . . . Once again he has organized disorganization into poetic flights of imagination, into film comedy that is classic in its purity and into a warmly human social commentary."

The reception generally afforded *The Knack* this author finds baffling, although it certainly fitted with Time's "Swinging Sixties" mythology. It's a movie I personally consider at best arch and at worst downright offensive, from the parody of a salesman idiotically uttering, "I must please you and I think I can" to Tushingham's "Lovely hands—and he raped me marvelous, super." That the movie found a ready response was undeniable.

Lester would quickly learn, despite *The Knack*'s success in Europe and worldwide rave reviews, just how little financial benefit the Cannes award bestowed. UA had a fallback strategy worked out with their European head of distribution, Elia Lopert. If for any reason a movie looked like a doubtful proposition, or was tainted with an unwanted certificate, it would be shuffled out of the glare of the parent label to the low-profile Lopert releasing banner in the U.S. It had happened before with *Mouse on the Moon* and would be utilized again for *The Knack* following its X-rating. Even *A Funny Thing Happened on the Way to the Forum*, "suggested for mature audiences," would receive the sideways shuffle. As a Lopert release in the U.S., *The Knack* lived up, or down, to UA's expectations by signally failing to catch on.

The Lesters, meantime, had celebrated the win at Cannes by dining at a fashionable restaurant in Beauchamps Place, where they glimpsed a signpost of nouvelle cuisine in the shape of a garnish of edible flowers. The times, it seemed, would keep on a-changing.

Jury duty at Cannes in 1966 struck Lester as distinctly Kafkaesque, with unknown individuals stopping him in the street, squeezing his shoulder and muttering epithets like, "We're counting on you!" before scurrying away. The normal number of jury members was boosted by the addition of several red-rosetted members of the French Academy, André Malraux among their number, with Sophia Loren as jury president.

A call from James Bond co-producer Harry Saltzman inviting him to his suite at the Carlton temporarily raised expectations of a job offer. Saltzman opened the door shoeless and in his shirt sleeves, affording Lester a tantalizing glimpse of the mother of all parties going on in the background. Stepping into the hallway and closing the door behind him, Saltzman glowered at him belligerently as he delivered his party piece: "Stop being rude to the other members of the jury."

"Harry, what are you talking about?" Lester spluttered. "I can only just say 'Bonjour,' let alone be rude to anyone."

"You know what I mean," Saltzman snarled. "Just live and let live—all right?" So saying, he opened the door, allowing Lester several seconds to assume he was about to be invited in, then slammed it in his mystified face.

Several days later, with the episode still unexplained, the jury assembled for decision time at the villa of the Begum Aga Khan, with a dip in the indoor pool organized before deliberations began. After a swim with the magnificent Sophia it was down to work, with Lester and several other members, Peter Ustinov included, opting for Henning Carlsen's *Hunger* for Best Film, with its star Per Oscarsson as Best Actor. "Yes, Oscarsson was wonderful, and *Hunger* is very fine," festival organizer Favre Le Bret agreed, "but let's stop talking Best Film for the moment and concentrate purely on Best Actor." With a majority in favor of Oscarsson, Le Bret moved on to Best Film nominations and was met, from Lester and Ustinov's corner, with a chorus of *"Hunger."*

"You can't do that," he protested.

"What do you mean?" Ustinov asked.

"You can't award two major prizes for the same film."

"Yes, you can," said Lester. "Last year *The Collector* got Best Actor and Best Actress."

As the argument raged back and forth two films that had barely been mentioned up until then were put forward. In the end *Hunger* was neatly eased out and a dead heat announced between *A Man and a Woman*, from France, and *Signore I Signori* from Italy. With his confrères busily dismissing any suggestion that the result had the remotest connection with the co-production deal the two countries had just signed, Le Bret's announcement that a lobster souffle was due to be served at 1 P.M. left precisely eleven minutes for the remaining five categories to be settled.

As for the gypsy's warning from Harry Saltzman, Lester discovered that Saltzman had produced Orson Welles's entry, *Chimes at Midnight*. Instead of the hoped-for Best Film prize, Welles was given a special award instead for his contribution to world cinema. Undeterred, the doughty Saltzman ran ads in both Variety and Screen International trumpeting that the film had won Best Film, refusing, in his own mind at least, to accept that it was for anything less.

During the last few days of the festival a young man approached Lester and explained that he had written and produced two low-budget films being shown on the Rue D'Antibes at midnight—would Lester please go and see them? He explained that this was difficult, since he and Deirdre had their three-year-old son with them and it was proving impossible to get babysitters. "No problem," the eager youngster assured Lester. "If you go and see my movies I'll babysit for you." He and his wife were thus able to see the two pictures, made for around $30,000 each, and were duly impressed. Fifteen years later Lester was padding down the corridor of the Bel Air Hotel in Beverly Hills when a well-known face approached him. "Richard!" he was greeted. "How are you? And how's Dominic?" Lester was amazed that Jack Nicholson still remembered his son's name and his babysitting activities after all those years.

Before the end of the trip Lester took a call from Irving "Swifty" Lazar, an agent legendary in his own lunchtime, offering representation. Over lunch at the Hotel du Cap the ineffable nattiness of his outfit of navy blazer, white yachting trousers, cap and tie was somewhat besmirched when young Dominic inadvertently spilled tomato soup, complete with croutons and a light sprinkling of basil, into Lazar's lap. Although the agent behaved impeccably, biting back his obvious annoyance as a welter of waiters instantly appeared with pristine linen towels. Lester remembers his first thought: "Uh-oh, this is *not* going to work!" (As a proud father his second was, "My son does *not* spill cheap soup!")

What the two men agreed to try was a loosely based "as and when" arrangement. If Lazar came up with an interesting project that reached fruition, he would collect his percentage. For several years thereafter a Christmas hamper arrived from the diminutive dynamo. These were initially spectacular, but grew less so with each succeeding year as the definition of "interesting project," not to mention "fruition," grew increasingly tenuous. In the end it was down to a modest bottle of bubbly.

CHAPTER SEVEN

"Let's face it, we just mutter a few words now and then and Dick Lester tells us how to do it."

—GEORGE HARRISON

With a meeting arranged at Annabel's nightclub with Paul, Ringo and Jane Asher to describe his ideas for the second Beatles movie, Lester made an appointment at University College Hospital to have a small growth on his head looked at. Having assumed they would merely examine him, he was distinctly nonplussed as a local anesthetic was administered and they proceeded to remove the offending lump there and then. Off he went to Annabel's immediately afterwards, a great wad of adhesive covering the wound. He remembers giving a woozily garbled version of *Help!* to an increasingly concerned group.

The first idea for the *Hard Day's Night* sequel was based on Ringo, unable to stand the pressure any longer of being "the one at the back," and deciding to end it all. When he wakes up in the morning he remembers meeting a stranger in a bar the night before who offered to do him in. Drunk, Ringo had agreed; in the cold light of day he panics. Furthermore, he can't remember the identity of his hired killer, so from now on everyone is suspect.

Unfortunately, it happened that a movie was being made in France with an almost identical plot. It was the sequel to Philippe de Broca's *The Man from Rio*, starring Jean-Paul Belmondo, eventually to languish unreleased as *The Chinese Gentleman from China*.

In many ways Lester was caught between the devil and the deep blue sea, squeezed from both sides by Shenson and the group. The boys, Shenson decreed, "should never be made to do anything in the film that will reflect badly on them, since kids will imitate them." And Epstein still wanted the Beatles to play themselves—but minus smoking, drinking and sex. Of all of them John was most vociferous that there was no question of any "corny teenage romance aspect." George also had his say: "We couldn't ever have made a film like the usual thing; we had lots of offers to have the group playing at the high school dance and that sort of rubbish and we just didn't want to know. We wanted it to be *our film*." In short, they had to be passive, innocent bystanders in whatever plot was dreamt up.

What the movie became was a pop art version of Wilkie Collins's *The Moonstone*, with Ringo stalked for a rare jewel in his possession. The original screenplay they found, entitled *Eight Arms to Hold You*, had first been submitted to Peter Sellers by Marc Behm, writer of the Cary Grant–Audrey Hepburn hit, *Charade*. "Have a go at it," Lester urged Charles Wood. Unlike *The Knack*, which had gone through several drafts, Wood spent just ten days on the redraft, which Lester was obliged to run past United Artists' Bud Ornstein.

Together with Shenson, he flew to Monte Carlo and made for the Hotel de Paris, where Ornstein greeted them with huge drinks served in enormous crystal tumblers. Immaculately dressed in a navy three-piece suit accessorized by gold cuff links, tie clasp and rings, and seated in an indoor swimming pool and sauna complex of Babylonian proportions, Ornstein was surrounded by a bevy of exotically beautiful females. "You look exhausted," he informed the new arrivals. "Have a swim first, then relax with your drinks."

As they emerged dripping, Ornstein sat them down and began the conference immediately, while the harassed, totally disadvantaged pair embarrassedly adjusted their borrowed bathing trunks, blushed at the surrounding girls and struggled to match the instant-business mode the executive had adopted. Lester had often heard the stories of how Columbia chief Harry Cohn had placed his desk so that the light blinded his victims, who already found themselves closer to the floor than they were accustomed since their chair legs had been cut down. This was the first time he had experienced the technique. Despite their enforced discomfort, however, he and Shenson carried the day and eased the script past Ornstein's list of concerns. Even as they left, Ornstein was still expressing reservations and would later describe the material as "fourth-rate Marx Brothers stuff, not really suited for the group's talents. But I guess the train was on the track and demand for a new Beatles picture was so great that I didn't get anywhere, not even with Epstein." ("It was just an assignment," says Charles Wood today. "I don't think I did a particularly good job.")

Following the grudging clearance, Lester failed to re-enlist his *Hard Day's Night* cameraman, Gilbert Taylor, who thoroughly disapproved of the hysteria the first movie had produced. The assignment was handed instead to David Watkin; it would be his and Lester's first feature in color.

Lester disliked *Eight Arms to Hold You* as a title and wanted to call the movie *Help!* before discovering that the title had been copyrighted in America. When it came time to shoot the title sequence, in February 1965, since no one had been able to come up with an alternative he decided to take a chance and go with *Help!* reasoning, correctly as it turned out, that it was such a common word they would never be sued. The Beatles left in their car that night and were driven home; by the time they reached St. John's Wood forty-five minutes later, John and Paul had the title song written. Next day it was recorded, and the day after that the film's title sequence was shot at Twickenham.

Perhaps bearing in mind the strictures of the formidable Groucho, Lester decided to exaggerate the differences between the four Beatles on this occasion, pushing their images further apart than they had been in *A Hard Day's Night*, making George both a romantic and a cheapskate who never pays for a drink; John ultra-sarcastic and satirical; Paul the sexually cocky individual the fans kept winking at; Ringo the lovable one stuck with an inferiority complex—little bits of business he could work into almost every scene. "In reality," Lester admits, "this was far from the truth. They were a mixture of all these things." Still and all, he reasoned, Jack Benny had lasted for years with his schtick of playing the violin badly and being miserly . . .

Most of *Help!* was shot with the group high on marijuana. Since they all had considerable difficulty remembering Wood's often complex dialogue as a result, Lester developed a technique of reciting one line at a time to them, which they repeated back. This time around, the acting competition was fiercer than on *A Hard Day's Night*. Victor Spinetti, Bruce Lacey and John Bluthal were back, the comic team augmented by Patrick Cargill and joined by relative heavyweights Leo McKern and Eleanor Bron.

Location filming in the Bahamas was chosen purely to avoid British tax liabilities, for which purpose "consultant" Dr. Walter Strach had taken up temporary residence. Epstein later began to have doubts about the purity of his motives in diverting cash to the islands when an associate of the good doctor's, James Isherwood, was alleged to have misappropriated funds from Woodfall Films. Advice was sought from the venerable Lord Goodman, who advised Epstein to pay the taxes and have done with it.

A Boeing 707 was chartered to take the cast and crew to Nassau. Flying first class were the Beatles, producer Shenson, Lester, Deirdre and three-year-old Dominic, Bron, McKern and Watkin. The Beatles lit up immediately after takeoff and never stopped giggling all through the entire five-hour leg of the journey to New York, with young Dominic heartily joining in the laughter. Unaware that they were high most of the time, Deirdre saw the group as "four silly boys." Of the four there was no doubt in her mind that John was "by far the sexiest."

The group were in for a shock when the plane landed, with a flight attendant informing them that they were required to disembark and go through U.S. customs in New York. They all flatly refused, John with particular vehemence. For a while, with a massive crowd and huge media presence on the runway, it was stalemate. In the end the Beatles and their stash were allowed to depart unexamined, a famous first victory against the U.S. Department of Immigration. The only extra baggage brought on board was a load of 150 teddy bears from Paul's fans (jelly beans having had their day). A delighted Dominic found himself buried for the remainder of the flight under the huge pile of teddies. As anticipated, the fastidiousness of Customs on the island was on a somewhat lower level than had been anticipated in New York.

Apart from the joints that had taken over from ciggies, the only time Lester had any hint of the drugs with which the group was involved came during location work on Paradise Island, while shooting a scene featuring models from America on Huntington Hartford's estate. There he accidentally overheard two of the most beautiful women he had ever seen, dressed in identical, stunning black swimsuits, try to coax Paul into taking heroin. The combination of their sexual come-on and enticement towards hard drugs was one of the most chillingly evil moments Lester has ever encountered, a numbing experience he will never forget. His sense of relief when Paul rebuffed the twosome was profound. Ringo unexpectedly presented a different kind of problem when one of his eyebrows turned white and he developed a distracting nervous tic, obliging Lester to constantly cut away even from long shots. It was symptomatic, he reflected, of the incredible strain under which the group constantly lived and worked.

He had a tense moment of his own filming a stuntman suspended from a Goodyear blimp and supposedly laying a trail of footsteps halfway up a wall for the Beatles to follow. Although the wire, couplet and supporting harness were normally more than adequate, the daredevil had overlooked the fact that the contraption's immersion in salt water on his last movie had rotted its webbing; when half of the harness ripped apart he tipped perilously to one side. Lester saw the whole thing from his vantage point in the blimp and yelled to the pilot through the cacophony—he describes it as like being in a steel box with a lawnmower engine going full throttle—to head out to sea before the harness collapsed altogether. Instead, the pilot was able to lower his craft so that the ground crew could disentangle their dangling colleague, with only light bruising to show for the episode. The spectacular emergence of the huge statue of the Goddess Kali from the sea posed a different set of problems. Built out of polystyrene blocks back at Twickenham and flown out in bits, it had to be weighted down until the time came for it to emerge hydraulically from the ocean floor. Lester was on the point of scrapping the notion when the riggers were finally able to surface Kali with some dignity and virtually no sign of the wobbles.

With George's twenty-first birthday looming during their stay, the ever-so-slightly sinister Dr. Strach organized a party in his honor without letting him know that in his kindly, highly manipulative way he had summoned press representatives from around the globe. Aware of the betrayal this represented, Lester watched apprehensively as George, his features like something cast in granite, approached the enormous cake Strach had laid out and accepted the knife he was offered. After cutting the first slice with icy calm, he hacked a second slice, stabbed through the cake for the third, then slowly demolished what was left. Laying down the knife quietly on the plate, he looked across the table at the startled Strach. "Thanks for the lovely party," he whispered, turned and walked out.

George's cake destruction apart, Lester witnessed several other occasions when all four of the group stepped out of character, often when extreme tiredness had set in. Ringo reached the end of his tether one day when one of the press poked a camera though a car window in his face. Startled and furious, he stubbed his lighted cigarette out on the photographer's wrist. (Ringo on the Bahamas: "I hate fucking sand.") John was the one who broke loose more than all the others combined. When he did, he could be especially cold and vicious, although the others were usually able to change his mood by drawing on their vast repertoire of in-jokes.

Lester shot a sequence in what he had been told was an abandoned and disused mental institution, which turned out still to have several patients held in particularly nasty conditions. The governor of the Bahamas gave a dinner in honor of the film crew that night, with Lester and the Beatles as special guests. John chose his moment and laid into the governor briefly but tellingly about the intolerable state of the inmates.

The general feeling of condescension towards the group, emanating especially from the officials' wives, cut deep. In conversation with Rolling Stone's Jann Wenner, John recalled "being insulted by these jumped-up middle-class bitches and bastards who would be commenting on our working-classness and manners. I couldn't take it, it would hurt me, I would go insane, swearing at them, whatever . . . it was a fuckin' humiliation."

During filming one day a little man stopped by, carrying a heavy bundle on a stick over his shoulder. Unwrapping this at the side of the road, he handed a book to Lester and one to each of the four Beatles. They were all to do with meditation techniques, the first contact the group had with Indian mysticism. When, much later, George tried to recruit everyone to follow the Maharishi Mahesh Yogi, he coaxed Lester and his wife to attend one of his classes. On her arrival Deirdre observed one of her ex-dancers in attendance; together they had a good giggle, spelling the end of Deirdre's involvement and, shortly thereafter, Lester's. While George was claiming he had met a man who was two thousand years old, John walked past and cracked "Yeah, and he's still wearing the same fucking suit." The exchange seemed to Lester to sum up both their personalities in a nutshell.

After moving the unit to Austria, Lester invited all of the cast and crew to a birthday party for his assistant, Clive Reed, taking over the entire downstairs of their ski chalet. Lester played piano, Paul drums, while George and John alternated on the guitars the house band had left behind, playing until four in the morning with the guests—Leo McKern, Victor Spinetti, John Bluthal and Eleanor Bron among them—all maintaining it was one of the best parties they had ever attended. As far as Reed was concerned, it was one of the highlights of his life. (Ringo on Austria: "I hate fucking snow.")

Lester discovered that if there was a choice Paul would always take the drums, for which he had a good technique, while John's choice would be piano. Ringo played piano as well, but with more bravura than style. A quarter of a century later, during the filming of Paul and his band's world tour at Wembley Arena, a sound check caused a half-hour lull. As Lester sat down at the nearest piano, Paul strolled up and said, "Okay, Dick, play 'My Funny Valentine' in C." Lester was astonished that, a quarter of a century later, Paul still remembered the incorrect key in which he had played it in Austria.

The sense of release Lester had captured in the "Can't Buy Me Love" sequence in *A Hard Day's Night* was duplicated in *Help!* with the ski sequence. Since none of the Beatles had ever donned skis before, Lester briefly toyed with the idea of using doubles in long shot. Instead, the group strapped on their skis and attacked the mountain with brio, fooling around with exactly the uninhibited abandon Lester wanted. During production of *The Knack* Lester had received an urgent call to forward a clip to the *Ed Sullivan Show* of "You

Can't Do That," a song that had been excluded from *A Hard Day's Night*. He was up to his ears at the time; so, for that matter, was his *Hard Day's Night* editor, John Jympson. The individual entrusted with the task was one John Victor Smith, who went on to do a first-class job. With Jympson again unavailable for *Help!* Lester turned once more to Smith. His cutting of the ski sequence, mixing "Ticket to Ride" on the soundtrack, confirmed Lester's belief that he had made a great choice.

All during the shooting of *Help!* there was always a piano around, on which Paul was constantly tinkering. He was working on one particular song that was slowly driving everyone mad as it came together piece by piece. Finally, Lester had had enough. "If I hear that once more," he told Paul only half jokingly, "I'll have that bloody piano taken away. What's it called anyway?" "Scrambled Egg," Paul replied. Lester heard no more about it until he was shooting his next movie in Spain, when an album arrived with a note from Paul: "I hope you like 'Scrambled Egg.' " The tune had emerged as "Yesterday," his most valuable copyright.

Back in London the Astors' Cliveden mansion doubled as Buckingham Palace, as well as Lambeth Palace for the meeting of the bishops. During a lunch break from shooting in their magnificent formal garden, the crew came up with the idea of a relay race between the production staff, electricians and actors, consisting of five sixty-yard dashes. Lord Astor, confined to bed as he was after suffering a heart attack, entered into the spirit of the event by offering a bottle of vintage champagne to the winners.

The Beatles at first ignored the mounting excitement of the competition, with John summing up what to them was a nonevent as "daft." Suddenly there was a change of heart as the group, with the addition of a gofer, entered their own team. "No chance," the crew scoffed, having watched them smoke like chimneys for weeks past. And they were wearing their ordinary street shoes!

Against all the odds, the Beatles wiped the floor with the competition. Ringo, who was extraordinarily fast, offered this explanation to the bemused crew: "If you'd done as many sixty-yard dashes as we have, picking up things that had fallen off lorries, you'd have won as well." With the champagne prize turned down, they settled instead for one of Lord Astor's canisters of oxygen and spent the rest of the lunch hour next to him, sitting on his bed and sniffing furiously.

In the middle of a day's shoot in Bond Street, Lester filmed the group drawing up outside Asprey's in an unmarked car, jumping out and running into the store. They were inside for a maximum of twenty seconds, with the camera left rolling since he planned to lay subtitles on the shot. Then they reappeared, jumped into their waiting car and were driven off before onlookers even realized the Beatles had been and gone. Before he left, Lester thanked the store manager for his cooperation. "Thank *you*," came the reply. "While they were here, John spent £800."

Charles Wood was asked along to watch several scenes that were shot in England and took his six-year-old daughter Kate out to Salisbury Plain, where she remembers sitting on both Ringo's and John's knees in their caravan between takes. For another scene, set in the corner of an Indian restaurant, Lester and Wood thought it would be amusing if they had a small Indian band playing a selection of Beatles hits, and set about finding an arranger who could transnotate between Indian and English scales and rhythmic structure. This individual was handed the sheet music of *A Hard Day's Night*, and as they began their run-through, Lester ordered a microphone wheeled in and recorded their first, absolutely hysterical attempt at sight-reading the Indian's notation on tabla, sitar and flute. George appeared just as the trio were finishing and stopped in his tracks, pointing at the sitar. "What's that?" he asked. Minutes later, fascinated, he was fiddling around on the instrument; within a few months everyone in the pop world was following his lead, and Ravi Shankar was filling the Festival Hall.

When the group was made up in their various disguises in *Help!* the idea was to make each of them look as they would in twenty-five years' time, complete with facial hair and Victorian glasses. Within just ten years, Lester noted with some amusement, they all looked uncannily like their movie images.

With the opening of *Help!* Lester's honeymoon with the critics ended. "Not up to predecessor's standards," Hollis Alpert maintained in Saturday Review. Suggesting comparisons now with Abbott and Costello rather than the Marx Brothers. Time magazine found the spontaneity of *A Hard Day's Night* replaced by "highly professional, carefully calculated camera and cutting." "Funny, though sometimes forced," thought Playboy. In London the *Times* detected "some sense of strain, more careless and slapdash, thus less funny." John Coleman in New Statesman found too many "cavortings and poses" while still finding the movie "charming and funny." Bosley Crowther in the New York *Times* felt that *Help!* lacked whatever had made *A Hard Day's Night* special despite the "interesting camera tricks," while Alan Dent in Illustrated London News was won over, despite what he described as the Beatles' "deplorable music," by the "zest and gusto" in the style of—guess who?—the Marx Brothers. "Hit or miss," thought Brendan Gill in the New Yorker, while Stanley Kauffman in New Republic felt that the movie's main problem lay in its easy comparison to *A Hard Day's Night*, since the emphasis on plot made *Help!* a different kind of film and one that succeeded "largely due to Lester's cinematic sensitivity." Variety found the camera work "a delight," but deemed that "in some sequences Lester overindulges himself."

Despite the praise heaped on the Beatles themselves in *A Hard Day's Night*, few reviewers singled them out in *Help!* In French Cinema Pierre Philippe's description of the group as "too passive" signposted John's disaffected comment that they had become "guest stars in their own movie," much of which he saw as "bullshit." And indeed it was in my view—frantic, forced, unfunny and plain silly, redeemed only by the group's songs. Lester's fondness for the movie, I guess, reflects the fun it was to make rather than what ended up on the screen.

Although *Help!* proved virtually critic-proof, with an identical worldwide take to that of *A Hard Day's Night*, it was considered a let-down in view of its vastly increased budget, more than double that of its predecessor, as well as the expectations it had raised that it might go through the roof. While UA's romance with Lester would continue for several more movies, their relationship with Shenson was, surprisingly enough, at an end. Several years after the release of *Help!* Shenson described UA's executives as "tough, laconic and intelligent, a shrewd bunch when it came to distributing profits, but fair and prepared to negotiate disagreements." His beef was with the lack of continuity he was offered:

They will "go" on a director almost every time if the experience with him has been good, whereas a producer's plight is one of proving himself afresh each time with a new package. You would have thought they'd have been at my door saying,

"What have you got?" Instead, the situation was simply that of saying, "Our door is always open." I think that these days when distributors do not develop their own properties they should get down on their knees and thank God for the producer, without whom they would not be in business. The money they pay one is not enough. A producer's pride, his mettle, his vision have got to be recognized just as much as a director's. If he weren't there, the picture wouldn't be there either.

Shenson continued to produce films over the years, from *A Talent for Loving* (originally acquired for the Beatles) to *Reuben, Reuben* in the eighties, without ever recapturing the same dizzy heights of success he had achieved with Lester and the Beatles. If you have tears, however, prepare to forget them now. With all of the residual rights to both *A Hard Day's Night* and *Help!* reverting back to him fifteen years after the movies were made, Shenson has earned a second fortune from television, theatrical and video rights to add to the original bounty they first produced. Today he owns 99 percent of both Beatles films—the other 1 percent he handed over to Lester several years ago as a bonus.

Lester acknowledges that, like Shenson, his association with the Beatles truly changed his life. If *A Hard Day's Night* had not been the success it was, Woodfall would never have offered him *The Knack*. He probably would have continued to make movies, but it would have been a longer, harder process before making his mark. What his hits with the Beatles provided was not only financial success, but emergence as a media personality in his own right. Between the release of *A Hard Day's Night* and *Help!* he was asked to pose for a succession of top photographers—everyone from Richard Avedon, Terry Donovan and David Bailey to Cecil Beaton and Lord Snowdon. Then there were fan letters from all over the world—hundreds from the States, a steady stream even from behind the Iron Curtain. He had emerged as a personality in his own right, a "happening," in-demand figure in the swinging sixties.

■

The problem with iconoclasm is that once the condition makes him famous, the perpetrator himself becomes an icon and subject to demolition by the media; live by the word and image, die by them. So it was that by September 1965, even as lines lengthened outside movie theaters showing *The Knack* and *Help!*, the satirical magazine Private Eye decided to have a go at Lester. The caricature of him accompanying the article, wearing a badge inscribed "I AM A BORE," gave a clue to its contents. They conceded that his "frenetic, pyrotechnic, gagpacked style" had framed the "up-to-the-minute authentic echo" of the Beatles fans' zeitgeist. He had even, they asserted, made the "dear dead days of Woodfall"—the working-class romanticism of John Schlesinger and Tony Richardson—look like something from another age (they seemed to have forgotten that *The Knack* had been made for "dear dead Woodfall").

After quoting Lester accurately as saying that he wanted his films to have instant impact—"for me there's nothing lasting"—they described *Help!* with its "jazzy photography, colored filters, zooms, speed-ups and hypnotic soundtrack" as two separate films—one with a fast-moving surface, the other a lumbering, painful, boring B-picture with a lousy, jokeless script.

They admitted that while *The Knack* was a different proposition, containing "vestiges of an imaginative play in its script," it followed the same distraction principle as *Help!*, overlaying "a ceaseless, unremitting, pile-driving cornucopia of half-remembered silent film gimmicks and unfunny sexual double-entendres, ill-timed pieces of slapstick and the sort of corny, repetitious jokes that one might expect from a fairly humorless ex-student of psychology at an American university." Private Eye's conclusion was stark indeed:

> The tragedy of Mr. Lester is that he thinks, as do his intellectual admirers, that he will go on being able to parade Instant Amusement for the Here And Now forever. He may espouse ephemerality. He may eschew the desire to be remembered in years to come. But he will still, himself, wish to go on eating and making films in the years to come. And he will be hoist by his own petard . . . He is a craze, a trend, a delusion. And his day will soon be over.

If the author of this awful warning (many of whose views I shared at the time) had but known it, Lester's alleged plundering of the film archives amounted to less than many filmgoers see in a good month, let alone a lifetime. And although his films indeed mirrored their time, surely that was their intention? Lester was being judged on his own, possibly ill-judged remarks as well as his movies, despite his potential for development. For the moment, however, he was clearly in the ascendancy.

CHAPTER EIGHT

Lester probably lost as much as he gained by his association with the Beatles; for years he was overshadowed by the pop-idol images he had done much to create.

—JAMES MONACO,
American Film Now

With the release of *Mouse on the Moon*, *A Hard Day's Night*, *The Knack* and *Help!*, Lester had made four hits in a row, two modest and two smash, for United Artists. For some time the company had been developing a film version of *A Funny Thing Happened on the Way to the Forum*, the Broadway smash with music and lyrics by Stephen Sondheim and story by Burt Shevelove and Larry Gelbart. Although comedy writer Melvin Frank was signed to write, produce and direct the movie, UA's confidence began to wane as rewrite followed rewrite with his collaborator Michael Pertwee. What if, they suggested to Frank, he stayed on as writer and producer but someone else was brought in to direct the $3 million movie? Although less than thrilled at this vote of reduced confidence, Frank was given little choice. When he approached Lester at UA's request, it seemed like predestination; Deirdre had even choreographed the London stage production.

Frank, together with his former partner Norman Panama, had belonged as youngsters to the squad of gag writers employed by Bob Hope. The legend was that Hope retained six teams of writers, each of whom separately wrote his entire half-hour radio show. The day before the broadcast, they would all meet at the comedian's house, their contributions laid out on a card table. With a razor blade Hope would cut out the gags he liked and throw the rest away. All twelve writers, known to the outside world as "Hope's Dwarfs," would watch the performance, in the process developing a series of nervous tics and other mannerisms that remained with many of them for life. Along the way Frank and Panama still managed to rack up an enviable list of film credits, writing and co-directing *Knock on Wood*, the hit Danny Kaye comedy in 1954 and receiving an Oscar nomination for their work, and continuing the Hope association from *My Favorite Blond* in 1942 to *The Facts of Life* in 1959 and *The Road to Hong Kong* in 1962. Frank's switch to Michael Pertwee as his co-writer on *Strange Bedfellows* in 1965 had proved less successful.

Although the tall, massive Frank was not exactly an old-age pensioner at forty-nine, Lester's impression was that Frank saw him as a very young man who would do precisely as he was told, interpreting his script on the button, exactly as written. He had no wish to comply, aware that UA's insistence on a fresh director had stemmed from their script concerns. It was simply far too long, theatrical and cumbersome, and this was producing serious budget problems. Quick as a flash, Frank provided the obvious answer. "How many pages can you shoot a day?" Lester was asked. "About two minutes a day, or two pages," he replied. Off Frank went to the production people. "How much does it cost to shoot each day?" Armed with this information, he concluded that he had to lose two weeks' shooting, or twenty pages. "Okay, leave it to me," a baffled Lester was informed. Frank then spent several days removing adjectives from the stage directions. If before they had read, "Pseudolus comes racing round the corner and suddenly turns tail as he sees the lecherous Lycus approaching," it was now amended to, "Pseudolus turns corner, meets Lycus."

"There," he announced triumphantly. "It's twenty pages shorter, we've saved the money." Lester swore that all he could do was to stare at him incredulously.

When he and designer Tony Walton traveled to Spain to check out the use of Samuel Bronston's standing sets for *The Fall of the Roman Empire*, they concluded that the cost of keeping the scaffolding in place was going to be higher than building a new set. They found another area thirty miles outside of Madrid that was more in keeping with their proposed style. Rather than attempt to duplicate the grandeur that was Rome in its heyday, they wanted it to look more like a latter-day Hounslow. The construction of a small village was planned, consisting of slum dwellings, a few two-story houses, an aqueduct, butcher's shops, slave markets—a *working* village, all higgledy-piggledy and authentic.

With Lester back from the trip and busily fine-tuning *Help!*, Frank asked Walton to show him around the proposed site. Frank was horrified at what he saw. "You can't build a set here," he declared. "This is a *musical* we're going to make, Tony, and you've chosen a hillside site . . ."

"I know. Richard and I talked it over and we decided it would be ideal."

"*Ideal?* You'll never get a crane up the hill. You've got to have flat ground for the crane."

"We talked about that. Richard doesn't intend to use a crane."

"That's *ridiculous!* You can't shoot a musical without a crane, for Chrissakes!"

Lester stuck to his last despite a torrent of calls from Frank. The working village was duly built and populated with the inhabitants of a nearby hamlet. The butcher chopped meat, the potter potted, the baker baked, while all of them filled the set with their families and animals, living their normal lives for the whole period of shooting. When Lester needed to film them, there they were doing what they were supposed to be doing, making and plying their wares. When flies and wasps obligingly descended on cue, Lester felt he had exactly the Roman slum he had been seeking.

Basically, because he wanted no changes made in his masterpiece, Frank adamantly refused to allow Lester another writer to work with. Co-writer Pertwee was especially out of bounds despite his familiarity to Lester from *Mouse on the Moon*. In an attempt to rework at least some of the script, Lester invited Nic Roeg, his focus-puller from the Danziger days, now a full-fledged cinematographer, to share his rented house outside of Madrid. Although they did what they could, with Roeg someone Lester could talk to, a friend he could bounce ideas off, their work was only half finished by the time shooting began. Several visual touches had been added that Frank had never intended, and his climactic chase sequence, which had gone on for almost two reels, had been heavily cut; the junior leads of Hero and his girlfriend Philia had been built up, with an element of parody introduced. What they had was the remnants of a Broadway musical with visual "bits." As far as Lester was concerned, any change had to be for the better. Meanwhile, Frank had drawn blood by having UA fire associate producer Denis O'Dell, an individual viewed as "Lester's man."

He began to demand additional sequences, like having all

the dancing girls in the brothel sequence gyrating to a background of the "flags of all nations." How do you tell someone, Lester pondered, that "flags of all nations" didn't exist at the time? And the superimposition of anachronism, *Boys from Syracuse*-style, was the very last thing he wanted.

By the time shooting was under way, the producer thoroughly hated his director. Lester was ruining his material, he railed to UA, and wouldn't agree to anything he suggested. Open warfare was avoided only when Frank was persuaded to stay away during filming. Instead, he busied himself as best he could, was always around to greet a new actor's arrival, and played poker with John Victor Smith, Lester's editor, who had worked with Frank before—quite happily, it seemed—on the last Hope-Crosby movie, *The Road to Hong Kong*.

A new problem emerged almost from day one. Joining Zero Mostel as Pseudolus, Jack Gilford as Hysterium, Buster Keaton as Erronius, Michael Crawford as Hero, Annette Andre as Philia and Michael Hordern as Senex was Phil Silvers as Lycus the brothelkeeper. If Lester thought he was bringing with him the rapid-fire wit and timing of Sgt. Ernie Bilko, he had another thought coming.

It was clear that Silvers was going through a terrible trauma in his life—his wife was leaving him because he couldn't stop gambling and his daughters were disowning him. After failing to turn up one day, he was discovered on the floor of his hotel room in Madrid reciting, over and over again, what he knew of The Lord's Prayer. "How about that guy?" Frank yelled when the news reached him. "It's not even his goddamn religion!"

When he eventually put in an appearance, he had trouble remembering his lines. And Lester had already decided, further eschewing anachronism, that Silvers must give up his trademark Bilko spectacles and wear contact lens instead, which many felt made him unrecognizable. When one of Silvers's contact lens dropped into a field during production, Lester and the entire unit were discovered on their hands and knees by a visiting battalion of UA executives.

Mostel had problems of his own during the first couple of days of shooting, with a severe case of Spanish tummy. Although Lester kept meaning to reshoot several of these early scenes, with Mostel visibly not up to form, this proved impossible in the rush to meet his schedule. When Mostel was restored to full health and strength, Lester was forced to watch his performance go stale as take followed take while Silvers struggled to master his dialogue.

He found Mostel a warm, delightful man, extremely protective of Silvers and covering up for him on every possible occasion. Although not a film actor per se, and despite his elephantine build, he had a balletic grace and moved superbly. Lester considered that this made him look best in long shot, the equivalent of his home turf, the stage; whenever the camera zoomed in for a close-up, all you saw was an old man with funny hair bobbing around.

The problem was that Lester was unable to stay in long shot in every scene involving Silvers, obliged to cut away instead from his constant fluffing of lines to Mostel in close-up. For one scene alone, in which he wanted the two actors to stroll down a street, talking in long shot, no fewer than eighteen cuts had to be inserted, with Silvers able to remember only one line at a time. Another of his phobias was a terror of heights, and Mostel gamely volunteered to grasp his ankles out of shot during a balcony scene.

A measure of comic relief was provided by Michael Hordern. Never having done a musical before, he suddenly found himself performing a dance routine with Mostel and

Silvers—and holding his own in their company. "If I could make a film with a part for Michael in it every year, I'd be a very happy man," said Lester. "He is amazingly talented, one of the best of the English school of acting. He understands insanity wondrously well, and plays with great conviction against terrible odds. He was thrown into *Forum*, yet came out, I think, the best."

While Nic Roeg's allegiance never wavered from his director, he liked Mel Frank personally and found him naturally funny and very bright, albeit a Hollywood diehard. He also, Roeg recalls, had an ability to laugh at himself. After Roeg had talked over with Lester an idea he had to reveal only gradually their village's main street, since sixty-eight pages of script were set there and he felt the familiarity might render it monotonous, his plan was rendered difficult after several days of shooting by a sudden change in the weather, since overcast skies posed a matching problem. Frank hated the earlier footage he saw and was well aware that Lester had approved the scheme. "Do you like what's happening here?" he asked Roeg one day.

"I think it's terrific," Roeg replied.

"Aw, gee," said Frank, throwing up his hands in frustration, "you're always taking his side. Why don't you have a mind of your own and think my way?" He then looked at Roeg, realized what he'd just said, and burst out laughing.

"Richard and Mel were poor casting," Roeg suggests today. "You wouldn't put Godard to work with George Lucas, it would be completely wrong. A division on the set brings things down, makes it more difficult for everyone. We just plodded on, there was nothing else for it."

Thankfully, the gods of comedy had decided that enough was enough, that Lester was due a break. His experience with Buster Keaton, long a hero of his, was to prove one of

"Where's my pay check, Lester!"

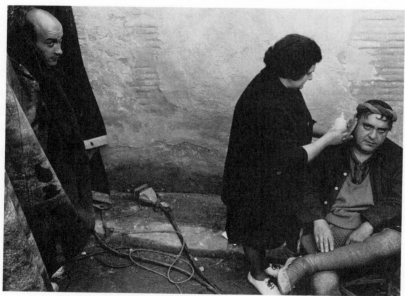

"One minute to showtime, Zero!"

Top: Buster Keaton and Richard Lester on the set of *A Funny Thing Happened on the Way to the Forum. Bottom:* Lester and Zero Mostel (seated) in *A Funny Thing Happened on the Way to the Forum.*

the most felicitous of his life. Everyone, for that matter, loved Keaton, although no one realized at the time that he was dying; what was thought to be asthma turned out to be cancer of the throat. His "asthma" meant that he was unable to run, and since he was playing the role of a man running seven times around the seven hills of Rome looking for his lost children, Lester was obliged to hire an ex-jockey to double for him. Keaton did the talking; his double did the running.

In one shot he was to "run" through a chariot race, Mr. Magoo style, and narrowly miss being run over. Then it was cut to a close-up of a near-sighted old man, deaf to boot, unaware of his hairbreadth escape and sighing as the chariots disappear, "Ah, the glorious breezes of Rome!" At that moment Lester thought it would be a wonderful piece of business if he started running again, just a few steps, and banged straight into a tree. With Keaton expressing great enthusiasm, Lester asked what he needed to set the scene up. "Where will the camera be?" Keaton asked. Lester told him. "I'll need two feet of black string and two makeup sponges," Keaton declared.

When these were duly produced, he marked off the distance with his foot, from the tree all the way back to the camera. Taking the string, he then tied his hat to his head so that it wouldn't fall off, carefully placing the makeup sponges underneath for protection. "Okay, I'm ready," he signaled Lester. As the chariots disappeared in the distance, he delivered his line, "Ah, the glorious breezes of Rome," turned, walked straight into the tree, hit it with a smack and keeled over.

"Terrific, Buster," Lester enthused. "Got it in one take." Only when Keaton failed to get up did they realize he had knocked himself out; perfect though his calculations had been, his eyesight was no longer what it once was. He had missed the sponges completely.

Lester learned a lot from the hardy, marvelously practical veteran. Keaton was no intellectual but a thoroughly mechanical-minded person who knew exactly what his body could do. He had, after all, been doing it since he was two years old and his parents had thrown "bouncing Buster" across the stage as part of their act. At the age of seventy-three he had legs like tree trunks.

A remark he made one day puzzled Lester: "We'll work on this until you preview it." Keaton was surprised to learn from his director that he had no intentions of previewing. "Oh, we previewed everything in my day," the veteran explained. "I had my own film company, with everyone on fifty-two weeks' salary a year. If a sequence didn't work when it was previewed, we didn't try to re-edit it, we'd just throw it all out and pay for the truck to take us back to the location and do it again."

"But Buster," Lester pointed out, "if this sequence we're doing now doesn't work and I want to shoot it again, Zero will be in New York, Michael Hordern will be in London, Phil Silvers will be God knows where and the set will have been struck. It would cost $500,000 to redo the one scene."

"I guess," Keaton drawled—and Lester could have sworn the famous deadpan almost cracked a smile—"that's why our films look so much better."

Keaton went on to vouchsafe something much more precious than gold, the driving force he had always kept in mind throughout his films—that his plots had all been propelled either by the love of a girl, an attempt to save her, a search for the perfect girl, or an attempt to prove his worth to her. He remembered shooting a scene for *The Navigator* that showed him underwater in a diving suit fixing the ship's

119

propeller. Halfway through he had an idea for an extra gag; spotting a shoal of fish about to pass by he grabs a starfish, clamps it on his chest, and waves them on. After filming this he cut it out, judging that the gag was extraneous. "I'd have given my left arm for a gag like that," Lester said admiringly. "Maybe you would," Keaton replied, "but it wouldn't have gotten you the girl. Fixing the propeller would."

One Sunday in the middle of Keaton's three-week stint, Lester suggested that Keaton, in costume, accompany him to the countryside with the second-unit crew and with a lavish picnic lunch organized. The idea was simply to sit around in a field most of the day, tell stories, reminisce, and if something emerged that could be used in the movie that would be fine; if not, they would have had a great day out. As it was, the day produced three shots that were fitted into the final movie.

Another highlight of the picnic was the arrival, in the middle of an otherwise empty field, of a big black Cadillac, out of which stepped Jack Benny. He'd heard his old friend was there and had stopped to say hello. For once free of schedules, Lester enjoyed a completely relaxed, memorable day.

Keaton's wife, an ex-nurse, was in constant attendance all through shooting, and always with a chair at the ready. The comedian's financial state, it seemed, was in better shape than it had been for some time. He had come from Rome, where he had been making a movie based on a screenplay by Samuel Beckett entitled *Film*, about which he was very dismissive. What a total waste, he muttered, hiring someone and having him act with his back to the camera all the time! As for his being "rediscovered" after his long fallow period, there was a distinct sense of too little, too late, which Lester understood completely.

At bottom Keaton was a plain-speaking, ordinary man, simple and measured in speech, someone to whom anyone employing the word "art" in conversation was immediately suspect. In his heyday the application forms for anyone wanting to work with him would certify, "I am a first-class crew technician, Grade One category" or "I am a first-class baseball player at second base," which represented precisely the basis on which they might be hired. While "art" was something he would grudgingly concede might emerge from the collective endeavors of these artisans, its bottom-line ethic was sheer hard work and dedicated professionalism. To Lester, Keaton remains the Guv'nor, the man from whom he learned most about the art of filmmaking and comedy.

Lester felt that the only parallel to Keaton in terms of physical dexterity on the movie was Michael Crawford. In one scene Hero slides down a grain chute inside a barrel and crashes into a passing chariot onto which he promptly clambers, all of it achieved in a single take. Crawford proposed to his girlfriend Gabrielle Lewis during production and requested that Lester arrange their December wedding in Paris and act as best man, two assignments he was delighted to accept.

He soon became aware that when Mostel was developing a performance he was another who could be extremely singleminded about his work. He had made Teyve his own in *Fiddler on the Roof* and was fairly dismissive of Topol's performance. Everything was over the top with the versatile actor and comic, but in a most endearing manner. A painter himself, he also collected pre-Colombian art. His wife, Kate, a wonderfully warm Irish woman, warned Lester: "He's such an enthusiastic collector. If you bent over right now, Zero would frame your ass."

Mostel loved nothing better than to tease and fool around

"Listen to that guy yell!"
**Lester with Michael
Crawford filming** *A Funny
Thing Happened on the Way
to the Forum.*
(COURTESY OF RICHARD LESTER)

"OK, move in Nic!"
**Lester with Nicholas
Roeg.**
(COURTESY OF RICHARD LESTER)

with the big, fat Spanish makeup girls, and in turn they adored this giant flirt of a man. At a meal with the couple Lester ordered squid, and, as was his wont, ended by soaking up the gravy with his bread. "It isn't bad enough, Richard, that all these hideous tentacles are sticking out," Mostel scolded, "but you've got to drain the ink as well!"

The tragic end of this remarkable man a decade later shocked Lester. Told by his doctor that he had to lose weight or risk damaging his heart, he went on a crash diet, shed forty pounds and within a week dropped dead. Lester often thinks of Kate and how silent their apartment must have seemed in the weeks and months that followed the loss of such a huge presence and personality. Another player in *Forum*, Jack Gilford, an old Broadway vaudevillian in the Mostel mold, went on to write an affectionate biographical tribute to his old friend.

When Lester is working on a movie, his concentration is on getting the job done. Tunnel vision precludes the intrusion of such incidentals as petty rivalry among the crew members, as well as the perpetual dilemma, for those with time and inclination to follow such shenanigans, of who's shacking up with whom. As a visiting celebrity, his eyes were well and truly opened towards the end of filming when he found himself inducted, together with Spanish musical star Marisol, into an organization entitled Companions of the Tuna. The group, mostly either law or medical students, dressed in university robes and sashes and visited restaurants and clubs playing guitars and tambourines and singing. Off they set one evening, together with their colorfully dressed companions, to sing and play.

Strumming as they strolled, the group passed through Calle Dr. Fleming, where editors, camera operators and many of the supporting cast lodged in rented apartments, the occupants pushing their windows wide and waving from their balconies to the players below. Looking up, what crossed Lester's mind as he spotted the first couple was, "Good grief, not *them*! He's old enough to be her father, he can't be with *her*!" Seeing more and more familiar faces, in the most unexpected couplings, Lester doffed his tricorn hat, revealing his unmistakable bald pate, and waved to the assembly. It was like a frame cut—as he was recognized, balconies emptied, windows banged shut, lights went out, and within a minute the entire apartment block was in total darkness.

Determined to stick to what Lester saw as a procedure that had worked in Hollywood's golden days, Mel Frank had hired fifty-five-year-old Irwin Kostal as the movie's musical director. (The "golden days" were in fact fairly recent; Kostal had supervised the music for *West Side Story* in 1961, *Mary Poppins* in 1964 and *The Sound of Music* in 1965, picking up two Oscars along the way.) The maestro's method was to lay down backing tracks for the vocals with a Spanish trio, with a full orchestra to be added later. Perhaps because of his habit of counting for the trio in Spanish and the quality of their timekeeping, all of the songs ended up with tempos that rolled up and down like waves. Lester's answer was to hire Ken Thorne to finish the job in the post-production process. Thorne tirelessly led a sixty-piece orchestra through the many tempi in a valiant attempt to produce a cohesive sound.

Lester inadvertently added to the confusion when he introduced a Roman instrument made from bone that produced a sound like the ram horn used in Jewish ceremonials, borrowed from a musicology museum at St. Albans. After the trombone players had taken one tentative look and immediately backed away, the trumpets and French horns quickly following suit, unprepared to lose their lips for their art. Since Lester was the prime mover, he ended up with the unenviable task of playing the antediluvian device, suffering a split lip in the process. In the middle of the final session the instrument itself, not having been played for 2,000–odd years and unused to the changes in tempo, let alone the moisture content of Lester's saliva, crumbled to pieces in his hand. Thorne's reward for his efforts was an Oscar, making *Forum* the only film of Lester's to have actually won an Academy Award.

Up until the very last moment Frank continued to present problems. Lester had shot a scene in the brothel, "the house of Lycus," in which eager-beaver Mostel is seen splashing through an ornamental pond without even noticing that his feet are getting soaked. Lester was informed that the scene had to be excised, since it was "lifted" from a *Road* movie Frank had made. (This came as startling news, since Lester had never seen a *Road* movie in his life.) The series was about to be sold to television, Frank explained, and Lester's "infringement" might jeopardize the contract. Several attempts to have the scene removed were successfully resisted. Frank's final act of defiance was to hire his own editor, Gordon Pilkington, with whom he fashioned a rival final cut. UA looked at both as a matter of courtesy and decided, in fairly short order, to go with Lester's version.

One more unfortunate encounter was in store, this time with Stephen Sondheim, composer of the original show's sixteen songs. Their meeting took place in London when the movie was in rough-cut form, and followed Sondheim's discovery that only five of his sixteen tunes had made it intact into the finished film. He took exception to everything, even to Lester's insistence on wearing a seatbelt for the short drive from the Hilton Hotel to a nearby restaurant for lunch.

Although Lester was driving an unfamiliar, extremely high-powered, two-seater sports model, Sondheim's smirk gave the impression that Lester's safety precaution clearly indicated deep psychological problems.

While admiring much of the composer's work, Lester found it hard to summon up much enthusiasm for the man himself, in whom he discerned an aggressive cleverness, together with a predilection for game-playing and trouble-making, pitting one side against the other on the tenuous basis that good things might emerge from the resulting dissent. To Lester the theory was nonsense. As he sees it, life is too short for such sophistry; if anger and jealousy have to be engendered to produce results, you're in the wrong business.

In the main the reviews for *Forum* reflected the backbiting atmosphere that had pervaded its execution. "Erotic errors," *Time* magazine headlined, going on to complain about Lester's "camerantics" and the conflicts between his style and Mostel's. In the New York *Times* Vincent Canby felt that Lester had gone "either too far or not far enough" with his adaptation, and agreed with Time that style was often at odds with the material. In *Take One*, Paul Ennis concluded that Lester had been "trying to reach the moon with a Zeppelin." As far as Brendan Gill in the New Yorker was concerned, "Lester's camera tricks (in many cases, they are *only* tricks)" were becoming "overfamiliar." To Pauline Kael the visual experience was "like coitus interruptus going on forever," while to James Maxwell of the Reporter the major faults lay in "draggy timing and the broad, theatrical performances of some of the actors." Richard Corliss in National Review gave moderate praise: "the pace varies, it is easy to miss some jokes, but it is also easy to become bored . . . still, at least half of its 568 or 574 jokes work, which qualifies it as a funny film."

Jules Feiffer headed the raves, describing *Forum* as "the best comedy . . . since *A Hard Day's Night* . . . the gags, vaudeville and bawdy humor congeal magically into art." Philip Hartung in Commonweal agreed, hailing the movie as "clever," the cast "outstanding" and the direction "freewheeling." Variety loved the "zesty scripting, imaginative directing and expert clowning."

In Britain David Castell in the Illustrated London News felt that Lester had imposed his style "without justification, reference or reverence on both the play and the actors, whose styles were at variance with his" (my view exactly, although if Castell had known of the problems involved . . .) while John Coleman in New Statesman found the movie "unexpectedly spellbinding."

For UA the box office figures proved less spellbinding. In isolated locations in Europe the movie seemed to work; in Madrid's Cinerama it ran for over a year. Elsewhere it bombed, and at $3 million it had cost more than all of Lester's movies to date *combined*. (At the same time, of course, his string of modestly budgeted films had grossed over $40 million for the company.)

After the rumbling disquiet engendered by his off-key relationship with Mel Frank and the virtually insuperable problems Phil Silvers had posed, Lester made what came close to a disclaimer. As for Frank, his writing/producing/directing ambitions were to strike paydirt two years after the clash of personalities with Lester. And his Gina Lollabrigida vehicle, *Buona Sera, Mrs. Campbell*, successfully featured Phil Silvers, recognizable once more with his glasses restored. He then produced a smash hit with Glenda Jackson and George

Segal in *A Touch of Class*. In view of this we'll give him the last word on *A Funny Thing Happened on the Way to the Forum*. "I could have forgiven Richard anything," was his eventual, heartfelt message to John Victor Smith, "if only the goddamn movie had made money!"

CHAPTER NINE

You can't say to me that Paths to Glory *is a pacifist film. The implication is that if Kirk Douglas had led the troops in the beginning, we would have been able to go out and kill the Germans more efficiently.*

—R<small>ICHARD</small> L<small>ESTER</small>

Lester bought Patrick Ryan's novel, *How I Won the War,* with Michael Crawford in mind as the leading character, Lt. Ernest Goodbody. He saw the book, which the Rank Organization tried to buy back as a vehicle for Norman Wisdom, as "pretty painless and rather condescending in that finally it made the working man only really interested in getting laid and having a drink." Although the book was also ostensibly disrespectful to the officer class, it still came across to Lester as having been written by one of them. In the end little was retained of Ryan's work except the title, one or two episodes and the names of a handful of characters.

Lester was appalled at the climate of nostalgia provoked by items like a BBC documentary that seemed to glorify Field Marshal Montgomery in particular and war in general, with the old soldier seen revisiting battlegrounds and reliving, if not positively revelling in, past glories. He wanted his movie to go beyond an antiwar stance and attack what he felt was the obscene Hollywood film that glorified death, sacrifice and suffering; *How I Won the War* was to be the first antiwar *movie* movie. There would be no repetition of the artistic conflict on *Forum*, since Lester intended to produce the movie himself for his newly formed Petersham Films.

He was equally determined not to portray a standard war film platoon, the typically all-around fighting unit of buddies, and deliberately chose a group of actors who were totally different in style from each other. He realized that Crawford would be required to give much more of a "real" acting performance than he had in either *The Knack* or *Forum*. Here he would be portraying an individual with three separate personalities and accents, one for his senior officers, another for his men and a third for the German soldier who captures him and who turns out to be the one person with whom he has an affinity. In Lester's mind, Crawford was fully up to the task. He next approached John Lennon for the role of Private Gripweed, explaining what he wanted to say and why he felt it was important, especially at a time when Britain was wallowing in nostalgia twenty-five years after El Alamein. That Lennon agreed to take part without even asking to see the script (just as well, for it did not exist at that point) and without bothering to ask how big his role would be told Lester two things—that he trusted his instincts and that he never for one moment saw the film as an acting career move.

To counterpoint Lennon's intuitive style, Lester cast the classically trained Jack Hedley (as the cowardly Melancholy Musketeer), Samuel Beckett specialist Jack MacGowran (as the mad-as-a-March-hare Juniper), Roy Kinnear (as the cuckolded Clapper), Lee Montague (as "good soldier" Troop

Sergeant Transom), Ronald Lacey (as the cynical Spool) and James Cossins (as the wishy-washy Drogue), dispatched under Goodbody by the weird and wonderful Lieutenant Colonel Grapple (Michael Hordern), on a mission to build a cricket pitch behind enemy lines for the benefit of a visiting VIP.

Charles Wood, the writer entrusted with adapting the book after his work on *The Knack* and *Help!*, maintains that Lester's approach to the movie was heavily influenced by *Dingo*, a play he had written for the National Theater that was turned down for a license because it was judged to have perverted and twisted fixed attitudes to war. It was eventually staged, first in Bristol, then in London at the Royal Court in 1967.

He and Lester came close to a falling out on *How I Won the War* as one complete draft demand followed another. "The problem is that Richard and I never work together," says Wood. "We'll talk, then I'll go away and put things down in order for him to say that he doesn't want it. I was never certain exactly what it was he wanted to say. He eliminates until he gets what he wants, and in the end it produces good work, but for a writer it's a thankless, soul-destroying process. I sometimes enjoy the product, but until I wrote *The Charge of the Light Brigade* for Tony Richardson I'd never done a piece I could point to and say, 'Yes, I wrote every word of that.' And even then the films weren't mine, I didn't feel any proprietorial interest, they're Richard's or Tony's films." Only after the seventh attempt, with Lester up to his neck filming *Forum* in Spain, did he declare himself satisfied. For a while Wood swore not only never to work with Lester again, but never to work on a film again. They were, he declared, simply too demanding.

Everyone roughed it on location in Germany, where the

"Where the hell's Lester?"

Jack Hedley (left), Lee Montague (third left), Michael Crawford
(right seated) and John Lennon (right) filming *How I Won the War*.
(COURTESY OF RICHARD LESTER)

unit first moved, living in tiny hotels with no creature
comforts whatsoever, with Lester on his usual tight schedule
to fit the $1 million budget. While shooting at Bendesdorf,
near Hamburg. Lester was third, after Crawford and associate producer Denis O'Dell, into the bath water. His room
was up a ladder, above the unit's chef, a man who rose at
five every morning and whistled and sang until everyone
else followed suit.

A reporter found John Lennon in reflective mood one
bitterly cold morning in Bendesdorf. "I was just a bundle of
nerves the first day," he admitted. "I couldn't hardly speak,
I was so nervous. My first speech was in a forest on patrol,

and I was supposed to say, 'My heart's not in it anymore,' and it wasn't. I went home and said to myself, 'Either you're not going to be like that, or you're going to give up.' I don't mind talking to the camera; it's people that throw me."

He was at the stage, he added, when he wanted to try everything: "And I'm lucky enough to be able to do it. I want to see which one turns me on. This is for me, this film, because apart from wanting to do it because of what it stands for I want to see what I'll be like when I've done it."

It seemed that John saw making *How I Won the War* as a form of therapy that might help relieve a growing identity crisis within the Beatles:

I don't want people taking things from me that aren't really me. They make you something they want to make you, and that isn't really on. They come and talk and find answers, but they're *their* answers, not *ours*. We're not Beatles to each other, you know. It's a joke to us. If we're going out the door of the hotel we say, "Right, Beatle John! Beatle George, now! Come on, let's go!" We don't put a false front on anything. But we just know that leaving that door, we turn into Beatles because everybody looking at us sees the Beatles. We're not the Beatles at all. We're just *us*. But we created that to an extent, and that's how it's going to be. That's why George is in India studying the sitar and I'm here making this. Because we're a bit tired of going out the door, and the only way to soften the blow is just to spread out a bit.

Having unburdened himself, he hailed Lester and joined him in line for tea, discovering to his annoyance that by the time he was served his favorite snack had sold out. "You don't have to be a star to get a cheese sandwich," he muttered to his director, "you just have to be first!" John went on to submerge himself completely in the role of the sycophantic Gripweed. Approaching Lieutenant Goodbody during a cricket match, he snivels, "May I rub your ball, sir? It would give me great pleasure!" The high point of the movie for him was filming his death scene after being shot. Cynthia was inconsolable when she watched the footage. It was, she told John in between bursts of tears, exactly how he would look when he died.

During one week's hectic location filming, Thursday was Alamein, Friday was Dieppe and Saturday was Dunkirk, with the skirmishes of Crawford's platoon matching and counterpointing the foul-ups of the major battles. Sunday was a rest day, then it was back to war, alleviated at supper parties in the evenings by Roy Kinnear's side-splitting impression of a one-armed golfer. The resourceful O'Dell came into his own in the move to Almeria when it became necessary to beg, borrow or steal military hardware. Although they had been half-promised a landing craft by the British authorities, a problem arose when it had to be towed past the Straits of Gibraltar, since relations between Spain and Britain were tense at the time. Lester continually postponed the scene, daily hoping that something would turn up.

While in his office one day in Almeria, O'Dell suddenly looked out the window to the sea and watched a destroyer and five support vessels of the U.S. Navy sailing past on maneuvers. Jumping into a car, he chased them down the coast and buttered up the officer in charge, coaxing out of him the name of his superior to whom he could apply for permission to use a landing vessel. Every time he got a no he got the name of officer up the ladder and in this way pleaded his case all the way to Washington, where he still got a no.

Armed with all of the names he had gathered and two crates of beer, he returned to the beach at Almeria and overwhelmed the individual in charge of the landing craft

"Lester never told me it would be like this."
John Lennon (left) in *How I Won the War*.   (COURTESY OF RICHARD LESTER)

with his knowledge of the chain of command of the entire U.S. Navy. If he could shoot the whole scene in a morning, he was told, he could use the craft. Since the original actor Lester had cast for the scene turned out to be unavailable, he was left with ten hours to find someone else and fly him out from London. Paul Daneman was given his pages of dialogue on the plane to Madrid. He was driven five hours by car to the location, where he landed at 5 A.M. Shooting began an hour later and finished at 1:30 P.M. Lester had his landing craft scene, with the destroyer and a full fleet in the distance flung in, completely unaware that filming had taken place. It was certainly one of O'Dell's finest hours.

A foretaste of the controversy their film would engender came when a visiting reporter stole a copy of the script and drove for five hours to Malaga airport. His article described *How I Won the War* as "a scurrilous film" that vilified the heroes of yesteryear and mocked their sacrifice. When English newspapers turned the story down—their turn would come later—it was published in Germany.

During their stay in Spain, where a much higher standard of accommodation was available, John asked Lester to come over one evening to the palatial villa he and Cynthia shared with Crawford and Gabrielle to hear some seven-inch forty-fives he was excited about. Distracted from the difficulties of the day's shoot, Lester found it hard to concentrate. "I don't like all that country-and-western shit," he informed a disconcerted Lennon after listening to Bob Dylan's earliest efforts. Crawford would often come across John sitting cross-legged on his bed with his guitar working on "Strawberry Fields Forever." Later a trip to the beach in his Rolls-Royce would be suggested, although the sea was only a few hundred yards away.

By the time Lester had finished shooting he had managed to inculcate his cast with his views on war and the insidious influence of war movies. Crawford was last to be converted, formulating his opinions only when the movie was in the can, and claiming that the film expressed his own philosophy that war was stupidly idealized. Both he and Lester still maintained that they would fight for their country if it were threatened. "If our fathers hadn't fought," Crawford pointed out, "we'd be sitting around with blue numbers on our arms." Only John carried the film's message through to its logical conclusion: "If there is another war I won't fight. I hate all the sham about war."

Lester made a conscious decision after *How I Won the War* to stop looking at daily rushes. He lavished praise on David Watkin's cinematography after looking at the rushes in a run-down local Bendesdorf cinema. Back at Twickenham, the movie still looked wonderful—but where, he agonized, were the flares and halations that had made it look so extraordinary back in Germany? When the answer was found to lie in the cracked lens of the fleapit's projector, the resourceful Watkin set about procuring a forty-year-old Ross Express lens, hoping to capture similarly picturesque enhancements on his next assignment, Tony Richardson's *Charge of the Light Brigade*.

During production Lester had extended the Greek chorus concept used in *The Knack* by filming scenes specifically to be spliced into dramatic moments. There was a cut from a graphic battlefield scene to a cinema, in which two old biddies (Dandy Nichols and Gretchen Franklin) are watching the action, with one muttering to the other, "The same thing happened to a son of mine, it was his eardrums." In the middle of another battle Lester ventured even further into Brechtian territory, having a soldier's wife appear in her apron after her husband's legs have been blasted off. To his agonized, "It hurts, Flo," her advice is, "Run them under the cold tap, luv."

Many critics chose to review not only *How I Won the War*, but their own feelings on war and war movies. The result was several passionate advocates, although John Coleman's "Magnificiently funny nonsense" review in New Statesman frankly puzzled and dismayed Lester. Had Coleman strayed into the wrong auditorium? "Brilliant, and rich with multi-leveled meanings, one of the most active and complicated movies ever made," declared Thomas Haroldson of Fifth

Estate. "Lester's anger is heavily felt. It forces us to laugh against our wishes and inclinations," said Brendan Gill in the New Yorker. "The best film of its kind since *Dr. Strangelove*. Brilliant, unnerving," raved Arthur Schlesinger, Jr. in Vogue.

Then there was the preponderance of conscientious objectors, led by Penelope Houston in Sight and Sound, who felt the movie was "undermined by its fragmented style, its simple message lost through technical indirection." Arthur Knight in Saturday Review described it as "a well-intended muddle." "By making war surreal rather than real, Lester trivializes it," wrote Richard Schickel in Life. "Film is forced, and substitutes motion for emotion, reeling for feeling, crude slapstick for telling satire," claimed Variety. "Lester's style works against the narrative," wrote Michael Billington in the London *Times*. "Its ultimate effect is to make audiences feel kicked in the teeth," said Bosley Crowther in the New York *Times*. "Lester mocks notable war films to prevent his own from becoming one of them," Richard Gillman declared in New Republic, while to Philip Hartung in Commonweal it was "episodic and alienating." Films in Review went further, describing the movie as "the product of possibly degenerate, probably traitorous 'mod-monsters' incapable of rationality."

Penelope Houston offered a more rational explanation to what she felt was its "strident, tense, exclamatory" tone: "*How I Won the War* seems to be stubbing its toes by kicking ferociously at an open door. Is there an audience here, of an age and temper likely to be affected by the film, to be thrown by its anti-militaristic attitudes?"

Writer Roger Eldridge noted that one editor had said of Lester and his collaborators, "They *hate* war . . . think of that! How unlike our beastly fascist selves who *love* war, believe it is a good thing in itself and quite the most enjoyable experience imaginable!" Lester refused to accept that he had overstated his argument. "But people *do* like war," he protested.

The older generation feel a comforting nostalgia at having survived the Second World War. They talk about their finest hour, they say "the army makes a man of you" and proudly tell you how many Germans they killed. Why else do they attend ceremonial dinners? All the major heroes in history have been soldiers. The first emotion in battle is glory, but glory implies heroism, and heroism implies killing. During the last war people were brought up on hate. Children were told that the Germans would come and rape their mothers. Nowadays, of course, the immediate shadow of war has been removed, but the sentiment is still the same. One of the major obscenities of war is the war film itself. It is treated as a big, colorful adventure story, with extras being mowed down like cowboys in a western.

In order to bring all this home to people, I had to make the film a violent statement. You are always made aware that this *is* a film. Most war epics create an illusion of reality, but in *How I Won the War* the audience is made to feel that this is some sort of documentary in which they have a part. Nobody is spared; in war the responsibility is shared. A lot of ordinary soldiers are not just following orders—they are actually enjoying the war.

Eldridge noted that even more than ordinary soldiers Lester had attacked war leaders like Churchill and Montgomery, portraying Churchill, in one eight-second scene, as a ventriloquist's dummy operated by the increasingly crazed Montgomery figure of Juniper. "Let's face it," says Lester, "Churchill was no deity. He made some colossal mistakes. The trouble is that the war has become irrevocably linked with Churchill as if he were the performer of miracles."

139

The Brechtian distancing Lester had chosen to adopt back-fired on him commerically. Alexander Walker said of what he termed Lester's "pious aim": "Alas for those who try to apply Brecht to the cinema. For all his sincerity, Lester's whimsicality has betrayed him."

During the first week of the movie's London Pavilion run the National Front let off a smoke bomb in the auditorium, halting the performance and clearing the cinema. The first week's takings remained encouraging, based on the controversy whipped up and Lennon's co-star billing, but slumped thereafter, killed by disastrous word-of-mouth. "I didn't realize that the alienation process would also alienate the audience," said Lester. "I also failed to understand that when you hire John Lennon, even when you tell the press thirty times that he is playing a straight role because he wants to, that people would still say, five minutes into the performance, "Why hasn't he played the guitar yet?" He didn't, and they felt cheated, that he had been brought in under false pretenses."

If in the Beatles movies Lester had relived his adolescence, many saw *How I Won the War* as his student protest, delivering his message via celluloid instead of the Western Union route recommended by Sam Goldwyn. Others accused him of willful artiness and obscurantism, especially regarding the puzzling reappearance of each of the platoon members after their deaths dyed in a variety of hues. It was left to Charles Wood to explain this particular detail:

> The idea was to have all the corpses together at the end of the film being transformed into the different colors of medals allocated to the various battles, but for some reason this was never followed through. Looking back I realize that the original novel was a better book than we thought at the time, but

I had a youthful innocence in such things. I still think it's probably the best thing Richard and I did together.

Wood is undoubtedly correct. The problem that was developing with Lester's work was its multilayered density, which required several viewings before his full message could be absorbed. Willful artiness and obscurantism? Well, he was certainly flexing muscles not previously apparent, perhaps in the process blunting the immediate impact. On a second and third viewing I found *How I Won the War* one of the most challenging films I've ever seen; cinema audiences unfortunately pronounce their verdict in much shorter order.

Familiar as he was with Ryan's original book, which he regarded as "perfectly innocuous and quite funny," James Garrett had filled a preview theater before the movie opened with 110 agency personnel, all eager, as indeed he was, to see "the latest Richard Lester movie." As it unwound Garrett sensed that it was dying by inches—on a scale of 1 to 100 he puts the eventual death factor at 100—and as the audience filed out he could feel their resentment; they were confused, puzzled and depressed, accurately anticipating later audience reaction.

The movie had considerable influence in a couple of directions, though hardly where Lester had expected. The first concerned Michael Crawford, for whom a meeting with Gene Kelly at *How I Won the War*'s San Francisco première led to a starring role in *Hello, Dolly* and a contract with Twentieth Century–Fox. And within months of its release thousands of youngsters around the world were wearing the National Health prescription glasses John had sported.

"If I fall under a bus tomorrow," Lester had declared before *How I Won the War* opened, "this is the film I want to be judged by. "One reviewer had his answer at the ready:

"My advice to you, Mr. Lester, is to look left, look right, look left again!"

■

Lester counts John Lennon as one of the handful of people who have affected his life most profoundly. For all the cruelty and willfulness on display from time to time, there was a power and innate intelligence, together with an ability—not always entirely welcome—to ground his flights of fancy when he began to drift too far away from reality. "Time and again," he says, "I'd rabbit on and John would just sit there. Then he'd say one sentence and I'd see what a fool I'd been. I'm not saying that he was the great white hope of mankind, but he did have a amazing gift to see through to the center of things."

John seemed to Lester to embody the idea that it was no longer necessary to slog your way laboriously through the educational system in order to be part of the establishment. This is a claim, he was convinced, that John had never deliberately set out to prove; rather, he had been used by a society forever searching for an easy way out, representing the idea that for anyone streetwise enough, success was there for the asking. He was writing, singing, playing, composing and illustrating—and he had had almost no formal training or education.

He struck Lester as having few pretensions but considerable perception, as well as an instinctive aversion to social injustice, cant and hypocrisy. "It just so happens that some group playing in England are making people talk about England, but nothing else is going on," John asserted.

Pop music gets through to all people all over the world, and in that respect youth might be together—the commie youth might be the same as us, and we all know that basically they probably are. But there's more talk *about* it than is actually *happening*—you know, "Swinging Britain," all of that. Everybody can go around in England with long hair, and boys can wear flowered trousers and flowered shirts, but there's still the same old nonsense going on. It's just that we all dress up a bit different.

The class thing is just as snobby as it ever was. People like us break through a little, but only a little. Once we went into this restaurant and nearly got thrown out for looking as we did until they saw who it was. It took me back to when I was nineteen and couldn't go anywhere without being stared at or remarked on. It's only since I've been a Beatle that people have said, "Oh, wonderful, come in, come in," and I've forgotten a bit about what they're really thinking. They see the shining star, but when there is no glow about you, they only see the clothes and the haircut again.

He freely admitted that in the early days of the Beatles they had been obliged to watch their step:

We weren't as open and truthful when we didn't have the power to be. We had to take it easy. We had to shorten our hair to leave Liverpool and get jobs in London. We had to wear suits to get on TV. We had to compromise. We had to falsify a bit, even if we didn't realize it at the time. I'm not a cynic. They're getting my character out of some of the things I wrote or said. They can't do that. I hate tags. I'm slightly cynical, but I'm not a cynic. One can be wry one day and cynical the next and ironic the next. I'm a cynic about most things that are taken for granted, about society, politics, newspapers, government. But I'm not cynical about life, love, goodness, death.

Lester regarded John's controversial "We're more popular than Jesus" remark as a casual line taken out of context and twisted into vitriolic anti-British sentiment by Southern fundamentalists. It also seemed to him to be entirely sensible; John wasn't saying that the Beatles were better or more important—simply that there were crazes, and they represented the hottest current craze.

Remembering a remark that Paul made to him in 1964— "Please God I don't become a thirty-year-old Beatle"—Lester was unsurprised when the group broke up. With John and Yoko Ono settled in America, John expressed the opinion that Paul would eventually follow, implying that anything he did Paul would sooner or later do and take credit for. It was an antagonism that lingered to the end.

Lester was in Oslo for publicity surrounding the première of *Superman II* when he was awakened by his secretary from London breaking the news that John had been assassinated. Minutes later, the phone rang again. It was NBC—could Lester be available for an interview? He replied yes without thinking about it, dressed and went downstairs automatically, where he was picked up and transported to a small office building housing NBC's studio. With just one camera and a chair in the room he was handed an earpiece and told to talk into the camera; when the red light came on he would hear a voice. Unshaven, not even having stopped to brush his teeth and still unable to take in the dreadful news, Lester thought to himself, "What the hell am I doing here?"

He had no idea to whom he was talking on the primitive link to New York, where they had the picture and sound and five other people dragged into the studio to discuss their reactions. All he remembers is staring at the unblinking eye of the camera, listening to the babble of voices from the U.S. and mumbling, "When is someone going to do something about gun control? Why are all these people wandering about with guns?" When someone pointed out that the gun had come from Hawaii, Lester virtually shouted, "What does that have to do with anything?"

In total shock, numbed by the subsequent press hysteria, he chose to pull the shutters down over the entire experience. As on a previous occasion years earlier in Philadelphia, the grief was contained inside. To this day he has never discussed the event, not even with Paul, George or Ringo.

CHAPTER TEN

San Francisco had become people in Mustang cars and three-piece suits changing into beads and badges just before they got into the city limits. Optimism and the flower movement were turning into hard drugs and anger.

—RICHARD LESTER,
talking to writer Neil Sinyard

The project that became *Petulia* arrived from producer Raymond Wagner while Lester was in the middle of shooting *How I Won the War*. The package consisted of a script by Barbara Turner and the book upon which it was based, *Me and the Arch-Kook Petulia*, by a Los Angeles dentist, John Haase. Lester hated both the book and the script, especially the cuteness of its leading character. But there was something about it, perhaps the challenge of bringing its archness down to earth and injecting a healthy dose of reality. *Petulia* would be his first grownup movie, his personal coming-of-age, and it would be a unique opportunity, as an American who had "been away" for fifteen years, to comment on the country's society with a detached eye. What one critic would dub Lester's "hate letter to America" was under way.

Having decided to set the movie in San Francisco rather

146

than Los Angeles, he and Charles Wood spent three weeks in the city with their wives, soaking up the atmosphere in Haight-Ashbury, driving over the Golden Gate Bridge and visiting the artists' colony of Sausalito. Lester had no desire to check out the marijuana that was constantly on offer, a few puffs back in his single days in Tangier having produced no discernible effect. As for hard drugs, he had lost enough of his jazz friends from the Studio Club—guitarist Dave Goldberg, drummer Phil Seamen, tenor saxophonist Tubby Hayes, all of them heroin addicts—to warn him off for life.

Wood kept a diary, detailing scraps of conversation picked up on the streets and in bars and cafés, which he later worked into a script. Slowly they found themselves enmeshed in a casual, ad-libby, surrealist way with the central character of Petulia and the men who featured in her life. The 120–page script Wood produced turned the original characters around, darkening the cuteness of the novel, desaturating the colors, diluting the sense of phoney charm.

Six weeks before shooting, Lester decided that Wood's version badly needed de-Anglicizing. The fruits of the "diary" were duly handed to Lawrence Marcus, who describes it as "the most liberating document it was possible to hand any scriptwriter." Taking it as his framework, he went on to fashion a final script that detailed Petulia's on-again, off-again infatuation with Dr. Archie Bollen, a man more vulnerable than he knows. He invested in the script his own painfully earned experience of divorce, a process neither Lester nor Wood shared. "You don't have to have one leg to imagine what it's like to have only one leg," says Lester, "but Larry had been there and wrote about that side of it extremely well. We transformed what had been a light, kooky comedy, written by this 'dentist to the stars,' into a disturbing piece of work."

His intention was to capture nothing less than the dying fall of San Francisco's "summer of love" and record the death of the hippie era, with disillusion etching its way through the endless love-in promised by the movement. What intrigued Lester was the contrast between 1966 and the new era, epitomized by the optimism of the Flower Power movement and its souring a year later when the druggies came along and the scene became violent, aggressive and vicious. It had all turned bitter and totally commercial; people were ripping each other off and inviting the tourists in. "Ray Wagner, a very sweet man, more gentle than most, started *Petulia* in a three-piece suit," Lester recalls, "and ended the movie in a flowered shirt with a hibiscus behind his ear. And he wasn't alone; a lot of people were doing that in 1967. Until the bubble burst, that is." (In his striped jester pants and mini-cloak, Lester might have added that he and Wagner made a pair.)

Casting would prove a problem, except in the case of his leading lady, Julie Christie, introduced to him by cinematographer Nic Roeg, who had worked with her on François Truffaut's *Fahrenheit 451* and on John Schlesinger's *Far from the Madding Crowd*. An Oscar winner in 1966 for her performance in Schlesinger's *Darling*, Christie was perfect casting for Petulia, transformed from an American kook into a distraught English girl.

Although James Garner had been set as Archie in Wagner's original concept, Lester was unhappy with him. The word spread like wildfire around Hollywood when Garner departed, and Lester demurred when Frank Sinatra expressed interest, having heard too many stories that Sinatra would give one take; and if it was good enough for him, that was it. Lester did not feel like giving away that sort of control.

Another interested party was Paul Newman, who had an hour of conversation with Lester on the phone. By the time the talking was over, they both knew it wasn't going to work. Lester had enormous respect for Newman as an actor but was not convinced he was Archie.

He had always loved the work of George C. Scott, starting with his television performances, and then on the New York stage in *The Andersonville Trial*. He had never seen Scott in a feature film, but had heard of his reputation for being difficult to work with; apparently he had punched out the director of his last movie. Undaunted, mainly because he was convinced that Scott was totally right, Lester met with and cast him.

He then looked for David Danner, Petulia's handsome, ineffectual husband who develops into a wife-beating sadist. Richard Chamberlain's claim to fame at the time was the *Dr. Kildare* television series, and a couple of movies, both of which had failed. After talking to him for two hours at Twickenham, Lester became convinced that Chamberlain could play Danner; the last thing he wanted was an obvious, slavering psychopath. Chamberlain had recently appeared on stage with Mary Tyler Moore in a desperately ill-advised musical version of *Breakfast at Tiffany's*; after struggling for weeks on the road it had closed on Broadway after just four preview performances. With this very much in mind, Warners' response to his casting was swift and sure: "The man is box-office poison. There is *no way* you can have him." At the height of the argument they virtually conceded that Lester could have any actor he wanted *except* Chamberlain. Leaping in, he seized the opportunity. "Fine," the studio was informed. "I'll have Andy Williams."

Terrified that he might be serious, they eventually gave in and agreed to Chamberlain on condition that he accept pittance of a salary. "This part," Lester argued, "is down for $75,000 in our budget and whoever plays the role deserves the money. He's the second male lead, the third lead in the movie, and you can't *do* this to him."

Although the battle for Chamberlain and the struggle over his salary was bitter for Lester and humiliating for the actor, the role would mark the beginning of his serious career in movies. "Physically he was perfect," says Lester. "There was a line in the original script about a man who would try to sell someone a million-dollar yacht while wearing no socks. Richard had that kind of physical charm and presence."

With veteran Joseph Cotten playing Chamberlain's father and Shirley Knight set as Archie's ex-wife Polo, Lester's major casting was complete. The supporting cast, apart from Arthur Hill and Richard Dysart, was mainly drawn from two improvisational groups in San Francisco, the American Conservatory Theater and the Committee, with early appearances by Austin Pendleton, René Auberjonois and Peter Bonerz. David Hicks was hired to design the interior decoration of the Christie/Chamberlain home and achieved exactly the chic, impersonal and totally false look that Lester wanted.

He saw contemporary music as a crucially important element in the movie, to the extent of setting the tone by having Quicksilver Messenger Service play at the pre-shooting party, with the Grateful Dead, Big Brother and the Holding Company and Janis Joplin set for the film itself. Lester shot at night for a week with Joplin, her sequence set in the lobby of the Fairmont Hotel, a huge, marble-pillared Victorian edifice that contrasted wonderfully with her personality and raunchy persence. She sang like a dream, looked like the back of a bus, and always managed to cover up whatever she had been up to with a heady perfume she splashed on liberally. All of the cast and crew loved Joplin and could smell her four blocks away. The unit was allowed into the Fairmont only for shooting after midnight; then it would take Nic Roeg four or five hours to light it. This left one hour to shoot, since they all had to disappear by 6:30 A.M.

Kim Hunter was cast briefly as Arthur Hill's wife until just before shooting began, when she called Lester in some distress. "I've got one more day to do on this other movie I'm shooting," she explained, "and I don't think I'm going to be able to get away." No matter how they tried to rearrange her schedule around it, Twentieth Century-Fox was adamant that she stay and complete her role. For the sake of a couple of days she had to drop out of *Petulia* and finish

Lester grooving (a term he detests!) with Janis Joplin and Big Brother and the Holding Company during the filming of *Petulia* in San Francisco. (COURTESY OF RICHARD LESTER)

Planet of the Apes—in which she was completely unrecognizable under her monkey makeup.

Two other movies being shot in San Francisco at the same time as *Petulia* were Mike Nichols's *The Graduate* and John Boorman's *Point Blank*. Lester had already been introduced to Nichols through his production designer, Tony Walton, while Boorman was part of the Bristol Mafia, consisting of Charles Wood, Tom Stoppard and Peter Nichols, and had made his own first feature, very much in *Hard Day's Night* style, with *Catch Us If You Can*, featuring the Dave Clark Five.

Lester and Mike Nichols ended up deeply depressed after their first meeting, convinced from a brief description of their respective ventures that they were shooting virtually the same film—an advanced case, both men later agreed, of creative paranoia. Out of their tête-à-tête came a suggestion from Nichols of an actress to replace Kim Hunter. While bowing to no one in his admiration for Nichols, Lester found the actress he recommended, after a day's wasted shooting, utterly wrong for the role. It was strange, he mused, how different directors envisage a role so differently. In the end the part went to local improvisational stalwart Kathleen Widdoes, the first and only time Lester has ever recast a role.

As filming began on Telegraph Hill, the area transformed from the bohemia of the 1930s to the high-rent area of the 1960s, one problem that quickly emerged was the contrasting styles of Scott and Christie. Scott was an instinctive actor who gave some of his best work on the first take, whereas Christie needed four or five takes to overcome her inhibitions before she could enter into the rhythm of her scene. Lester solved the problem by shooting several of their encounters separately, with Scott busily practicing his golf swing by the time Christie was on her best take.

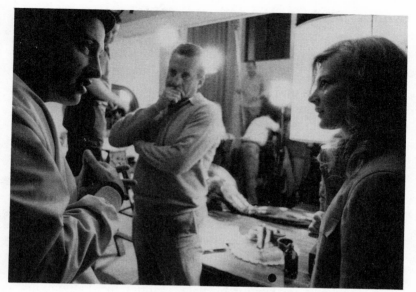

"Here's how we do it."

Richard Lester with George C. Scott and Shirley Knight on the set of *Petulia*.　　　　(COURTESY OF RICHARD LESTER)

When John Haase, author of the original book, traveled from Los Angeles to San Francisco hoping to write an article on the making of the film, he had reckoned without Lester. "The last person we need is the spurned writer," he decreed. "Tell Haase—tell everybody—it's a closed set." This was far from new policy for Lester, who believes it unfair to subject the actors, technicians or himself to the split in concentration visitors inevitably force. Furious at being barred, Haase returned home in a fury, vowing to file suit against the company to compensate for the "rudeness" he had encountered.

Having filmed a scene that graphically depicted Danner's attack on his wife, Lester eventually cut the footage from the finished movie. It was enough, he decided, to show the awful results of the beating without presenting the overt violence on screen. "Danner represents the quality of American life I understand fairly well," says Lester.

> If you are born and raised in a country where you stand up every day and pledge allegiance to the American flag and say, "We are the chosen people, we are the best of everything; we are the saviors of the world; we have the standard of living that is worth having," you set a certain standard for yourself which you can never live up to. And when it is proven to be impossible, then there develops a kind of gratuitous violence, because of an intellectual impotency. I tried to parallel that with this character who was told by his wife, "You are the most beautiful thing I've ever seen, you are the most perfect man, you are everything." He could never live up to what was expected of him, and became sexually impotent, resorting to violence and beating his wife. Through him I attempted to show the threshold of violence that occurs in America—the argument in the supermarket over a can of sardines, the sudden explosion of unnecessary violence because nobody can live up to the image.

"There's nothing hard and fast with Dick Lester. Petulia's character is evolving all the time," Christie observed between scenes. "Lester doesn't always tell you why he wants something," Chamberlain added, "and you never know what camera is on you. What he gives you is a sense of importance. He takes each scene terribly seriously." Scott's two cents' worth was an eloquent tribute to his director. "I don't know what this film's about," he claimed. "But I know *he* knows!"

If ever a scene in one of his movies justifies Lester's twin-camera technique it is the episode in which Archie, in the middle of their argument, hurls a bag of cookies at Polo when her back is turned. After rehearsing, Lester took Scott

Richard Lester and George C. Scott hitching a ride during *Petulia*.

to one side and told him to hurl the cookies with a real vengeance. With one camera filming a wide shot and the other close up on Knight, the moment of impact and her startled, enraged face as she spun around was perfectly captured. "She was physically stunned," says Lester, "and, being a wonderful actress, showed it. If I had tried to shoot her reactions separately, she would have known what that bag of cookies was going to do, the force with which it was going to hit her, and she would have been braced, expecting the blow. This way, although she knew he was going to throw them, she had no idea what it was going to be like, and we captured her surprise perfectly on film. You could never get that impact shooting separately."

Nic Roeg felt distinct optimism as filming on *Petulia* proceeded.

> I could sense that Dick was doing great work on this movie, and Wagner was a bright, adventurous man, Larry Marcus a very clever writer. Dick's very good at letting actors give of themselves. A director's like a jockey, the horse is the film and everything in it. You can encourage it, you can try to hold it, but it can still get out of control. There was never any question of that on *Petulia*. There was a terrific exchange of thoughts, Julie, George, Shirley and Chamberlain were all working well, and there was such an agglomeration of talent. I remember thinking, "maybe—somehow—this is really going to work!"

Warners' was dismayed at Lester's notion of filming several scenes on the sidewalks of San Francisco "on the fly." "You can't just photograph people on the street without proper clearance," they protested. "Why not? I'm not portraying them as axe murderers," Lester replied, "and extras won't look as authentic." The company's response was to send large quantities of baseball caps, sweatshirts and

T-shirts, all of which were emblazoned with the Warners' logo, and which Lester adamantly refused to distribute; the last thing he wanted was for passersby to know there was a movie being shot in the vicinity.

Although Warners' power base was only a few hundred miles away in Los Angeles, Lester treated the head office as if it were on the moon. Used to working independently and handing over the finished movie completely scored and dubbed, he treated with some contempt the regular dispatches they sent; *Petulia* was, after all, being made as a British picture on location in the States, rather than an American movie. When Rudi Fehr, Warners' editor at Burbank, forwarded memos like "Sound on Slates 32, take 4, unacceptable. Reshoot," Lester simply ignored them—reshooting was against any religion he had ever known.

During his one and only visit to Burbank, a half-day trip to confer with Wagner, Lester found himself being pursued down a thickly carpeted corridor by a short, elderly man. Thinking it was either a case of mistaken identity or a favor about to be called in, Lester increased his pace and lost his pursuer in the maze of offices. Leaving the building later, he passed a huge photograph of Jack Warner and recognized him as the individual he had outrun. The two never did meet, for soon after their not-so-close encounter the company became Warner/Seven Arts, with Eliot Hyman and Robert Solo among those in charge and the legendary Jack no longer part of the company he and his brothers had founded.

■

Early in the New Year Lester took a call from Joe Losey, in the middle of making two films back to back with Elizabeth Taylor. He was unhappy with the voices, the score and the entire dub of *Boom!* he told Lester, but was committed to starting the second movie, *Secret Ceremony*. Lester agreed to help, since this was, after all, his favorite part of the filmmaking process, and he had a lull of a few months while his next project was being developed. Redubbing *Boom!* took him eight weeks, his efforts rewarded by three cases of vintage champagne from Losey and the promise of a "gift" from the movie's producer, Taylor's ex-agent, John Heyman.

"Do you like Francis Bacon?" Heyman asked when they met. "I think he's wonderful, an extraordinary artist," Lester replied "Fine," said Heyman, "there's an exhibition of his work coming up soon. We'll go and see it together and you can pick any painting you want." Lester was thrilled—until the exhibition started and he discovered that Heyman was nowhere to be found. By the time the two met again, about ten years later, the moment had passed. Lester thinks from time to time of the Bacon he might have brought home; whichever one he picked would be worth several millions today.

Petulia's editing was in the hands of Anthony Gibbs, working for the second time with Lester after *The Knack*. He said:

> One reason I like working with Richard is that he, like Tony Richardson, prefers you to go away and "surprise" him with an assembly rather than giving you definite instructions. After all, it's possible for an editor to bring out of a film something the director had not even realized was there— another viewpoint. And if the editor's viewpoint proves disastrous, there is always the director's own concept to return to . . . In *Petulia* the difficulty was to find a suitable style. For all its highly original treatment, and despite all the flashbacks and flash-forwards, it was deliberately edited in a flat, unobtrusive fashion; there were no pyrotechnics, no subliminal

effects. It was this cool approach, I think, which paradoxically prevented the film from appearing cold.

Petulia became the American entry at the Cannes Film Festival in 1968 and ran straight into the infamous May riots, the disturbances having rapidly spread from the wrecked streets of Paris. No sooner had the festival begun than the entire structure started to fall apart, with strikes everywhere, shops and restaurants closed and transportation disrupted. The organizers desperately tried to carry on, despite the increasing violence on the streets that culminated in a police baton charge against demonstrators massed outside the main festival theater.

Deciding it was time to stand up and be counted, Roman Polanski took a stand against what he described as the "Mafia of Communists" behind the riots. Railing that this kind of pressure was exactly what he had left behind in his native Poland, he was adamant that his film remain in competition. At the other end of the scale there were the bully-boys within the festival committee itself, typified by Jean-Luc Godard, whose attitude was simply that everything had to be destroyed, society had to stop—nothing less than total anarchy would do.

During the baton charge Lester was a guest of reformed heroin addict and filmmaker Conrad Rooks on his luxury yacht. With the sounds of conflict from the mainland loud and clear while his guests ate and drank, and with a piano player on board tinkling merrily away, Lester overheard another guest turn to his host with a suggestion: "Conrad, couldn't you get him to play a few revolutionary songs?"

With movies being withdrawn on a daily basis from the competition, Lester decided in the end to go with the flow. His announcement in English was offered in an unfortunate

French translation to Warners', who expressed anger at what they regarded as solidarity with the anarchists. Whether his message was distorted in translation or not, Lester finds it hard to argue with their reaction, except to point out that he had no wish to remain one of the sole competitors in a festival that had been so thoroughly debased, with the streets and theaters blazing. "The sense of pessimism and despair involved was extraordinary," he says. "The cynicism that was being displayed was monstrous. There was a well-known French film director setting fire to the curtains during the day, but by the evening he was at a party with United Artists saying, 'This won't affect my three-picture deal, will it?'"

And Lester had more to lose than most. With *Petulia*'s screening planned for the Thursday before the festival's Sunday closing, the movie was placed second-favorite to win the Palme d'Or and repeat the success of *The Knack* three years earlier. It would have been an unprecedented honor. With the cancellation at Cannes and the continued riots in the capital, the opening was delayed in France for six months.

Since the French air traffic controllers were on strike, even getting out of Cannes proved difficult. On the day *Petulia* should have been shown, Lester was on his way to Genoa. From there he circumnavigated France and flew to London, where he was due to start *The Bed Sitting Room* the following Monday.

If the demonstrations produced one benefit it was in sharpening Lester's attitude to the satire informing his new movie. Following the theory that if you blow up a Greek temple what remain are perfectly formed pieces of that temple, he was about to portray a world where, although only twenty people are left alive, they all continue to behave in the same ridiculous manner they did before the holocaust destroyed their civilization. No matter where movies are set, Lester reflected, they remain mirrors of our time.

With their country waking up to the ongoing horrors of Vietnam and the sour aftertaste of the drug- and sex-influenced "night before," Americans did not care for the nihilism of *Petulia*, especially filtered through the news of Robert Kennedy's assassination the week it was released. Although Petulia did have its critical supporters, it was shunned by the public, spurred on by the likes of Newsweek's Joseph Morgenstern, who described it as "a rotten, dishonest comedy, leaving doubts as to whether Lester loves or hates his characters." Petulia was, he declared, the work "of an opportunistic, deracinated entertainer, who keeps up with the affairs of his homeland from London by going to see *The Loved One*." Judith Crist in New York magazine thought Lester was becoming "a captive of his style," which he was "exploiting for its own sake." Renata Adler, on the other hand, described *Petulia* in the New York *Times* as a "strange, lovely, nervous little film." Time magazine, while conceding that "Lester enjoys himself satirizing San Francisco and contemporary society," complained that "the actors have little to do." Penelope Gilliatt, writing in the New Yorker, described Lester as "a visibly brilliant director" producing a "passionate" film whose accuracy in portraying contemporary sensitivity was "grieving and distinct." For every Richard Corliss, however, who described *Petulia* as "relevant and revelatory" in National Review, there was a Pauline Kael who found it "obscene, disagreeable and dislikable" or a John Simon to whom it was "a soulless, arbitrary, attitudinizing piece of claptrap."

Reaction abroad was similar, if a little less extreme in its praise and condemnation. According to Michael Billington

161

in the London *Times*, "Lester's mannerisms are becoming intrusive," with *Petulia*'s style at odds with its content. John Coleman in New Statesman disagreed, describing it as "Lester's most vulnerable and best film to date." Not unexpectedly John Haase complained long and loud about the transformation Lester had achieved. "The love story has been destroyed," he claimed. "There are a lot of things Richard Lester put in to show his talent—scenes in a roller rink, bullfights, two doctors having lunch in a topless restaurant. Doctors don't eat in topless restaurants. I'm damned if I can figure out the story. Petulia was a very warm person in my original book; in the movie she comes out as an irresponsible nut."

"They are not the same people as in the book," Lester agreed.

> There is something delicate, very interesting and, I hope, very real in the film about two people trying to get through to each other. I feel that Petulia is very vulnerable, sad and desperate. Nothing happens in the movie at all, there is no dramatic high point, and people just keep missing each other. It's really about all of us. Petulia keeps *imagining* possibilities. She has premonitions of things happening all the time, but *when* they happen, they're dreary and sad. In my own life my hand gets caught in my sleeve in most of my dramatic exits.

The normally reticent Lester had clearly been moved by Petulia into a rare bout of introspection.

Many, this writer included, place *Petulia* among the all-time classics of the cinema. Lester had been premature in asking that *How I Won the War* decide his place in cinema history, fine movie though it was. Had he done nothing else, *Petulia* places him in the pantheon of great filmmakers.

The movie has been constantly rediscovered and reevaluated over the years; in a survey of the best American films made between 1968 and 1978, it emerged third behind Coppola's *Godfather* and Altman's *Nashville*. Several years after its release, Sheila Benson in the Los Angeles *Times* wrote, "Lester's films cry out for more than one viewing. I settled into my sixth look at *Petulia* with the sense that I might have overdone things; perhaps it was possible to overdose on *Petulia*. Eight minutes into the film I wriggled contentedly in my seat, caught all over again." In 1985 critic Joel Siegel wrote, "*Petulia* is, without question, my favorite American movie, perhaps my favorite of all movies. I've seen it at least twice a year since it was released and each viewing has yielded fresh insights and pleasures."

These assessments lay in the future. At the time, Lester had delivered his third flop in a row, was about to embark on a fourth, and had to endure the inevitable backlash that was made all the more bitter. In the otherwise innocuous columns of Holiday magazine, Burt Prelutsky quoted "a friend of Lester's" claim that he was now the most self-assured fellow in the world:

> The last time he worried was the evening they previewed *A Hard Day's Night*. He was scared stiff at the time. Now he says, "Any movies I'm connected with, I'm the star of . . ." As a writer who has had experience with Dick, I can tell you he has absolutely no respect for words. He doesn't even *understand* word jokes. He makes a very conscious effort to be zany, which can get to be tiresome. He has one great fear, that of being considered old-hat or traditional. I think that keeps him up at nights.

Then Stephen Sondheim evidently still smarting over *A Funny Thing* . . . took center stage. "Dick is terribly immature," he coolly informed Prelutsky, "and that's both a plus and a minus. It's a plus when he's making Beatles movies, but a definite minus when he's trying to deal with something of substance. He can't tell a story . . . He's a very nervous fellow and also very nervous-making. My most vivid memory of him is that he once put on double safety belts for a one-minute drive . . ."

Sondheim's litany was leavened by praise, however faint:

> What I like about his *Forum* was that it was a movie and not a photographed stage play. Unfortunately, Dick doesn't care about plot, so he ruined the book. The plotting of the play was brilliant, but he ruined it by throwing it all out the window. I'd have to say he has even less respect for the story than for the word. He's full of statements; he's really a very pompous fellow. Although he may claim he is only going to stay in films for ten years, as he only stayed in TV for ten years, I would guess he'll remain in films, because he's getting better at them. His latest, *Petulia*, was his best.
>
> Would I work with him? If the property depended on its story, I'd be very reluctant. If it depended on spontaneity and invention, he'd be my first choice. I personally admire someone who has the courage of his own arrogance; that's why I think Dick is growing . . . He's not an auteur director; he's just got a set of gimmicks. He's a tricky director, but there's nothing personal about his films. That's why he's a second-rate, make that a *second-echelon* director."

Sondheim graciously conceded that *Petulia* was "a very hopeful, very encouraging sign. It's the first time he's used gimmicks to illustrate characters. Content dictates form, as Fellini and Truffaut know; when Dick learns that lesson properly, maybe he will be up there with them."

While Lester's "I'm the star" remark turned out to be entirely fictional, it was true that at one point he had threatened to give up movies after ten years—until, that is, he had wandered in from working in the garden one day to find his wife savoring the quote. "What's this?" she asked. "Oh, you know I've always been a frustrated musician," he replied. "If things hadn't turned out as they did, I'd like to have played piano, or composed or conducted." As Deirdre chewed this over, her eyes fell on her husband's hands, filthy and scratched up from his morning's work. "With *those* hands?" she asked, sending them both into gales of laughter.

Ray Wagner had the perfect put-down for Sondheim. *"No respect for words? He's the wittiest man I've ever met. And in fact, after Larry Marcus, who wrote* Petulia, *saw the movie, he said, 'It's ten times the film I wrote.' Dick doesn't have a style. What his films have is* him.*"*

CHAPTER ELEVEN

Richard Lester has a way of making a film your friend.

—JULES FEIFFER

After *A Hard Day's Night* and *Help!*, the Beatles had one more movie to make for United Artists to fulfill their three-film contract. Despite the success of the first two, they were impatient to move on and no longer be "guest stars in our own movies," as John saw it. For a while they toyed with a novel of Richard Condon's, *A Talent for Loving*, then switched to commissioning playwright Joe Orton to fashion a screenplay. "Basically," Orton wrote in his diary, "the Beatles are getting fed up with the Dick Lester type of direction. They want dialogue to speak. Also they are fed up with actors like Leo McKern stealing scenes. Difficult, this, as I don't think any of the Beatles can act in any accepted sense." Orton went on to produce a script entitled *Up Against It*, and subtitled *Prick Up Your Ears*, which Shenson, Epstein and the group read, disliked and promptly vetoed. They wanted material that was different, but not *that* different.

Oscar Lewenstein had staged several of Orton's plays in revival, including *What the Butler Saw*, with Ralph Richardson, *Loot* and *Entertaining Mr. Sloane*, and heard of the discarded screenplay. When it was shown to Lester, his response was, "Get a young Dick Lester to direct it." To many the remark smacked of an arrogance that was not intended: "What I was saying to Oscar was, 'Get somebody in who's up for it, someone who will bring an energy and enthusiasm to the project and have no sense of responsibility or critical reputation or bugger all else to live up to, someone who can be as anarchic as I was when I was doing the *Goon Shows.'* "

When Lewenstein persisted, Lester took a second look and decided that, while far from being a finished piece of work, *Up Against It* might be converted into something that was fun—like a musical-political frolic for Mick Jagger, Ian McKellen and a couple of young girls. Meanwhile, the Beatles had decided to take the easy way out with a documentary that would complete their contract with UA. Amidst constantly squabbling and several fistfights, *Let It Be* was shot at Twickenham and on the roof of their Apple headquarters by director Michael Lindsay-Hogg. The strains were becoming terminal; a complete break-up seemed to be only a matter of time.

Lewenstein agreed to a deal with Peggy Ramsay, Orton's agent, that the playwright would report to Twickenham to work with Lester on a musical adaptation of *Up Against It*. Twiddling their thumbs over coffee on the appointed Monday morning, Lester and Lewenstein received a call from the driver Lewenstein had dispatched to collect Orton. "I rang the bell," they were told, "but there's no answer."

"He *must* be there," they insisted, "Keep trying, have a look around and call us back." Looking through the letter slot, the driver glimpsed a pair of naked legs stretched out on the floor; Lester and Lewenstein promptly called Peggy Ramsay, who summoned the police. When Orton's flat was broken into, he was found battered to death by his lover, Kenneth Halliwell, who had then taken his own life.

Once the shock of Orton's death had subsided, Lester continued to pursue the project, working first with Roger McGough, then with Charles Wood. *Up Against It* simply refused to happen; Orton's work proved virtually impossible to adapt. The problem for Lester was that he had already received a verbal go-ahead from UA for "a Mick Jagger musical."

A switch to *The Bed Sitting Room*, a play by Spike Milligan and John Antrobus that had impressed Lewenstein in its stage version, now loomed as a more immediate possibility. Lester took Milligan and Antrobus's screenplay and handed it to Wood for adaptation. Since Lewenstein had already paid him a generous fee for his work on *Up Against It*, Wood had what he described as "a crisis of conscience" and offered to adapt *The Bed Sitting Room* for no fee. When Lewenstein insisted that he had to be paid something to secure the copyright, Wood accepted a £1 note, which he promptly framed. "My conscience was a assuaged," he says today. "I must have been rather mad in those days! Although I rewrote the script I kept all the original gags."

Although he had read Rachel Carson's *Silent Spring* in the late fifties, Lester thought that *The Bed Sitting Room* was the first film that made him aware at first hand of environmental problems. It is set after the Third World War has ended (duration: two minutes, twenty-eight seconds). The bomb has been dropped, and there is nothing left alive except for twenty human survivors, all of whom are about to mutate. Much of the black comedy in the piece arises from the survivors behaving as if nothing had happened.

Lester prides himself on having taken a major step forward in the history of movie billing by introducing cast credits in order of height. He had doubts as to whether he could get this past the multitude of agents involved, representing (not in order of size) Michael Hordern, Arthur Lowe, Rita Tushingham, Spike Milligan, Mona Washbourne, Sir Ralph Richardson, Harry Secombe, Peter Cook, Dudley Moore, Roy Kinnear, Dandy Nichols and Marty Feldman. He prevailed and had a clause inserted stipulating that "in cases of argument, the decision of the producer shall be deemed final and binding."

In the concentric circles of relationships that constitute show business, Lester had known "Pete and Dud" for years. Judy Scott-Fox, later to become Cook's agent, had been his secretary at the Establishment Club in the fifties; he also had a mutual friend in Jonathan Miller. And Lester had made a commercial for James Garrett with Cook, Moore and Ursula Andress, intended to promote some totally undrinkable product of Cadbury's that would have been better exploited as a wood finish, capable as it was of transforming an oak table into an instant antique; the results of the test marketing had been an unmitigated disaster. The commercial upon which the foursome embarked proved great fun, however when Andress, set to play a bikini-clad figment of the pair's imagination, turned up five months' pregnant, Lester promptly wrapped her in a borrowed fur coat with the contractual bikini underneath.

He was dismayed at the ease with which he was able to find locations for *The Bed Sitting Room*—like Port Talbot, near Swansea, where industrial waste poured from Imperial Chemical's plant, turning lakes and trees into dead things. Lester's cast had to be hosed down to avoid hospitalization after wading in the goo. Then there was Stoke-on-Trent, bang in the heart of the industrial Midlands, which provided a quarter-mile vista of blue-and-white cracked porcelain

Lester and Dudley Moore stuck in the mud filming *The Bed Sitting Room*. (COURTESY OF RICHARD LESTER)

plate, and St. Austell in Cornwall, with its endless clay pits. Shooting for ten weeks, from May through the summer of 1968, was an eyeopener not only for Lester but for his entire cast and crew.

The casting of Sir Ralph Richardson as Lord Fortnum of Alamein afforded at least one delight, although it was no less hazardous a process than his transmutation to the bed sitting room of the title. Their first meeting took place when Lester was invited to Sir Ralph's Nash Terrace house overlooking Regent's Park. Sitting in his fourth floor study, the veteran commented, "I like to think we are all God's bees, don't you?" Lester thought, "Christ, it's a trick question. If I fail, I'm out." He survived—to this day Lester still regards himself as at least *somebody's* bee. Sir Ralph's next pressing

170

concern was to discover how his character would walk. "Once I know that," Lester was informed, "I've got him." Having studied his work over the years, Lester found this hilarious, only because the one thing Sir Ralph never changed was his walk.

Opening up his copy of the script and picking out one of the weakest lines, Sir Ralph intoned the words with lip-smacking relish. "How can I *not* be in a film with a line like that?" he demanded to know. "It's *sheer brilliance*. I say, would you like a drink?"

Next to his study desk was a small table with a silver salver on which sat two crystal decanters of gin and whiskey, matching glasses and a small crystal bottle of Angostura bitters. "What would you like, dear boy?" Sir Ralph asked his guest.

"I'll have a whiskey, thank you," Lester replied.

"Excellent. Would you like some of mine while yours is coming?"

Puzzled, Lester stammered, "Y-yes, please," whereupon Sir Ralph began to fill one of the tumblers. Just then, an extremely aged butler entered the room. "Ah, Lucky!" Sir Ralph greeted him. "Just in time!"

Noting that Lucky bore another silver salver, on which lay two identical decanters and crystal glasses (but no bitters), Lester watched as the two began an exchange of tumblers and decanters that stopped just short of a squabble.

As Lester was nervously contemplating being asked to hold their jackets, the phone on Sir Ralph's desk gave a sharp ring. "Answer that, dear boy," he asked Lester, elbowing it across so as not to lose his grip on the crystalware. When Lester picked up the receiver and gave a nervous hello, he found it was Sir Ralph's wife on the other end of the line. "Who the hell are you?" she demanded to know.

"It's . . . why, I'm . . ." he managed to get out before the good lady cut in with, "Oh, never mind. Just shut those bloody lift doors!" When Lester finally set foot on the pavement outside he was able, for the first time in his life, to imagine how Alice must have felt after emerging from her subterranean adventures.

At the last moment Sir Ralph almost walked out of the movie after a pre-production costume fitting where he learned he was to appear in morning dress, topped by a black silk hat in which was planted a battery-operated early warning radar system. "I can't wear that!" he exclaimed as he tried the outfit on. It turned out that what he objected to was not the Heath Robinson implant but the color of the hat, which he pointed out should be regulation daytime gray.

Location work on the movie took Lester and his crew to Torquay, where they found themselves booked into a truly terrible mausoleum of an old English hotel. Lester was concerned that he would be blamed for landing everyone in what amounted to a badly run dump reeking of the stale smell of body odor, moldering carpets and overcooked cabbage. At breakfast the first morning Sir Ralph eased the pain of it. "It's so wonderful what you do for us," he told Lester. "It's one of the pleasures of filmmaking. How wonderful to be taken to a place that reminds one of one's schooldays!"

One of the most moving scenes in the film, in which Tushingham delivers a soliloquy about her new boyfriend, sprang from a feeling Lester had that a quiet, reflective moment was needed amidst the surrounding madness. Wood telephoned the dialogue through the morning after it was requested, where it was taken down in shorthand by the script girl, memorized by Tushingham and shot later that day, watched over by her parents, Washbourne and Lowe.

Far from a marriage made in heaven, theirs was confined strictly to the movie and Wood's dialogue. "Moaning Washbourne" and "Arthur Slowe," as they nicknamed each other, did not get on terribly well.

Even though he was used to Lester's speedy filmmaking technique, David Watkin was still taken aback at the alacrity with which he tackled *The Bed Sitting Room*, especially after the construction of one set temporarily nudged the production over its $1 million budget. "I make a deal with myself," Lester explained. "If United Artists lets me make the movie I want to make, without interference, in return I stick to the budget they lay down."

Rita Tushingham had seized the opportunity to work with Lester again, and was one cast member who took his policy of never showing rushes in her stride. "It makes perfect sense to me," she says, "because that's the way I started out with Tony in *A Taste of Honey*. 'Thank God he did that,' I said to myself at the end, for I realized that if I had seen them I would have been 'adjusting' my walk, my stance, the way I move my arms—everything!—as the movie progressed. Because half the time when you look at rushes you're not looking at your 'performance,' but at different aspects of the way you're looking and moving and most of the time it's best not to see that."

Tushingham's sense of fun came out when she saw Michael Hordern deep in conversation with Sir Ralph and teasingly asked him, "Picking up some hints on how to be a knight, are we, Michael?" Knowing he was a staunch Conservative, she sent Hordern an invitation to be a special guest at a party for the Labor party. "Look at this!" he huffed and puffed as he arrived on the set the following morning. "How dare they send this to me!" Next she dispatched a parcel containing a tiny build-it-yourself model yacht with a note from Buckingham Palace: "We are sending you this kit, which we'd like you to assemble and sail in all the Royal Parks, then come back and advise us on your progress. It might then be possible that you will be in line for a knighthood." Tinkering about on a pile of trash one day, Tushingham found a wooden leg that contained a stack of extremely old £10 notes. She still called her director over and excitedly showed him the treasure. "Will this put us back on budget?" she asked solicitously, instantly dispelling his gloom. Unfortunately, the notes were out of date.

Only when he had a rough cut of the movie, with no score, did Lester finally consider a screening for the heads of UA. With Arnold and David Picker, editor John Victor Smith and Lewenstein joining him, they sat in the preview theater and unreeled *The Bed Sitting Room*. Halfway through, prompted by the constant fidgeting from the Pickers, Lester suddenly realized that he had neglected to warn them not to expect a musical with Mick Jagger. Oops!

Around reel eight, Arnold Picker removed his cigar from his mouth, turned to him and asked, "How much longer is this *shit* going on?" As soon as the movie ended he walked out without uttering a word, leaving his nephew to wave Lester a decidedly fretful farewell. The word that filtered back, although it was hardly necessary, was that the senior Picker loathed the movie.

Lester decided the best, indeed the only thing to do, was to keep his nose down and press ahead. With a Kurt Weill–inspired score composed by Ken Thorne, he entered the film at the Berlin Film Festival, where it won the Gandhi Peace Prize in July 1969. Even with this accolade, admittedly a few steps down from the main prize, the Silver Bear, the film did poorly.

While in Germany, Lester and Deirdre, together with Rita Tushingham, the David Pickers and Sir Ralph, were guests at a luncheon thrown by Berlin's mayor. After several glasses of wine Richardson delivered, in his inimitable style, one of his great put-downs. It began innocently enough as the mayor was informed, "I do so love your city." At this his host leaned forward, beaming, awaiting the great man's reasons. After an impeccably timed pause, Sir Ralph explained, "It has the most magnificent . . . escalators."

From Germany the group traveled to the Moscow Festival where a locally dubbed print of the film was screened in a 4,000–seat cinema, with every seat filled. Unfortunately the film was neither dubbed nor subtitled; instead, the soundtrack was turned off and a translation of all the lines was read out in stentorian tones. This was greeted with utter silence until a visual piece of business produced thirty seconds of hysterical laughter: a Van Gogh painting is hung in a room covered with floral wallpaper, whereupon Mao Tse-Tung enters and covers it with a piece of identical wallpaper. Although Lester had only intended the piece as a throwaway, the Russian audience took it as a statement on Maoism, which they found extremely funny. After that one reprieve, it was back to silence.

Judith Crist greeted the American opening of *The Bed Sitting Room* in New York magazine by describing it as "a flatulent, snail-paced series of *Goon Show* discards." Pauline Kael in the New Yorker found the "chaos" of the movie "numbing." While complaining of the "odd script which Lester seemed content to fumble along with," Stanley Kauffman in New Republic at least conceded the unassailability of the photography and acting. The movie, according to Joseph Morgenstern in Newsweek, was a "dim post-war farce," too "remote" to reach audiences. Time magazine, on the other hand, found it "hilarious." There was isolated support on the fringe as well, notably from the Los Angeles *Free Press*, who hailed it as the "culmination" of Lester's work. Frederick Goldman in Film News later described the dialogue as "brilliant," while conceding that the demands it made of its audience might account, in part at least, for its ignominious box-office failure.

In Britain the movie received a mixed, slightly more upbeat reception. In the Spectator, Penelope Houston saw it as "a solid filmmaker's idea that had gone wrong," suffering from a "dated theme." Richard Mallet in Punch was disappointed to find some of its "best jokes thrown away," while John Coleman in New Statesman grudgingly conceded that the "film has its moments." The Scotsman saw it as "a wild movie, funny, bawdy and sometimes rather sad." Alexander Walker in London's Evening Standard offered moderate praise, at the same time suggesting that "sustained Goonishness" at ninety minutes was rather hard to take. While the Guardian paid tribute to "an honorable failure," Dilys Powell in the Sunday *Times* was the film's chief supporter, describing it as "funny at a first look, at a second uproarious" and "Lester's funniest work."

Brilliant though I find the movie, it undeniably made little attempt to reach out and beguile its audience. Lester's ambition to bring Beckett to the masses succeeded no better than *How I Won the War*'s Brecht-for-all, its release affording both his admirers and critics a chance to summarize his career to date. Like the reviews of his movies, they ran the gamut. London's What's On critic had clearly had enough:

> I shall not be reviewing *The Bed Sitting Room* next week or any week. My own sense of humor is so utterly at variance with Mr. Lester's that I feel it would be unfair to him and to you,

the reader, if I did. So I shall pass the chore on to someone else. In truth, I have so disliked Mr. Lester's films (and latterly the term "dislike" has become a strict understatement) that I have come to the conclusion, in view of their popularity, that somehow or other, however uninvited and unwelcome, prejudice must have taken over or at least colored my judgment.

Margaret Hinxman was next out of the closet in the columns of the Sunday *Telegraph*. After admitting to finding Lester's early "comic cuts" often "droll, but also deeply irritating, like the pranky larks of a gifted adolescent allowed to show off for too long at a stretch," she had fallen happily on *Petulia*, which seemed to indicate he had left his "antic capers" behind to find maturity as a film artist. Now, it seemed, *The Bed Sitting Room* had brought her back down to earth with a thud.

Penelope Houston also chose to jump ship, complaining that in *The Bed Sitting Room* Lester "still uses incessant restlessness as a substitute for pace. Anything goes, so in the long run nothing much goes. . . . It's all timing, and at the moment one of us seems to be out of step." The Financial Times also felt that a summation was in order. Even as they conceded that Lester was "quite evidently a very considerable talent," they went on to suggest that "none of his films have been totally successful." The oddest paradox, they suggested, was that "his worst shortcoming is a sense of timing at odds with the kind of comedy in which he prefers to work. He seems to be an artist caught in a wrong situation between the poles of comedy and philosophy." One glimmer of hope was held out: "If ever he resolves his dilemma, he will be an auteur to be reckoned with."

Vincent Canby's contention in the New York *Times* that "Lester's movies seem to get worse in direct relation to the seriousness of their intentions" was countered in the columns of Time magazine: "Lester shows few signs of fatigue," they claimed in their glowing review of *The Bed Sitting Room*. "In fact, he gets better with each film. The two Beatles movies and *The Knack* had a glossy, TV-commercial cleverness about them that made the chaotic brilliance of *How I Won the War* all the more surprising and gratifying. Last year's *Petulia* was one of the few successful American attempts to tell an adult love story . . . There has been no director of such prodigious comic invention since the halcyon days of Preston Sturges." A Lester film was, they maintained, "the product of a passionate, painful comic vision that is helping to establish him, more and more, as one of the world's most original filmmakers." (In the eighties, when twenty United Kingdom critics were asked to present lists of the ten best British films of all time, three chose *The Bed Sitting Room*.)

As cinematographer to both men, David Watkin saw parallels between the careers of Lester and Tony Richardson. "Tony upset the critics by denying them a press showing of *Charge of the Light Brigade* and the usual champagne and caviar that goes with it. Richard outraged the establishment with *How I Won the War* and *The Bed Sitting Room*, both of which were really significant, great things to have done, but subversive pictures. What the two had in common was a complete refusal to compromise on what they wanted to do. And both, in their own way, paid the price for that."

The question for Lester in view of these summations, some of which bore all the exhilarating hallmarks of career post mortems, was: Whither—forward, backwards or sideways? UA's answer was colored by their own crisis. Tony Richardson had followed his *Tom Jones* triumph with several lossmakers for the company—*The Sailor from Gibraltar*, *Mademoiselle*, *Charge of the Light Brigade*. Sean Connery had temporarily retired as James Bond. Following the smashes with Lester, the Beatles' *Yellow Submarine* and *Let It Be* caused scarcely a ripple. After being taken over by the Transamerica Corporation in 1967, UA was hit just three years later with losses of $45 million and began frantically canceling pictures, even pulling the plug on Stanley Kubrick's long-planned *Napoleon*. If Lester had been coming off several hits, events might have been very different. He wasn't, and the result was a last-minute cancellation of his next two projects that yielded a yawning five-year gap without a single movie. "Who would have thought," Lester later mused, "that within a year it would be as if I had the plague?"

In December 1954, Peter Sellers had defied a theatrical matinee audience expecting *Goon Show* antics. He arrived on stage wearing baggy leopard-skin tights (normally reserved for a balancing act performed with Secombe and Milligan as Les Trois Charleys) and, armed with a record player and an album entitled *Wally Stott's Christmas Melodies*, he greeted the assembly: "Good afternoon, brethren. I want to play you some quite lovely melodies. They are particularly endearing to me and I hope you will find them enjoyable also." He then proceeded to play "White Christmas," which received polite, if puzzled applause, then followed up with "Jingle Bells." After the third number he picked up the player, bowed graciously to the audience—no applause this time, but several boos and catcalls—and walked off. The response of the furious theatrical management to the uproar that followed was to invoke the famous "as known" clause inserted in all performers' contracts under "description of act." Sellers had "performed," but not "as known."

In financing *How I Won the War* and *The Bed Sitting Room*, UA had expected Lester to perform "as known" in the zany, highly profitable style of *A Hard Day's Night*, *The Knack* and

Help! His refusal to do this led to an immediate reappraisal that was directly related to the bottom line.

■

Ella Lester's death from cancer in the middle of her son's shooting of *The Bed Sitting Room* came as a terrible blow, even though he had been aware of her illness for over a year. Stressful as his upbringing had been in many ways, he was able to recall, amidst memories of perfume wafting from the cellar, the waxed flowers and the stewed food, a mother who was devoted to him in her no-nonsense, unsentimental fashion. Besides her gift of a lifetime supply of perfume for Deirdre, another of Ella's legacies was acknowledged by her son: One day he blurted out to his editor, John Victor Smith, "I know I'm stingy," adding rather touchingly, "but I can't help it! I got it from my mother!"

"Stop squinting, try shades, Dick!"

George and Lester on location in Switzerland for the filming of
Help! (COURTESY OF RICHARD LESTER)

"Oh, no! There goes John sky-diving again."

Lester and Paul McCartney. (COURTESY OF RICHARD LESTER)

The tables turned: Paul
filming Richard Lester on
location in Switzerland.
(COURTESY OF RICHARD LESTER)

"Why hasn't Paul got shades?"

Lester with George, John
and Paul in Switzerland for
the filming of *Help!*
(COURTESY OF RICHARD LESTER)

"Having a good time, Ringo?"
"Oh, the greatest, John."

Ringo and John on location in Switzerland filming *Help!*
(COURTESY OF RICHARD LESTER)

Paul, John, Lester and George trying out the slopes.
(COURTESY OF RICHARD LESTER)

"I can see you!"

John, George, Richard Lester and Ringo (top) filming *A Hard Day's Night*.
(COURTESY OF WALTER SHENSON/APPLE)

"Bon voyage, Paul."

Paul McCartney and Richard Lester filming *A Hard Day's Night*.

Richard Lester, "clean old man" Wilfrid Brambell and Paul McCartney filming *A Hard Day's Night*.

*"Well, it happened this way,
Dick. . ."*

Ringo and Richard Lester
filming *A Hard Day's Night*.

"I can't hold my smile forever, Dick!"

Ringo Starr and Richard Lester filming *A Hard Day's Night*.

Richard Lester with Ringo, Paul and John about to bust loose on location for *A Hard Day's Night*.   (COURTESY OF RICHARD LESTER)

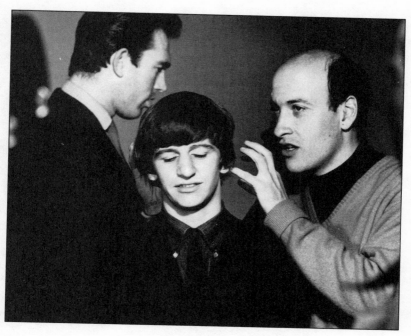

"You are feeling sleepy."

Ringo Starr and Richard Lester.   (COURTESY OF RICHARD LESTER)

"Look, Dick! Ringo's lighting up his tenth ciggy this morning. . ."
(COURTESY OF RICHARD LESTER)

John says: "Look, I could direct this picture."

John Lennon with Richard Lester and the camera crew on the set of *A Hard Day's Night* at Twickenham Studios.
(COURTESY OF RICHARD LESTER)

Richard Lester, Ringo Starr and Patti Boyd swapping comic books while filming *A Hard Day's Night*. (COURTESY OF RICHARD LESTER)

Richard Lester auditioning Paul McCartney. (COURTESY OF RICHARD LESTER)

"Where's that tape of 'Can't Buy Me Love?'"
(COURTESY OF RICHARD LESTER)

Jam session with Lester and Paul McCartney.
(COURTESY OF RICHARD LESTER)

Lester and Paul McCartney playing "My Funny Valentine in C."

George Harrison joins in the fun.

"I didn't know you made movies with other people as well!'

George Harrison and Richard Lester at the World Charity première of *The Knack* at the London Pavilion, June 1965.

(COURTESY OF RICHARD LESTER)

Deirdre and Ringo giving Dominic Lester music lessons.

(COURTESY OF RICHARD LESTER)

"Where's my drums?"
(COURTESY OF RICHARD LESTER)

"Waiters! There's a fly in my curry!"

George Harrison, Leo McKern, John Lennon, Richard Lester, Ringo Starr and John Bluthal on the set of *Help!*
(COURTESY OF WALTER SHENSON/APPLE)

Paul acting as Richard
Lester's unpaid assistant
on location in the Bahamas
filming *Help!*
(COURTESY OF RICHARD LESTER)

Trying desperately to cheer
John up while filming
Help! in the Bahamas.
(COURTESY OF RICHARD LESTER)

John and Paul wondering what on earth Lester is up to.
(COURTESY OF RICHARD LESTER)

"Climb in! Sorry there's no room in the front."
Organizing a car boot sale to balance the budget.
(COURTESY OF RICHARD LESTER)

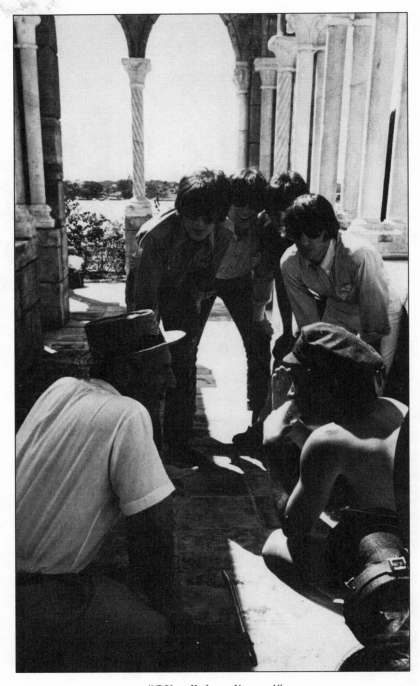

"OK, roll them dice. . . !"

Producer Walter Shenson with George, John, Paul, Ringo and
Lester on lacation in the Bahamas filming *Help!*

(COURTESY OF RICHARD LESTER)

CHAPTER TWELVE

"He's [Lester is] oddly remote, a perfectionist and probably a most fascinating hell to live with.

—IRMA KURTZ

After the end of shooting *The Bed Sitting Room* in 1968 and David Picker's departure from United Artists shortly thereafter, Lester's desert of discontent stretched until 1973 as one project after another collapsed. *Send Him Victorious*, a political thriller by the future British Foreign Minister Douglas Hurd together with Andrew Osmond that was due to be shot in Rhodesia in 1969, was rejected by UA with the rationale that "nobody even knows where the goddamn country is." With Ralph Richardson, Jeanne Moreau and Ian McKellen lined up to star, Lester continued to pay a crew of thirty for several weeks, hoping to find another backer. Very soon the bank account he had built up during the sixties had melted and he was forced to abort the venture.

An adaptation by Charles Wood of George MacDonald Fraser's *Flashman* was the next project to collapse. Lester had always realized the difficulty of filming the book, from both a technical and financial point of view. One sequence, depicting the entire British army of the Indus in retreat from Kabul in a blizzard, blew the idea of a modestly budgeted movie on its own. Despite this, *Flashman* was initially green-lighted by UA, cast with John Alderton in the lead, and came within four weeks of shooting in 1970 near Granada, where the plan was to utilize the ancient dungeons beneath the Alhambra. The deal fell apart when a company representative turned up and informed Lester that Alderton had a triangular-shaped face, whereas he and his colleagues had always pictured Flashman as someone with an oblong visage. UA, it seemed, wanted out; down went *Flashman*.

Lester was given a novel about religious fanatics in the American South entitled *Wise Blood*, eventually directed by John Huston. It was not a subject that Lester felt he could bring anything to, but he met with lawyer-turned-producer Jack Schwartzman and was impressed. Schwartzman offered to help set up a director's cooperative, in which each member would share in the profits of the others' films. With UA lined up to finance the co-op, six directors agreed to join Lester—John Boorman, Tony Richardson, Lindsay Anderson, Ken Russell, Joseph Losey and Karel Reisz (John Schlesinger was approached but declined; he was up to his neck in offers following the success of *Midnight Cowboy*). The concept fell apart when UA blackballed two on the list, Tony Richardson and Joe Losey—and there went Lester's remaining contact with the company that had backed seven of his first nine films.

"There was a dangerous assumption in the sixties that we all helped each other and joined forces and worked on each other's material and were mates, which is far from the truth," he points out.

> John Schlesinger I knew because he shot a lot of his movies at Twickenham. He was always wildly depressed when he was shooting and his films seemed to me to last forever—there I'd be shooting for six weeks, John for twenty-odd. He could

never say he was going to do a film quickly for you, he couldn't help himself, *Sunday, Bloody Sunday* was small-scale, but he still shot for twenty-eight weeks. He's a very amusing man, great fun, although some of his choices are probably as unwise as mine. *Midnight Cowboy* I thought was a stunning movie, it had the best of John, it was real and yet operatic, it was heightened reality, everything fell into place.

The others I knew best were Tony Richardson and John Boorman, both people I've been sociable with and whose work I've admired. Tony is another who made some films he really shouldn't have. It was getting harder for him from *Tom Jones* onwards, yet there were parts of *Charge of the Light Brigade* that were so impressive. Tony adored the day-to-day filming, he loved being on the set, winding up the actors, stirring up trouble and playing God, he had a wonderful time on the floor. Totally unlike me, who can't wait to get to the editing room.

I think John Boorman was at his best when he was writing and creating something out of existing material. *Point Blank* and *Deliverance* are terrific movies. I don't know whether it's a lack of intellectual rigor on our part, it's dangerous to blame the system and say that it's because we live in the outback that our strike record is less good, whether there is less commercial material floating past our noses from either the cocktail parties or agents' offices on the West Coast. Tony was never really happy in England, yet couldn't come to grips with subjects in America. He was still very much on the outside and I think in a way both Boorman and Schlesinger are the same. Me too."

Although Lester made no actual movies between *The Bed Sitting Room* and *The Three Musketeers*, he was far from idle. Apart from the multitude of offers to direct movies he didn't want to do, all of which had to be at least considered, he spent a lot of time developing scripts for projects that for one reason or another never got made. One of the things that kept him solvent was making a series of Italian *Carouseli*, two-minute-and-twenty-second black-and-white television commercials containing two minutes of entertainment before the twenty-second "message" at the end. There could be no relationship, the Italian TV authorities dictated, between the subject matter and the advertising, so no crawling about in deserts could end with a plug for Perrier; no car rally episode could end with a sales pitch for the latest automobile. Five different *Carouseli* were gathered in groups each night on Italian TV between 9:00 and 9:15 P.M. and regularly drew the week's highest audience ratings.

Another ruling that suited Lester perfectly was that each clip had to be ritually destroyed after a single showing. This left him free to shoot even the most outrageous gags, knowing they would be seen only once, unthinkable with endlessly repeated commercials. Lester flew known and trusted regulars like John Bluthal, Ronnie Brodie, Joanna Lumley, Peter Butterworth and Jenny Hanley off to various locations and worked out a group of ten short films at a time. One series was shot with the cast of three men and one woman quartered in the center of the Sahara Desert at a Foreign Legion fort, improvising ideas with limited props. Lester took his own editor along, a young man named Peter Boyle (most recent assignment: *Robin Hood—Prince of Thieves*) and together they sat around cutting and trimming their *Carouseli* down to size in the cool of the evening. What others might see as a black hole in his career had its compensations.

Another lucrative commission came from Braniff Airlines, whose budget of $250,000 for a commercial was unheard of at the time. The finished film, shot on Shepperton Studios' largest stage and lit by Nic Roeg, lasted precisely three minutes and depicted a world of the future in which people behaved on airplanes as badly as on present-day subways. Only later did Lester discover that Braniff had never intended the commercial to be shown—they were bidding for routes and intended to use his footage to help achieve this. (As it happened, they were awarded elsewhere, while Lester received that year's award for the World's Best Commercial.)

The biggest sense of regret is knowing that for five years of my strongest time physically, with my stamina and energy at a peak, I was making, for the most part, two-minute commercials in Italy that were being destroyed after one showing. I was like an athlete being underused; it was like constantly practicing backhand strokes instead of playing a full game of tennis. At the end of it I had no vendetta against any individual, I didn't have that paranoia that any group had been out to destroy me, I just felt that my life had been wasting away. All through that time there was always a film I was trying to get going, working with a writer—usually Charles. There was never a point where I wasn't going in and working a full day to prepare something, but they just didn't happen. You could say that it drove me slightly up the wall. The only consolation was that I was in good company; several very talented people were up the small wall. Almost everyone I knew was down and depressed, for nothing seemed to be happening, there was complete stagnation. In discussions with Alan Parker years later when we did a TV show together, he couldn't get over how even-handed I was about the experience and some of the individuals concerned. Compared to him, he reckoned I was Mother Teresa.

Still without any likely movie offer in sight, Lester was in Paris completing a commercial when he received a call late in 1972 from a young man named Ilya Salkind. Would he consider directing a film version of Alexandre Dumas's *The Three Musketeers*? After Lester replied that he didn't really think so, Salkind persisted: Had Lester read the book? He was sure that he had but retained only dim memories of it from childhood. As he tackled the paperback Salkind insisted on sending, he realized that what he remembered were the various film adaptations, which only covered about one third of the actual plot and left out the darker, savage side of Dumas.

When he ran the 1921 Douglas Fairbanks silent version, he found it so delightful he felt it would prove impossible to top. Then he saw MGM's Lana Turner/Gene Kelly Technicolor remake, which he disliked intensely. This, together with a Don Ameche/Ritz Brothers musical comedy version, he felt that he could probably surpass. Within a week of Salkind's call he was on a plane to the south of France to discuss the project.

The genesis of the *Musketeers* remake can be traced to one evening in September 1972, over dinner at the luxurious Colombe d'Or in St. Paul de Vence, the former artists' colony overlooking the Riviera. Fifty-seven-year-old Alexander Salkind, descendant of Russian emigré and film producer Michel, and his son Ilya were an odd-looking twosome, both little more than five feet tall, the father resembling nothing so much as a Troll doll with his pot belly and startling shock of swept back gray hair, the son darkly handsome and mustached, conveying a constant sense of restlessness. After working for several years out of Mexico, where Alex had begun his film career by producing a movie with Buster Keaton in 1945, the family was now based in Paris, although Alex retained at least a toehold in Latin America courtesy of an honorary consulship of Costa Rica. Working with his son, Michel Salkind had produced his last film in 1959, *The Battle of Austerlitz*, enlisting no less a luminary than the fabled but down-on-his-luck French director Abel Gance for the French/Italian/Yugoslavian/Liechtensteinian project. This was the "international" co-production Alex Salkind would come to specialize in as he roamed the earth, like his contemporary Dino De Laurentiis and the emergent Menahem Golan and Yoram Globus, Cannon's go-go boys, in search of production money. This was often obtained from the most unlikely and, on occasion, downright suspect sources, although it was claimed to be done by pre-selling territory by laborious territory. (Or "by mirrors" as the system became cynically known, before all three teams, and a host of others besides, found themselves grouped together under the single accommodating umbrella of Frans Afman at Credit Lyonnais.)

The Salkinds had a third partner in soft-spoken, bearded Pierre Spengler. As an eleven-year-old he had been taken by his stepfather to audition for a role in *The Ash Cathedral*, a play written by Alex's wife, Bertha, and directed by Abel Gance while *The Battle for Austerlitz* was being prepared. In Gance's absence young Spengler was taken on by his deputies and attended rehearsals for several weeks, befriending Bertha's son Ilya while they hung around backstage. Gance eventually turned up and demanded a run-through while picking at his dinner from a tray set in front of him. No sooner had Spengler walked on than Gance laid down his fork and motioned him to stop. "That little boy doesn't look Mexican at all," he declared before returning to his tray. It was certainly a point overlooked by his assistants, and one that Spengler was in no position to deny. (His next encounter with Gance took place many years later, with the maestro, in his ninth decade, planning a twelve-hour version of the life of Cervantes. "Don't you think that's rather long for a movie?" Spengler dared to ask. "Not for an Abel Gance movie!" came the unhesitating reply.)

Although his acting career was over, the friendship with Ilya endured, and at seventeen Spengler left school and asked Alex for a job. "If you're prepared to make tea, answer the telephones and mail letters, yes," came the reply. From this start both Ilya and Pierre visited sets, met film people, started to learn about movies and deals and gradually got their feet wet under Alex's guidance. Besides working on the patriarch's movies they gained outside experience as well, notably as second assistants at Nice's Victorine Studios on Bryan Forbes's *The Madwoman of Chaillot*.

By the early seventies the "dead hand" of Alex Salkind had become the stuff of legend, the only wonder being how he carried on despite his every involvement flopping, usually both commercially and artistically. The undoubtedly ambitious *Battle of Austerlitz*, at $4 million a huge film for its time, proved unexportable, variously described as "stultifying" and "hopelessly cluttered" whether in its full 166–minute version or when slashed to 123 minutes. His other highlights included the British *Ballad in Blue*, featuring blues singer Ray Charles (a curious sentimental drama), the French/Spanish/German/Italian *Kill! Kill! Kill!* (its purple prose and direction supplied by Romain Gary), Orson Welles's French/Italian/West German version of Kafka's *The Trial* (gripping but muddled) and the French/Italian/West German *Bluebeard*, starring Richard Burton and Raquel Welch (totally off-putting, which nonetheless did what Spengler calls "honorable" business). Although by 1968, according to Ilya's best estimate, they were down to their last $10,000, this did not deter the team from offering Kirk Douglas $1 million for their next venture, *The Light at the Edge of the World*. They were saved, he maintains, by "a providential lawsuit" that gave them a fresh injection of capital. With one bound—however puzzlingly—they were back in business.

During dinner at the Colombe d'Or the discussion between the Salkinds *père et fils* centered on possibilities for their future movies, and in typically ambitious manner considerable time was spent thinking up a project that would reunite the Beatles. What about *The Three Musketeers*?

"Great idea, son," the patriarch may well have remarked, although whether these are the actual words he used and in which of the five languages at his disposal he uttered them, must remain a mystery. Despite their bubbling enthusiasm, the duo soon crashed back to earth, realizing that the reunification of the Beatles was unlikely. So in their absence, whom else could they cast? The Salkinds' feeling was that an all-star comedy team along the lines of Bob Hope, Jerry Lewis and Danny Kaye would be a riot in a burlesque version of Dumas' temptingly out-of-copyright tale.

Spengler was not present at this historic meal, finessing a deal in Budapest at the time. But he dissented when the idea of a broad comedic version was put to him, convinced that none of their investors would back such an outdated idea. Incredibly, several did, enabling the Salkinds to raise advance cash for the concept. When it came to pinning down the required old-time stars, however, they proved elusive. Then Ilya had a stroke of inspiration: "Let's make *Dumas*. Let's make it *real*." Another tour of investors was duly made to explain the change in emphasis. Now the movie would be high adventure, stuffed with stars, extremely sexy—oh, and in exchange for your quarter-million upfront, whom would *you* like to see in it? Leonard Whiting (hot from Zeffirelli's *Romeo and Juliet*), Ursula Andress (just plain hot), Richard Burton (cold, but not yet ice-cold despite *Bluebeard*) and Raquel Welch (ditto) were at the top of the backers' wish list.

Hoping for another *Tom Jones* and planning a version that would stop just short of an X-rating in the U.S., the Salkinds and Spengler first thought of Tony Richardson to direct and invited him to talks in Paris. Before the oysters had even arrived at lunch Richardson said, "You are aware, of course, that I always get final cut." Alex looked first at his son, then at Spengler, finally at Richardson. "We never give final cut on our pictures," he replied, shaking his head, "but *bon appetit*." Although all of them knew there and then that the deal was off, this did not stop the irrepressible Richardson informing a colleague on his return to London, "They said they wanted to make *The Three Musketeers*, whom they named as Athos, Porthos and D'Artagnan. I certainly wasn't going to work with people who didn't even know who the fucking musketeers were!"

Now the name of the director originally mentioned in connection with the Beatles cropped up. Of course! If they could coax Richard Lester to direct the movie it would be not only high adventure, stuffed with stars and sexy—but funny as well! Lester was aware that the Salkinds had already approached Richardson for their Sexorama version. By the time he had convinced himself—and them—that he was the man to tackle the assignment, the movie was designated as a three-and-a-half-hour roadshow spectacular. *Flashman*'s George MacDonald Fraser was contacted to write the screenplay and turned out what Lester considered a truly astonishing piece of work in just five weeks. In his hands the emphasis had been moved away from the predominantly sexy towards a rip-roaring comedy adventure, albeit one informed by the darker tones previous movie versions had chosen to expunge. One aspect of the Salkinds' deal was location shooting in Hungary, where arrangements had been made to accommodate the cast and crew with maximum economy.

During Lester's few weeks there in the early spring of 1973 scouting the 104 locations—100 were found, with Austria's Schonbrunn Palace selected for one scene—it was obvious that red tape would almost certainly strangle the lighthearted feel he was striving to achieve. A set-up sketch that should have taken a couple of days took a week to deliver. An art director knocked on Lester's door one night to say he was about to be fired by the government-run studio because he had used a tiny amount of petty cash for a bottle of beer following a meeting at Schonbrunn. Now he didn't have the Austrian schillings to repay the studio, and no other currency, it seemed, was acceptable to them. With everything from beer money to location authorization, the iron hand of authority was in evidence, personified by dour government officials waving forms and withholding permits, and marked by a distinct lack of enthusiasm allied to an apparent inability to say yes to anything the first time around.

Lester decided that rebellion was in order. With six weeks to go before shooting was due to start in May, he left the snows of Hungary behind him and flew with two associates to Madrid. The local film industry suffering from a dearth of activity, and he was assured that everything could be set up in the required time frame. Although he had made enough movies in Spain to know that the film board was as good as its word, there was one tiny snag—it considerably increased the cost of shooting. The Salkinds told Lester that the move to Spain would virtually double the budget.

In his recollection it was lengthy discussions with the team, who were otherwise happy enough with the change of location, that led to the decision to scrap the idea of a three-and-a-half-hour "hard ticket" roadshow and go for two separate films, *The Three Musketeers* and a sequel, *The Four Musketeers*, to be shot simultaneously. Spengler disputes that this was the reason and puts the increase in costs in moving from Hungary to Spain at no more than 20 percent. In his version the rationale behind splitting the movie was that no child would sit through the PG-rated version Lester and Fraser had produced—not with a length of three and a half hours. Whatever the reason, the Salkinds decreed that the change of strategy had to be withheld from the cast in case word leaked back to the U.S. distributor, who would be informed that a "sequel" existed only when the team decided it was politic. As far as the actors were concerned, they were making the "project" (the term used in their contracts) in which they had signed to appear.

Lester's first choice for Athos was Charlton Heston, who turned the role down, unwilling to spend the entire summer "hanging around in Spain," as he put it. Instead he suggested he would be willing to do a "bit." Lester took the cue and suggested Heston consider playing Cardinal Richelieu, a part so far outside of the actor's range that he hadn't even considered it. Attracted by the much shorter time frame, and reluctant to forego the chance of working with a director he admired, Heston accepted, placing himself completely in Lester's hands regarding interpretation. "I haven't made as many comedies as you have," he told Lester. "How much of a comic adjustment do you want me to make to Richelieu?"

"None, for God's sake," Lester replied. "You're the villain in this piece and you have to be absolutely credible and genuinely threatening, otherwise it won't work."

Already impressed with Heston, in whom he detected an unexpected sense of self-deprecation, Lester was delighted at their next meeting when the star invited him to his hotel suite, then refused to appear until every detail of his Cardinal Richelieu costume and makeup was correct. When he did make his entrance he was walking with a slight limp to de-emphasize his height—Richelieu was a short man—and was sporting a wig, cloak and false nose. He stood there for a moment to let the full picture sink in before wryly cracking, "Yep, the same old boring Chuck Heston!" (Later he would

*"Lighten up, Charlton, twenty years from now
Disney will be doing this."*

"Milady" Faye Dunaway and "Cardinal" Charlton Heston in *The Three Musketeers*.   (COURTESY OF RICHARD LESTER)

say, "I did the picture because of Dick Lester. The director's the most important thing about a movie, then the part itself." With a broad grin he defined his "cameo": "That's what you call it if it's not the feller the film's about.")

Michael York was cast as D'Artagnan after Lester saw Joe Losey's *Accident* and Zeffirelli's *Romeo and Juliet.* York arrived with his photographer wife, Pat, who proceeded to take what seemed like several thousand pictures of him at every conceivable stage of production, which everyone considered just a bit much.

Frank Finlay was physically the least suitable for his role of Porthos, being neither "huge" nor a "gaudy, noisy fellow" as laid down by his creator. Although Finlay was known neither as a comic nor a Falstaffian character, Lester felt that with a combination of padding and theatrical bombast Finlay could carry it off. He had never met Oliver Reed, but following Dumas's description of Athos as "burly" and a man who "lives hard, drinks too much" reckoned that Reed might bring something to the role even Heston might have missed. Richard Chamberlain he considered excellent casting for Aramis; in Dumas's version he was a priest-killer and a fop, with an overemphasis on style and grandeur, by far the most mannered of the musketeers. Although his film career had never caught fire after *Petulia*, the actor was coming to Lester on this occasion from a great personal triumph on stage as Cyrano de Bergerac.

Faye Dunaway as Milady de Winter and Raquel Welch as Constance Bonancieux satisfied the Salkinds' glamor quotient, although Lester regarded Welch's casting as an imposition. When the team insisted he gave in with reasonably good grace, he determined to invent some physical comedy that would "give her something to do" and, bearing this in mind, cast Spike Milligan opposite her as M. Bonancieux.

Despite the fact that Lester had already chosen Christopher Cazenove for the Duke of Buckingham, the Salkinds substituted Simon Ward and paid Cazenove off, chasing the extra marquee value of his success in *Young Winston*. It was left to Spengler to explain the situation to Cazenove, who flew to Spain at his own expense to protest that he had been promised the role. "I'm sorry," Spengler told him, "but the distribution people want a name." Roy Kinnear was a natural for D'Artagnan's underling, Planchet; Christopher Lee was cast as the dastardly Rochefort. Lester had admired Jean-Pierre Cassel's work in Renoir's *The Vanishing Corporal* and felt he would be ideal as Louis XIII, while Geraldine Chaplin struck him as perfect for Anne of Austria. (Later it turned out that although she looked every inch the part, her voice came over less impressively. For a while Lester intended to use another actress to revoice her role but was prevented from doing this when Chaplin pointed out that she had the right of redub in her contract.)

From the beginning of the project Lester sought to make the enterprise as authentic as possible, down to what people wore, how they behaved, what food they ate—including the filth, and the rat catchers. (The Salkinds and Spengler did not share his quest for authenticity and were initially alarmed when Lester insisted on dirtying several of the costumes. When they saw the results on the screen, however, they swiftly changed their minds.)

Since Dumas's novel was set in 1627, Lester researched major discoveries and inventions in farming, medicine and astronomy. If Harvey in 1610 had discovered that blood circulation was pumped from the heart and not the brain, as previously supposed, how many people in 1627 would have known that? Some, perhaps, but the lesser informed would still be applying tourniquets to necks to stem the flow of blood.

In one of the movie's scenes Lester staged the action around a game of real tennis, having discovered that it had become so popular in seventeenth-century France that finally the king had had to order all tennis courts closed—the game had become *too* fashionable (Moliere's theater had been built on a shut-down court). Then there was the passion for Dutch tulips, with individuals paying thousands of francs for a single bulb. (This particular piece of research paid off in *The Four Musketeers*, when D'Artagnan, having bedded a wench, wakes up in the morning to confront a limp tulip.)

Further plumbing of the archives yielded information on swordfights of the period, with Lester and fight arranger Bill Hobbs studying the seventeenth-century book by Thibault on the art of fencing and faithfully employing his moves. The first thing Lester realized was that seventeenth-century blades were extremely thick, heavy and long. Instead of balancing on the back foot and lunging forward as in standard fencing, his combatants had to place their weight on the front foot and hack, using a dagger and cape to fend off their rival's blade while they slashed down.

This led to some extraordinarily impressive scenes, like the spectacular battle in the laundry, where all did not go according to plan. The Spanish fight arranger set to do battle with Oliver Reed was unprepared for the actor simply hurling himself at him the moment Lester yelled, "Action!" He came close to throwing up with fear and from then on refused to fight Reed. He was replaced by a young gypsy boy who acted as Reed's stunt double as well as playing his adversary. He turned out to be as streetwise as Reed and was the only person with nerve enough to face up to "dreaded Olly."

■

On the eve of filming, Lester retreated to his hotel apartment, ate an early dinner and went straight to bed. Just as he was about to fall asleep, Pierre Spengler called. "What are you up to?" he asked. "I'm in bed," Lester replied, "sucking my thumb and crying."

"Really? Look, I'm having my twenty-sixth birthday party but I've told everyone it's to welcome Faye Dunaway to the picture. You've got to come."

"Happy birthday," said Lester. "I'm going to sleep." Fifteen minutes later, after much cajoling by Spengler along the lines of "duty" and "you are the director, after all," he was dressed and psyched up for anything. It was just as well. Following the introduction to his Milady de Winter, he sat for a while chatting about the great adventure on which they were about to embark. Lester watched fascinated as Dunaway had four glasses of champagne set up on the table in front of them, then produced a silver pillbox from her bag and placed one pill beside each glass. As each pill was downed with a champagne chaser, Lester felt constrained to ask, "Faye, what on earth are you doing?"

"Oh, don't worry," the diva replied. "They're only aspirin. You see, champagne gives me a headache." (Several years later Lester met playwright Israel Horovitz and his star, Al Pacino, to discuss the possibility of Lester's directing a movie entitled *Compliments of the Author*. At dinner afterwards Lester told the champagne-and-aspirin story to his hosts, thinking it would suit the flaky actress in their movie. He then declined the assignment after he and Pacino failed to click. Three years later, sitting in a hotel room in New York, Lester caught a commercial for what had become *Author! Author!*, directed by Arthur Hiller, and watched as the Dunaway episode was faithfully re-enacted by Dyan Cannon.)

He detected in Dunaway, who did not prove the most popular member of the cast, a veneer of hardness and bitchiness that suited Milady. One of her problems, Lester was convinced, was an apparent lack of enjoyment of the filmmaking process. She invariably turned up an hour late every day, then had to undergo three or four hours of makeup with her own staff. Since the most flattering light was from dawn until 9 A.M. she proved her own worst enemy, for as soon as the sun came up dust began to fly and pupils to contract. When she finally arrived she would be carrying a tray that held Blistex, a lip salve, and separate glasses of cola and ice water. With everyone waiting and anxious to proceed, she would take a sip of cola, followed by ice water to take the taste away. By this time her lipstick required touching up, followed by another application of Blistex. Then she would start the process again—sip of cola, ice water, more lipstick, more Blistex. Lester began to get the feeling she could not bear to expose herself and actually begin a scene.

If Dunaway could dish out grief, she could also take it. In a flashback sequence that showed her being branded as a harlot, the camera was first to focus on a brazier full of hot coals, then the branding iron being applied to her upper arm. At this point the special effects department were to blow a puff of smoke through a tube inside the iron, with a realistic *s-s-s-s* to be added later by Gerry Humphreys back at Twickenham. Lester decided he had better allow a few extra seconds for the flashback dissolve, and slowly counted "one, two, three, four, five" while the branding iron languished in the coals. When it finally reached Dunaway, she gave an impressively realistic scream before turning on Lester and shouting, "It's only a fucking *film*, you know!" as he stood there, shocked and profusely apologetic. The scar, he heard later, lingered for several years.

■

David Watkin began to realize something about Lester when he looked at the piece of paper stuck to his camera magazine, where he routinely had the various actors, doubles and stuntmen on a film sign their names. There at the end of the *Musketeers* list was *Richard* printed in large letters. "Who the fuck's *Richard*?" he asked his deputy. "Your director," came the reply. Lester had clearly decided to have done with "Dick" for good; if his name was Richard in the credits, he now wanted to be addressed as such. "I thought he was just being pretentious," says Watkin, "until I suddenly remembered how much I hated being called Dave or Davy!"

The name change was not confined to professional circles, but included even the Lester household and Deirdre, who had for years called her husband "Dick." Several longtime acquaintances were puzzled, especially James Garrett, who recalls Lester's eyes "glazing over every time someone called him Dick," although he finds it difficult to pinpoint when the transition took place. The truth was that Ella Lester was responsible, having expressed her considerable dismay to her daughter-in-law during a visit to England, a year before her death, that her son was being improperly addressed.

To many it was as if Billy Wilder had suddeny insisted on being called William or Al Pacino had become Alfred. It says much for the respect in which Lester was held that everyone acceded in the end to his wishes and those of his mother, although to this day the odd "Dick" still slips out—at least from Paul McCartney.

CHAPTER THIRTEEN

"I know the Salkinds talked to Tony before me on Three Musketeers. *It's never bothered me—that's part of the game."*

—RICHARD LESTER

With a tight budget, each episode of *The Musketeers* costing around $3.5 million with the schedules intertwined, the entire cast and crew were quartered in Madrid, a decision necessitating long and arduous daily journeys to locations. The rationale was twofold: the Salkinds worked out that the Madrid-based crew would be unable to claim its expenses if they returned home each night; and in each move to a fresh location, a day's shooting would be lost. On balance, their decision was probably the right one in strict financial terms, but it ignored the wear-and-tear on individuals through early starts, constant traveling and late finishes.

One morning Lester and his troupe left the city at six in the morning in a convoy of cars and drove all the way to the Plain of Urbaza in the north to a site production designer Brian Eatwell had chosen for the Duke of Buckingham's deer hunt sequence. As they decamped four and a half hours later, Lester remarked, "You realize we'll never be able to do a full day's shoot here." "But you must admit it *looks* like

England," his associate countered. "God, the distance we've come, it should *be* England!" said Lester. Just then a blanket of fog descended; they managed just two and a half hours of shooting that day before having to face the return journey.

Another interminable drive took the unit east to a National Treasure monastery at Uccles on the road to Valencia, where they were allowed to build a false wall covering three levels and attached to the building itself. Later they were able to set fire to this for the climactic siege of La Rochelle. The same pattern, if not the same distance, prevailed for the entire shoot, with the unit traveling to Aranjuez, La Granja, Segovia, Toledo and Pedraza, in all of which they were unable to stay overnight. Brian Eatwell's hardy vehicle clocked 85,000 kilometers by the time he was through, with the movie dubbed "Travels with My Aunt" by the Spanish crew.

As architect of the move from Hungary, Lester had considerable compassion for the art department when they protested a shortage of funds. "We stumbled at the beginning after six wasted weeks in Hungary," Eatwell declared, chafing at having been given half his normal preparation time, "and staggered all the way through."

One of Lester's trickiest tasks was in attempting to coordinate the schedules of the huge cast flying in and out, their contracts all over the place. Heston was around for only a few weeks, Faye Dunaway for six, Jean-Pierre Cassel for two weeks in batches of days. As a result Lester found himself constantly working with doubles, having Heston in Madrid looking down on a scene to be shot several months later in Toledo, or Michael York passionately addressing a long-gone Dunaway. The investiture scene was shot several times, from different points of view, over four months, Heston making his contribution during May before he departed, Cassel

Richard Lester and award-winning cinematographer David Watkin arguing over whether it's "Dick" or "Richard" while filming *The Three Musketeers*.   (COURTESY OF DAVID WATKIN)

filming his in August, followed by Raquel Welch in September. (At one point, to the accompaniment of much good-natured ribbing from the crew, Lester himself was got up in wig, mustache and robes to double over-the-shoulder shots of the absent Cassel.) As the strain of directing the mammoth operation began to tell, Lester found his weight dropping from an already lean 147 pounds to 129 pounds through sheer exhaustion.

Never particularly renowned for his gregariousness, he surprised his crew one night by inviting them out for a meal at a local taverna. Of the thirty who were served paella, all of them—except for their host—came down with varying degrees of food poisoning. "It *must* have been the paella," one of them told Lester a few days later. "It can't have been," Lester replied. "*I* didn't become ill." Following the incident the crew came up with a nickname for their director: The Bionic Man. It reflected his apparent invincibility as well as his dogged determination to battle his way through the countless difficulties he encountered at every turn on *Muske-teers*.

Lester was sound asleep one morning at 3 A.M. when the telephone rang. The police had arrested Oliver Reed a few hours earlier after he had clambered into the fish tank in the dining room of the Castellano Hilton. There, much to the consternation of the other guests under the impression that some disgusting drunk was biting the heads off live fish, he gnawed large chunks from several carrots he had stashed in his trousers. When Lester arrived to sign him out and drive him back to his hotel, Reed was the picture of sheepish apology.

Heston's admiration for Lester grew as the weeks wore on—from his multiple-camera technique ("makes a lot of sense, especially with comic stuff; you're sure to have the good accident on all angles") to the easy wit constantly on display. His diary entry of June 7 gave several of Lester's critics a hefty sideswipe:

> Lester worked very quickly. He's very sure of his setups and blockings; so far he hasn't used a moving camera once on the film . . . His ultimate simplification of film technique illustrates the technical ignorance of the critical community, since they laud Lester in terms of the brilliance of his camerawork. What they mean, of course, is his cutting. I'm enormously impressed with his talent and find his method very easy to respond to as well.

In Segovia he approached Lester and declared, "God, I've really been in this trade too long. I recognize this location. We shot here on *El Cid* back in 1961."

"Really, your Grace?" Lester replied. "Now if you could just remember where you put the cameras . . ."

Heston's final diary entry on location read, "I'll be damn

surprised if it doesn't turn out. The script is very good, the cast at least that, and Lester a lot more. I have a good feeling about this one."

■

During the months of filming Lester was afforded ample opportunity to observe the Salkinds in action. He never felt that they learned anything from their mistakes, and they would cut corners financially in a way that produced antagonism amongst the hardworking crew—like hiring someone with little experience as chief of production because they could control him, or appointing one of the least reputable caterers against everyone's advice. Lester could see that this was how the Salkinds functioned: if something looked like a bargain, they would never stop to think about the consequences.

Lester also learned a lot from his association with the Salkinds about evasion. If he was discussing some technical problem with them and was in danger of stepping on their toes, they would suddenly slip into French. Then they would notice Lester's eyes following the conversation, and he could see them figure that although he didn't speak good French, he obviously understood enough. They would carry on, but only until figures came into the conversation, at which point they instinctively switched to Russian, losing Lester completely. What struck him as particularly funny was the fact that whenever he first suggested a joke it was invariably met with stony silence. Then they would walk down the corridor, and suddenly he would hear them laughing; they had translated from one language to another until they finally got it.

For whatever reason, Alex Salkind had one particular idiosyncrasy that he invariably enacted every time he asked Lester out to one of the luxury hotels in which the team lodged. After encouraging the rest of the party to order whatever they liked, he would request a simple plate of boiled rice or spaghetti for himself and eat a few mouthfuls while they were talking, before calling a waiter and pointing to his plate in disgust: "I can't eat *this*! Take it away." He would decline any offer of an alternative dish with a disdainful, "No, no, just take it away, *please*." One assumption would be that Alex ate what he needed to keep his small body and soul together—for free—in some of the finest restaurants in the world.

■

Reportedly bubbling over with enthusiasm about her role in the picture and having expressed her delight at the prospect of working with Lester, Raquel Welch discovered in short order that he was no schmoozer. He had turned in for his customary early night, hoping to get enough sleep before the four o'clock jitters struck, when Welch telephoned from California: "Hi, how are you? I'm really looking forward to seeing you next week. There are a few things I'd like to discuss first about the script."

Lester sat up, bleary-eyed. "When you come over, Raquel, won't that be time enough?"

"I'd like to discuss a couple of them now just to put my mind at rest . . ."

"Well, what?"

"There's this joke while I'm shopping with D'Artagnan and I pick up two melons and I say, 'Do I need melons?' and D'Artagnan does a double take between my breasts and the melons and says, 'Absolutely not!' "

"So what's wrong with that?"

"Frankly, I don't think it's in very good taste."

"No? I find it funny."

221

"Well, I don't. There must be something else we could do instead."

"Look, isn't this a matter we can sort out when you arrive?"

"I'd rather we did it now."

"I'm sorry, Raquel, but I've had a long day and I've an early start tomorrow. I suggest you take these points up with the producers if you're not satisfied." He replaced the receiver, turned over and struggled to get back to sleep.

Ten minutes later it was Pierre Spengler's turn to take a call from California, only this time it was from Barry Hirsch, Welch's lawyer. The message was instantly panic-inducing: "Pierre, Raquel's off the picture."

"What do you mean, what are you talking about?"

"Your director has been rude to her. She's out."

Minutes later Spengler was on the phone to Lester: "What have you done to Raquel Welch?"

"Look, Pierre, I'm exhausted. I'm not about to discuss script changes and jokes with the woman over the phone."

"Well, right now we have a big problem on our hands. She's walked off the picture."

"Really? Maybe you should get someone else instead. Goodnight, Pierre."

Spengler was left with no alternative but to phone his court of last resort, Alex Salkind, in Geneva. After explaining that the situation was utterly deadlocked, he asked, "Alex, shouldn't we at least think of replacing her?"

"Are you mad? Are you crazy?" Salkind exploded. "All our contracts with the distributors guarantee Raquel Welch. Absolutely not! You will fly to Los Angeles first thing in the morning and sort this out. And Richard's got to learn to be more of a diplomat."

In Los Angeles Hirsch was unmovable; Welch was "disturbed, nervous, highly upset"—and gone. "Barry," Spengler pleaded, "we have a contract with Raquel and we don't want to get into a horrible lawsuit, but . . ." At this point Gunther Schiff, Hirsch's partner, entered the discussion. (He represented Richard Chamberlain, who was working perfectly happily with Lester in Spain.) "Why don't we ask Raquel exactly what it is she wants," he suggested, "and what would make her happy to make the movie?"

The result was a lengthy list of conditions: Lester was forbidden to give the star any direction on the set; if he wanted to change any part of her performance it had to be done out of earshot of the other actors and crew. Then she had total control over photographic material or press releases. And the Salkinds, Spengler and Lester had to sign this list of demands before she officially agreed to return. In view of Alex's "contracts," they had little alternative.

On the evening Welch was due in Spain a highly apprehensive Spengler informed Lester that he and Ilya, in the interests of cementing relationships, would wine and dine her in the finest restaurant in Madrid, and it was essential that he attend. When Lester impatiently tried to wave this away, Spengler insisted: "Richard, come *on*, there's no point in having a war." Within ten minutes of the group sitting down in the bistro all fears were dispelled as Lester and Welch unexpectedly chatted away like old friends while Spengler and Salkind heaved heartfelt sighs of relief on the sidelines. "What can I say?" Lester asks. "She was just delightful."

"I'll confess something that will probably surprise you," Welch informed a reporter soon after her arrival on the picture, with an entourage that included her personal photographer Terry O'Neill. "Raquel Welch is one of the most hated actress in the world. You know why? Because I do not tolerate errors or unprofessional behavior. My hardness is my only weapon." When Ilya Salkind went on to add, "Raquel is very big in the small countries," it was with a deadpan that Lester felt would have done credit to Buster Keaton.

Welch's original insistence on having her own costumes made had been a particularly tough condition to swallow even before the clash, since Lester and Yvonne Blake, his costume designer, had worked for months to make the clothing as authentic as possible, researching undergarments and how cloth was cut in the seventeenth century. On the first day of shooting Welch turned up wearing a Lurex creation that was spectacularly wrong; when she looked around at the other players she realized she had made a terrible mistake. Ron Talsky, her designer, insisted that he had carried out his own extensive research—in the MGM library, where he had found sketches and swatches of Lana Turner's crossover bra. (When the movie was nominated for an Academy Award for Best Costumes, to everyone's consternation Talsky received top billing over Yvonne Blake, who had clothed everyone else in the cast.)

Before Welch's first scene, in which she was to hide in a closet with Michael York, Lester and David Watkin had one of their many amiable exchanges. "How are you going to light her?" the cinematographer was asked. "I'm not," Watkin replied. "She's inside a closet, and there's no light there."

"Look, David. This woman's flown eight thousand miles to be here, with a list of conditions longer than your arm. Put a light in there."

"It's not a fucking fridge, you know."

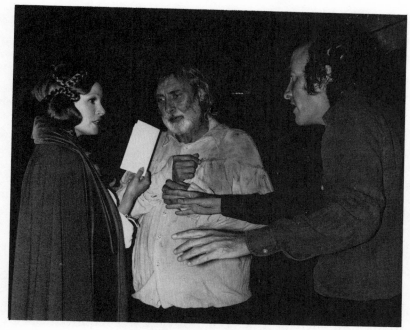

"This is my husband?"

Raquel Welch and Spike Milligan with Richard Lester on the set of
The Three Musketeers. (COURTESY OF RICHARD LESTER)

"It bloody well is as far as I'm concerned."

At this the laconic Watkin turned away, shrugged and
muttered to his assistant, "If *Richard* says let there be light,
there shall *be* light."

One of the things that struck Lester as odd was how
Dunaway came across on screen as fine boned and delicate,
in contrast to Welch's more than ample presence. In reality
it was quite the reverse, with Dunaway larger in person than
she appeared on screen, while the stunning Welch had the
most delicate hands, wrists, ankles and feet. After all the
initial brouhaha, she also turned out to be one of the most
popular members of the cast.

225

By the time the tussle between the two women was staged, Dunaway had clearly decided it was the best of three falls and hurled Welch to the marble floor. Lester was taken aback at the aggression on display and was about to step in when O'Neill rushed forward and began taking photographs of his stunned client. "For Chrissakes, Terry, have you no shame?" he asked. "She'll kill me if I don't get this," O'Neill replied. (Soon after filming, he switched allegiance in spectacular fashion and married Dunaway.)

Despite the frantic schedule there was occasional evidence that Lester was taking just a little more than his usual time to luxuriate in the wealth of detail he was capturing. There were other occasions, one during night shooting in the chateau where Welch and Dunaway had their set-to. When this scene had been captured, in a first-floor room with distinctive yellow walls, an exterior shot looking into the room from Michael York's point of view was required. David Watkin had set up lighting towers posted at regular intervals around the building; unfortunately, the nearest was several rooms away. "I'll have it moved," Watkin suggested. "No, it'll take too long," said Lester. "We'll simply go to the nearest tower and shoot Michael looking into that room instead." When they did, the continuity girl was the first to protest. "We can't film here," she declared. "The room might be identical in every other respect, but it's got green walls. We can't have an entire scene shot against a background of yellow, then Michael looking into a green room. "Yes, we can," Lester insisted, knowing full well that York hurling a bag of diamonds into the room would sufficiently divert everyone's attention. "Richard, are you *sure*?" Watkin asked. "David, I promise you—no one will ever notice," Lester replied. (To this day, as far as we know, no one ever has.)

Lester took considerable pleasure in his reunion with Milligan, although he was certain Welch took it as a personal insult when she discovered he was cast opposite her:

He recalls, when they first met, she had a *very* quizzical look on her face: "*This* is my *husband*?" Spike was wonderful in a sequence we shot in La Granja, where we filmed the exterior of a seventeenth-century palace at night, with fireworks illuminating the scene while the ball is taking place inside. He was supposed to be watching all this in hiding, using a periscope, and every time I approached him he was in tears, so moved that the film had the power to recreate something as beautiful and poetic, the ability to bring an epic back to life.

Milligan had been in considerable awe of Charlton Heston, with whom he played several scenes. It was Heston who took the initiative with his introductory piece: "Spike, I'm absolutely overwhelmed at the thought of playing a scene with you. I've always loved the Goon Shows and the breakthrough in comedy you achieved. I really want you to know what a thrill this is for me." Heston detected in Milligan an undercurrent of pain he traced all the way back to Shakespeare's fools, who laughed to keep from crying.

If someone, on the other hand, had to be the unit bore, Christopher Lee earned that particular distinction hands down—in some quarters, at least. "He'd show you a mark on his hand and tell you that was where Basil Rathbone got him," one of her fight arrangers recalled. "He'd had his fights with Errol Flynn, and with anyone else you could name. He was a veteran, he could do it all, and would tell you about it at the drop of a hat and at enormous length. Chris likes to chat just as Olly likes to drink. The trick was to ensure that the two of them were never in the same car

227

together on the way back from location." ("He does have endless stories to tell," Spengler confirmed. "Our first meeting was at noon one day and ended at 11 P.M. that night; he had a lifetime of stories ready for me. But I found his company *extraordinarily* interesting.")

In all, what Lester refers to as a "technical horror story" went on for seventeen weeks. "As soon as shooting begins there is a kind of blind hysteria that takes over, from which you aren't free until the very end," he says.

> "People don't seem to realize how much hard, grueling physical labor is involved in the shooting of a film, to say nothing of the mental anguish. Only after you've finished do you realize that you've had really quite a good time, and you begin to look back on the experience with a sense of nostalgia, almost as if it were your childhood. During shooting, the main sense is the pressure, every morning, of one hundred pairs of eyes staring at you, waiting for you to *produce!* If you get by that, filming is marvelous fun. You have some of the nicest toys for adults outside of a nuclear laboratory and you don't have to have much special intelligence to play with them. And of course you meet a lot of people with wonderfully adaptable imaginations, a sense of fantasy, and that certainly is worthwhile. Back then I still had a kind of childish wonder at it all."

The movie had had more than its fair share of casualties. Michael York often seemed to be leading with his chin in the dueling scenes and received several deep cuts; in the saddle he was constantly being thrown by his mount. Oliver Reed took a sword clean through his wrist and was hospitalized for several days. "You feel the actors getting tired," says Lester, "and you don't know whether or not you've shot enough material and you wonder whether to try again, whether you're taking an undue risk, or whether to say, 'It's only a bloody film' and call it off, not take the gamble."

Looking back today from the long series of films in which he has been involved, both in and out of the Salkinds' fold, Pierre Spengler recalls how impressed they all were with Lester's performance on *Musketeers*:

> "First, he's fast. Second, all the ideas he had in pre-production, many of which we pooh-poohed, were realized so magnificiently that we instantly changed our minds. His ideas of showing half-constructed buildings with old scaffolding, soiled clothes, and his constant quest for authenticity—all of it paid off in a look for a period film that had never been achieved before. He really knows what he wants, there are no second thoughts—sometimes too much so."

The particular instance Spengler has in mind involved the first location Lester chose for *The Three Musketeers'* climactic ballroom sequence. When he and Ilya Salkind turned up after a couple of days' absence they were dismayed that the scale of room Lester had picked, sumptuous though it was, and hung, like the other apartments in the chateau, with priceless tapestries was—well, small. "Richard, this is one of the most important scenes in our picture," Spengler protested. "We need a much bigger room than this."

"Don't worry, Pierre, I'll make it *look* bigger." Lester assured him.

After a huddle with his colleague, Spengler came back: "No, no. We're going to cancel this, it doesn't matter what we have to do instead, or how much it costs. . . ."

While the two were pondering where else they could shoot—eventually a set was built in a studio in Madrid and the priceless wallhangings borrowed—Lester went zooming ahead and filmed close shots at Heston and Dunaway in a corner. (He had to; Heston was about to leave.) Later these scenes were matched up with the incontestably grander studio-based ball that did full justice to the elaborately be-wigged dancers and Yvonne Blake's astonishing costumes.

Instead of a respite after seventeen frantic weeks of shoot-ing, Lester was given less than three months for post-production, the Salkinds having already announced a De-cember premiere in Paris for *The Three Musketeers*. Spengler came into his own with John Victor Smith, inviting him to spell out the number of personnel he needed to edit the mountain of film Lester had shot. "However many you need," Spengler assured Smith, "you've got them."

Lester came close in the process to driving Gerry Hum-phreys and his team up the wall with his usual insistence on further packing an already crowded soundtrack. Several actors, including Michael Hordern (recalled from a fishing expedition), aided and abetted him in the process. Whenever a scene had a couple of peasants on the sidelines, whether participating in the action or innocently standing by, the order of the day was to think up amusing lines to plant in their unsuspecting mouths. One disadvantage was a movie that had a multitude of overdubs, ranging from the main characters, who were often revoiced, to these sideline mut-terings. The reward was some of the biggest laughs in the picture, as in one scene where two characters carry Milady upstairs in a sedan chair, one saying to the other, "Christ, she's put on weight!"

With a major score for period instruments contributed in record time by Michel Legrand, working in conjunction with musicologist David Munro, *The Three Musketeers* was rushed to completion in both French and English versions. It was the cue for the Salkinds' publicity machine to rev into top gear, and the première they organized in Paris proved partic-ularly memorable. Troops of horsemen in seventeenth-cen-tury costume rode up the Champs-Elysées, and the cellars of the fifteenth-century Orangerie were hired for the opening night party, for which a period orchestra was in attendance. Unfortunately the team had sent out invitations willy-nilly without bothering to take into account the seating capacity of the theater concerned. Instead of the "Version Originale" they expected to see, around 500 overspill guests were invited to walk a little farther down the Champs-Elysées, and view the movie in its "Version Française."

Unknown to Lester or Deirdre, Jean-Pierre Cassel had once been known as France's Fred Astaire; unknown to Cassel, Deirdre had been a top dancer and choreographer. As they danced together at the Orangerie, the floor dramatically cleared like the parting of the Red Sea for two thrilling professionals, each one delighted at unexpectedly finding a partner of matching ability. Cassel has remained a good friend of the couple over the years; whenever they are in Paris he happily acts as their interpreter.

Since many of the advance articles in Paris had protested that Michael York, with his height, blue eyes and fair hair, was ridiculously cast as D'Artagnan, Lester was amused to note that the Duke of Armagnac—who contributed magnums of liqueur to the opening party—was even taller than York, and a blue-eyed blond to boot. During the festivities at the Orangerie, news arrived that the movie had been chosen for the Royal Command Performance in Britain the following March.

Once it emerged that the "project" they had filmed was split to make two movies, there was a variety of reactions from the cast, the mildest emanating from Charlton Heston, with whom the Salkinds had employed their own version of the domino theory, overpaying him to come on board and playing up the added luster he brought to persuade the rest to sign on. "I had only worked a short time," Heston rationalized, "been very well compensated and had an absolutely marvelous part." Lester, he added, had "done an excellent job." Faye Dunaway was the most aggrieved, since she hardly appeared in the first movie and came into her own only in the "sequel."

"There's no question we were a bit naughty in not telling the participants," Spengler admits.

> "There were a variety of very good reasons, the main one being that we wanted to sell *The Three Musketeers* on the strength of its cast, and negotiations would have been much more difficult with the distributors if they'd known there were two films—it would have been "Fine, we'll take the two for the price of one." And we didn't sell the rights to the first film to Twentieth Century-Fox until they saw a promo reel, and even then we were paid just $2.5 million for all English-speaking territories, not enough to cover the negative cost.
>
> In English law we had the right on our side in that we owned the performances they had given, but regardless of this Fox had us over a barrel when we offered the second movie. They knew that the cast were unhappy and insisted that we had to settle with them first. We did, offering profit points in *The Four Musketeers* that would guarantee them a minimum of an extra 20 percent on top of their original salaries. In the end they all got more."

Early in the New Year director Peter Bogdanovich kicked off *The Three Musketeers'* critical reception in the U.S. with a spectacular review in New York magazine. "Lester's is the best of all the film adaptations of the book," he declared, "and his best film." Vincent Canby in the New York *Times* was less convinced: "The movie looks like an evening in a bump-o-car arena, with magnificently costumed people in place of cars." While conceding that it was "generally amusing and interesting," Canby complained it was also "light on character" and that the fight scenes "lacked spontaneity." Not at all, Time magazine countered, the movie was "a surfeit of pleasures" that "careens along on its own high spirits." Judith Crist agreed in the columns of New York magazine, averring that Lester had updated the story "in the best way," adding "a contemporary twist while retaining the elements that distinguished its source." To the New York *Daily News* the movie was "clever but tedious"; to Rex Reed in the Washington *Post* it was "idiotic." Michael Korda in *Glamour* magazine would have none of that. Lester was "a comedic genius," he declared, the movie "a maniacal tour de force, beautifully acted, costumed and directed."

In Britain the reception afforded the movie was much the same—mixed, but on the whole extremely favorable. In *Films and Filming* Gordon Gow found much "beauty and humor" and "York successful as both clown and earnest youth. Aside from some very occasional laboriousness, Lester keeps the pace lively." Although Benny Green in *Punch* found "gags that are false to Dumas," Dilys Powell found the movie "bang on target . . . while it may not look serious, I think its style and mood are to be taken seriously." The London *Times'* headline ran: "Richard Lester recovers the knack."

With the excitement of the openings behind him, the film a certified worldwide smash, his career in movies firmly reestablished, and *The Four Musketeers* set to follow a year later, Lester set about the tricky task of collecting his profit points from the Salkinds. Unable to extract any information from the team, he met with Alan Ladd, Jr., then head of Twentieth Century-Fox, who explained that under his contract with the Salkinds, he wasn't allowed to show Lester profit figures. He then visited his executive bathroom obligingly leaving the books open on the table.

When Lester persisted in raising the question with the Salkinds, he was informed that both *Musketeer* movies had been made by a Panamanian company to which all profits accrued; Lester's contract, alas, was with their profitless Liechtensteinian company. Deciding to sue, he was advised that the only way to bring the Salkinds to heel was to confront them with a powerful Mafia lawyer. After approaching this worthy through an intermediary, Lester explained that there was probably a million in the deal—did he want to work on a percentage? "I don't do anything for a million, kid," he was informed, sounding the death knell of his litigation, as well as his percentage. Lester had the cold comfort of knowing that he had probably made the best Panamanian film of all time.

■

The theme of most reviews of *The Four Musketeers* is a direct comparison with its predecessor; depending entirely on which critic you read, the film was either a worthy successor, or much better, or much worse. According to the Los Angeles *Free Press* the movie lacked "the charm of the first film." The St. Louis *Post-Dispatch* found it "not quite so funny and clever as *Three*," although "still delightful." The rest ran the gamut: "Worthy successor to *Three*" (*Oregonian*); "almost as funny as *Three*" (Dallas *Morning News*); "funnier than *Three*" (Pittsburgh *Press*); "lighter, funnier, less burdened by exposition than *Three*" (New York *Times*); "inferior to the first movie" (Cleveland *Plain Dealer*); "less raucous but more satisfying" (New York); "every bit as exhilarating as its predecessor" (Films and Filming); "less slapstick and more swashbuckle than the first movie" (New York *Daily News*); "It looks like a clumsy carbon of a bad satire on the original" (Variety); "better than *Three*" (Films in Review). A rave from

Sheila Benson in the Los Angeles *Times* seemed to transcend all the conflicting notices and offer healing balm for the unkinder cuts: "Even more than its predecessor, *The Four Musketeers* has a depth and richness almost impossible to absorb in one sitting. So go once and then go again. Savor the juiciness of every single line and be grateful that we have Richard Lester—yesterday we would have Cecil B. De Mille."

Although Lester had set out to make the sequel, or second half, darker in tone, recognizing its need for development, he had basically made the three-and-a-half hour epic that was always envisaged—and, in my judgment, succeeded magnificently. The only departure was in its screening in two halves—and with an intermission of a year instead of the usual fifteen minutes.

CHAPTER FOURTEEN

*If I'd made all the films I've turned down and
turned down all the films I've made, I'd have
come out about the same.*

—DAVID PICKER

Lester was back in Spain following the successful release
of *The Three Musketeers*, looking for a suitable location for a
battle scene that would complete the sequel, when he took a
call from Denis O'Dell back at Wickenham. "How involved
are you?" he was asked. "I'm on the final push," Lester
replied. "Why?"

O'Dell explained that he was sitting at his desk with ex-
United Artists executive David Picker. Now an independent
producer, he was about to embark on a bomb-scare-at-sea
movie, *Juggernaut*, vaguely based on a true incident that took
place on the *QE2* in mid-Atlantic. Bryan Forbes, the original
director, had jumped ship. With his replacement, Don Taylor, about to be cast adrift and shooting only four weeks
distant, Lester's name had come up. After his long dry spell,
it seemed he was on a roll.

Almost before he knew it he had signed on, although he
first had to obtain a leave of absence from the Salkinds,
assured that he would return to film their final scene once

Juggernaut was in the can. Walking back from negotiations at Twickenham's Turk's Head pub with Picker, having agreed to "help out" by accepting a ridiculously low salary, he made a mental note to find himself an agent. Then, as now, a "percentage of the profits" more often than not turned out to be illusory.

Since *Juggernaut* had been written by Richard Allan Simmons, who was to co-produce the movie, there was a negative reaction when Lester informed everyone that the entire script had to be rewritten from scratch. It took two weeks of working night and day with Alan Plater before Lester was reasonably satisfied. Although the basic plot and action sequences remained, new characters had been inserted, motivations and attitudes changed, plot points and mood sharpened. What fascinated Lester was that the only people who had anything in common in the movie were the bomb disposal men and the bomber. These characters were playing for real, whereas all the others—the shipping line owners, the police and the government—were simply playing games. Displeased with the changes, Simmons had his name taken off the picture. The final credits have the movie produced by his nom de plume "Richard de Koker," with a screenplay by de Koker and additional dialogue by Alan Plater.

Richard Harris had already been set to star as the bomb demolition expert, together with Omar Sharif as the ship's captain and David Hemmings as Harris's assistant. Lester cast the rest—the ship's owner, Ian Holm (and his real-life son, Barnaby, playing his screen son); Shirley Knight as Sharif's romantic entanglement; the ever-reliable Roy Kinnear as the quaintly named "Mr. Curtain," the ship's social director; Anthony Hopkins as a Scotland Yard officer; and Freddie Jones as the rather confusingly named "Juggernaut," the bomb mastermind of the title. Michael Hordern accepted a spit and a cough, as did Cyril Cusack, another consummate professional who came in for half a day, glanced through his script and immediately delivered a performance containing every particle of shading and nuance Lester could have wished. Roshan Seth, who later played Nehru in *Gandhi,* was cast in his first film as a steward with a Peter Sellers–Indian accent for the patrons and broad cockney for his fellow crew, while twenty-three-year-old Simon MacCorkindale made his debut as "No. 1 Helmsman."

Picker and O'Dell had already hired a 25,000–ton Russian ship of German origin that had been sold to the Soviets and renamed the *Maxim Gorky*. The Russians had just taken possession and negotiated a deal with the film company that seemed reasonable at the time. Since this was February 1974, and oil prices were soaring daily as the oil crisis intensified, what the Soviets ended up with represented a total loss. As far as Lester was concerned, it was a similar arrangement to his takeover of a train in *A Hard Day's Night*, with the *Maxim Gorky* temporarily rechristened the S.S. *Brittanic*.

In their recruitment drive for economical extras, the unit had placed an advertisement in the local newspaper that ran, "Would you like a *free* two-week holiday cruise? Although we cannot guarantee the weather (on the contrary, we'll be looking for storms!), all meals are complimentary and every time you are filmed you collect £5." The campaign was such an outrageous success that a near-riot broke out when the 2,500 applicants had to be whittled down to the 250 required. The boat's embarkation, with captain, crew and passengers waving a fond farewell to relatives on the docks, was filmed simultaneously by Lester's cinematographer Gerry Fisher, an old Joe Losey hand, and by the BBC,

alerted by the recruitment ad, for a documentary they entitled *Voyage to Nowhere*.

Although at first the Russian crew were wary of their
bourgeois capitalist passengers, the atmosphere soon
thawed, with Soviet port making an appearance at meal-
times, followed by vintage claret, then vodka. Fraternization
beyond this was frowned upon; when one of the Russian
waitresses was discovered dancing with a film electrician she
was promptly confined to quarters for the rest of the voyage.
And there was always the obligatory, thinly disguised KGB
agent around every corner. One individual, as far as Lester
could see, did nothing but stir porridge all day in the galley,
while keeping a watchful eye on the diners.

Lester needed a force-eight gale for the spectacular scene
in which the naval bomb demolition team arrive by helicopter and are dropped into the sea before perilously clambering
up rope ladders to the deck. Off they went to the North Sea
for the required conditions. Once the stuntmen involved had
been helicoptered on board, they proceeded to ignore Lester's warnings of the rigors involved in the scene and tore
into the plentiful vodka on hand. "Stuntmen don't often
listen," says Lester. "Thank God we had ten Zodiac helicop-
ters circling around next day, because they were dropping
like flies off the ladders. Since we had to keep the stabilizers
off, we lost nineteen TV sets when we hit one really big
wave." Unlike most of the other landlubbers aboard, Lester
managed to avoid seasickness, thanks to a tip from his
regular second unit photographer, ex-navy man Paul Wilson. A sip of whiskey in the morning followed by regular
chewing of dry bread did the trick.

One scene with which the Russian captain adamantly
refused to cooperate was the blowing up of a ship's funnel,

Juggernaut's "demonstration" to the ship that he means business. Lester went ahead with plans to shoot this as his last scene just before docking at Southampton. He would film both from the deck, to capture the shock of the impact, and from a helicopter in long shot, assured by the resourceful O'Dell, who had somehow managed to smuggle a quantity of explosives on board, that everything would work on the appointed morning. A formal end-of-picture presentation was organized to the captain of one of the first digital watches, suitably inscribed; at the moment of acceptance O'Dell gave the signal to blow a false funnel he had built. The captain was furious, but by then it was too late—Lester's cameras had been rolling and the shot was in the can. It was back to Twickenham after sixteen days at sea for studio interior work on comfortingly dry land.

After a hard night's drinking Harris was due to film a sequence in which he attempts to dismantle a bomb unit. The actor was working with a hairpiece woven into his own locks by the makeup department to disguise the fact that he was almost totally bald in front. Since he was virtually unconscious when the toupée was fitted, the makeup people had no way of knowing that it was tied on far too tightly. Harris was in agony as he sobered up during the long, arduous take, gamely finishing the scene. Then there were groans all around when Lester demanded a retake for a key moment. "It's impossible," Harris informed him. "This fucking rug's killing me."

Lester agreed that the wig would have to be removed, but not before he came up with the kind of ingenious solution that typifies his keep-things-moving attitude to filmmaking. "You reach into your pouch," he explained to Harris, "and pull out the lucky little woolly hat you keep for such occasions. And you stick it on your head and off you go!"

"But Dick," Harris protested, "that means we'll have to shoot the entire second half of the scene all over again."

"It doesn't," Lester replied. "You whip the hat off again a few seconds later. You've had all the luck you need. And I'll simply splice the clip into the middle of the scene."

Lester enjoyed filming *Juggernaut* about as much as he has ever enjoyed making a film. There were several factors at work, besides his affection for everyone in the cast. It wasn't his project; he was doing David Picker a favor and so the burden of the entire enterprise did not rest on his shoulders. He completed the twelve-week schedule in just seven weeks before nipping back to Spain to finish his assignment for the Salkinds.

Juggernaut was rushed into release in September 1974, neatly sandwiched between the two *Musketeers* movies. According to Films in Review, Lester had produced a *"quiet disaster film, witty, human-orientated, and understated"* in contrast to *"The Poseidon Adventure* brand of Hollywood grandstanding."* Gene Siskel in the Chicago *Tribune* agreed that the film was far removed from the usual Hollywood disaster movie and was "witty and fast-paced, until a very abrupt denouement." Time magazine described Lester as "a filmmaker of satiric skill and carbolic wit unsurpassed in the contemporary English-speaking cinema" and "a superb stylist" who had made *Juggernaut* into "an amazingly engineered entertainment. *The Poseidon Adventure,* by inevitable comparison, looks like something staged by a kid in his bathtub just before bedtime."

Pauline Kael in the New Yorker complained that Lester's characters lacked warmth, but had "black-hearted existential bravado" instead; she admired the "nifty" way he had undercut the clichéd situations. McCall's magazine found the film tolerable only because of the humorous touches be-

"Still sea-sick, Omar?"
Lester, his wife Deirdre and Omar Sharif at the London premiere
of *Juggernaut*.   (COURTESY OF RICHARD LESTER)

tween tense moments; according to Variety, Lester had created only "moderate" human interest and "fair" suspense,
with the dramatic potential undermined by restrained filming and underplayed acting. The *Christian Science Monitor*
found *Juggernaut* a "nifty bit of what's-gonna-happen-next
movie making" with clever direction and "some sterling
performances." Newsweek's Paul Zimmerman found the
week's other thriller, *The Taking of Pelham 1-2-3*, "pedestrian"
compared to *Juggernaut*, whose imagery was "beautiful" and
whose bomb was "elegantly convincing." In London, the
Times saw the movie as a "well-machined piece of entertainment." At a press party, David Picker came out with what
Lester considered a classic line. "I think Dick Lester can do

any movie he sets his mind to," he declared. "I may be smiling," said Lester as he stood nearby, his years of film-making inactivity all too fresh in his mind.

Although given to melodrama at times, with Harris and Holm in particular indulging in occasional bursts of scenery-chewing, *Juggernaut* had surprisingly tender passages that punctuated the superbly mounting suspense. We are really made to care about Shirley Knight's "other woman."

For his part Kinnear eagerly seizes his juiciest-ever role, unexpectedly breaking out of his jovial persona by muttering to Knight at one point, "Don't patronize me, lady." His smile freezes when the passengers fail to respond to a Lambeth Walk lesson he offers: "Oh, *sod* them." And it's certainly possibly to detect the fine hand of Lester behind the dignitary who says, "If I go down with the ship, I'll get three lines in the Philadelphia *Inquirer*." One scene, in which the police superintendent visits a master bomber in prison, seeking clues to the methods and motivations of *Juggernaut*, uncannily presages a similar episode, almost twenty years later, between Jodie Foster and Anthony Hopkins, as Hannibal Lecter, in *Silence of the Lambs*. The twist is that Hopkins played the equivalent of the Jodie Foster role in *Juggernaut*, interrogating the evil genius of Cyril Cusack. ("I might tell you lies, tantalize you a wee bit. It's up here in my head, and that's where it's staying!")

The movie did modest business in the States without ever remotely achieving blockbuster status; just a fraction of the box office generated by the much-ridiculed *Poseidon Adventure* would have been most welcome. It performed considerably better overseas, where a change of title helped in several markets. After initially playing as *Juggernaut* in the non-French-speaking section of Belgium, it was released as *Terreur sur la Brittanic* elsewhere in the country and doubled its business. When first shown on BBC television it emerged as number one in the week's ratings, with an audience of 19.2 million.

Several cynics had difficulty fitting *Juggernaut* into what they saw as the "canon" of Lester's work. What had happened to the erstwhile darling of pop artistry in the Beatles movies, the purveyor of "Swinging Sixties" Britain in *The Knack,* the iconoclast who made *The Bed Sitting Room,* the pacifist of *How I Won the War*? Nothing he maintains:

> The one thing I've learned is to take a very skeptical attitude towards "canons." I would certainly never try to judge my own work as a group of films. I think it would be very dangerous if I started thinking, "Well, in the *genre* this will fit in here . . ." It may be pure self-deception, but it means not really paying much attention to that sort of categorizing, or saying, "Where is your style in reel four?" I don't think I *have* a style.
>
> This is not Gary Cooper rolling a hat in some sort of false modesty—I really don't think I have any particular way of working. As the job comes up, as the day comes on, I shoot it in the way it seems right to do it. It's a very instinctive reaction. With *Juggernaut* I was not able to spend three months developing the idea, and I estimated wrongly in thinking it would be possible to rewrite the script in ten days, as well as partially recast, and in that time get what I wanted to put into it. I think I got *some* of it, but I realized I couldn't mess about with the basic structure. If I had taken enough bits out of the thriller plot to put in what I wanted, the thriller aspect would have fallen apart. But I would love to have been able to do more. What I don't know is how different it might have ended up, or how much like my other films it might have been— because I really don't know where the part of *me* goes into the film. Whether it goes into the planning stage, the writing stage, the editing stage, or the shooting, I just literally get on and do it.

With Bob Fosse's *Lenny*, starring Dustin Hoffman, under his belt along with *Juggernaut*, David Picker asked Lester what he would like to do next. With agent Judy Scott-Fox appointed to field this and future offers, *Flashman* was about to re-enter the picture.

With his novel George MacDonald Fraser had been one of the first to pluck a minor fictional character from the pages of popular literature—Flashman was the bully in *Tom Brown's Schooldays*—and create a separate life for him. In Fraser's hands he left Rugby and became a habitual liar, womanizer and accidental army hero, turning whatever happened to him into success with both women and the establishment. The first *Flashman* book was printed in the form of a Victorian pastiche, a long lost diary, which American academics mistook for the real thing when it first appeared.

Lester had been deeply impressed with Fraser's work on the *Musketeers* movies and astonished at his abilities in and understanding of the language of cinema. With the original *Flashman* novel still considered too expensive to mount, Lester felt that the moment had passed. "After putting so much work into it originally," he says, "I felt that I'd already made the film, even though it had never reached the shooting stage. It was dead." He decided instead to go for the second in Fraser's series, *Royal Flash*, in which the antihero was involved in a *Prisoner of Zenda*-type plot, called upon to impersonate an aristocrat.

With more time to think about casting the second time around, Lester looked at the possibilities. Despite Flashman's failings—he was someone who would take credit for anything, hide under the bed, cheat on women, lie about his past and jeopardize his colleagues, an arrogant coward totally without honor—he needed to be played by someone who could bring off the "Jack the Lad" insouciance, displaying equal amounts of charm and insolent nerve. Looking back at his original choice of John Alderton, Lester had a change of mind; excellent actor though Alderton was, he now felt he could do better. And David Picker was demanding a name.

Although the role was considered by many to be virtually uncastable, Malcolm McDowell seemed to Lester to come closest. Fresh from the futuristic violence of Kubrick's *A Clockwork Orange* and the picaresque adventures of Lindsay Anderson's *O Lucky Man*, the actor was attracted to the project by the idea of sending up historical romance with the social commentary that he saw as typifying Lester's work: "It's like what England *was*," said McDowell.

> In a way Flashman resembles what we would all like to be. It's to do with what we remember reading in our history books about Victorian England. But we can't do anything anymore, we're a great nation in decline. And I wanted to bring a feeling of that into Flashman's character. Of course he's deplorable at the same time, a complete and utterly ruthless shit. And the way I chose to do it, he's knowingly so.

With Alan Bates cast as Rudi von Starnberg and Oliver Reed as Otto Von Bismarck, the cast of top British talent was completed by Tom Bell, Joss Ackland, Christopher Cazenove, Lionel Jeffries, Bob Hoskins and Roy Kinnear, with the two leading female roles awarded to Britt Ekland (Duchess Irma) and Florinda Bolkan (Lola Montes). Future luminaries included David Jason, Rula Lenska and Bob Peck, with Michael Hordern producing a priceless cameo as Flashman's old headmaster. When the conquering hero modestly proclaims, "I'm just a simple soldier," Hordern's "Oh, *far* from it!" is worth its weight in gold.

"Olly, you must stop terrorizing Malcolm!"
Lester and Oliver Reed on the set of *Royal Flush*.

(COURTESY OF RICHARD LESTER)

Aware of the danger that the movie might look like another *Musketeers* episode, Lester deliberately sought a fresh production design from *Juggernaut's* Terence Marsh, as well as different camerawork in the shape of veteran Geoffrey Unsworth. Maybe, he would later reflect, he had concentrated too much on the stylistic aspects of the movie. And despite David Picker having set the movie up with his old firm, United Artists, they again pulled out at the last minute—on this occasion, just four days before shooting. Lester's track record on *Musketeers* facilitated a providential, speedy transfer to Alan Ladd, Jr. and Twentieth Century-Fox.

With shooting under way in Germany and perfectly capturing the fairy-tale castles on the Rhine, Lester sent a driver to Munich Airport to pick up Oliver Reed. The actor was due to begin rehearsals for his major fight scene with McDowell in which the object was to inflict cuts—the *schläger* method of dueling. Noticing that the driver had only one eye and one arm, Lester returned to setting up the episode with McDowell and calming his nerves. Although McDowell had never met Reed, he had heard about his no-holds-barred fencing antics on *Musketeers*.

Picked up at the airport shortly after 10 A.M., Reed took one look at the chauffeur and decided he was someone he could deal with. "I want a drink first before we go any-where," he informed him. "Take me to the nearest tavern." Ignoring the protestations that it was a three-hour drive and that he had to be on the set at one o'clock, Reed drank solidly until noon. Standing up, he stared balefully into the driver's single orb. "We're leaving now," he declared. "And I should tell you something. *I am never late for an appoint-ment.*"

Moments later, the car was careening all over the Auto-bahn, with Reed in the passenger seat yelling, "Faster! Faster! *Faster!*" When a car in front refused to yield, he wound the window down, leaned out and screamed, "I'm your Emperor, Count Otto Von Bismarck! Get out of the fucking way!"

With the journey completed in under two hours, and the driver slumped in a quivering heap, Reed marched towards the restaurant where McDowell and Lester were having a delayed bite of lunch. Towering over his co-star, who was still anticipating the duel with mounting trepidation, he roared, "Ah, *McDowell.* I'm going to hurt you, little man. I'm going to hurt you *very badly!*" Then, turning on his heel, he walked out. McDowell never recovered from the shock, although the scene was eventually shot without major injuries being incurred.

Not the least of McDowell's concerns was the control of his facial contortions as he ducked and swerved to avoid Reed's blade; it was fine to portray cowardice, but not outright terror. For another duel, he and Alan Bates had to exchange several hundred thrusts, spread over four shooting days. During the scene, McDowell recalls, Bates had to drive him back towards an open fire:

> They put some petroleum jelly on my bottom so that it would catch alight. And it didn't work at first, although it seemed to me I was putting my bottom right into the fire. So they put more and more jelly on, until eventually I was larded with so much of the dammed stuff that when I got within ten feet of the fire my whole body burst into flames. Alan, who was supposed to be my deadly enemy, got such a shock that he rushed forward and said, "I'm terribly sorry. Are you all right?" So there had to be a retake.

Lester found the technical aspects of the movie difficult, and although the setups, lighting, costumes and sets did eventually come together, *Royal Flash* was not a happy shoot. "It was hell to make," he says, "not because of the actors—I liked the cast very much—but let's say I was less happy with the crew. I think Germany is a difficult place to shoot in. Or it was then."

Following a less-than-enthusiastically received sneak preview in Los Angeles, Lester and Picker jointly agreed to reduce the running time from 121 to 98 minutes, achieved in the main by shaving sequences rather than junking entire scenes. As a result of this pruning Roy Kinnear ended up with his entire contribution on the cutting room floor. Many

*"Look out, here comes
Olly!"*
Alan Bates and
Malcolm McDowell in
Royal Flash.
(COURTESY OF TWENTIETH
CENTURY-FOX)

felt that throwing out the footage was a mistake, that the
longer form had given the tale more scope and allowed the
gags a smoother integration with the plot.

When the movie had its Royal Première at London's
Odeon, Leicester Square, McDowell was appearing around
the corner at the Duke of York's in a revival of Joe Orton's
Entertaining Mr. Sloane. Both *Royal Flash* and McDowell were
due for a rough critical ride, although the international
pundits were in their usual collective disarray.

What to the Florida *Times* was "a Royal treat," with "imaginative comedic situations" and "a superlative cast,"
amounted, in the Denver *Post*, to a "big fizzle." What the
Baltimore *Sun* perceived as "rousing fare, superior to the

Musketeers movies—fresher, less ponderous and visually beautiful" was viewed by the Cleveland *Plain Dealer* as "labored," with Lester "insistent" in trying for laughs. What the New York *Times* described as "good comic fun" in which Lester "throws away more gags than some comedy directors think up in an entire career" was perceived by Michael Billington in the Illustrated London News as "a heavy-handed mistake." Vancouver's Georgia Straight praised "a diverting film, with everything done right," which was blasted by Films in Review as "sophomoric, unevenly paced and silly." Candice Russell of the Miami *Herald* saw the film as "better than the similar *Musketeers* movies—a rousing satirical swashbuckler," but according to the Spectator, it was "the least of Lester." What to Liz Smith in Cosmopolitan was "wonderfully ridiculous," was to John Simon in New York, "boring from direction to acting to photography." The movie with the "mordant nerve of the novels of Fielding—and Thackeray" in Cinema magazine was, in the Washington *Star-News*, "vacuous," with "repulsive" characters and "heavy-handed" jokes.

The public voted with its feet and stayed away from *Royal Flash*. Coming so soon after *The Three Musketeers* and its sequel, it looked as if they had had their fill of swashbuckling and derring-do. Apart from anything else—and I found much of the movie enormously entertaining—*Royal Flash* was let down by an inexplicably limp ending, almost as if Lester had grown tired of the enterprise and simply wanted to have done with it, unprepared to go the extra mile that would have given it the necessary flourish.

■

During the renaissance that followed in the wake of *The Three Musketeers*, Lester was asked if he was more in love with the camera and its possibilities than he was in exploring the labyrinth of human character. Admitting that was a "reasonable comment," he addressed what he—and Charlton Heston—regarded as an unjustified critical reputation for camera antics:

> If you look at most of my films very analytically, there is practically no camera movement, nothing that I would say is visually arresting, practically no zooms, practically no camerawork at all. If you look at *The Three Musketeers*, I think the camera moves three times in the whole film, yet they say, "Ah, yes. It's that *Running, Jumping and Standing Still Film-*style of camerawork." It *isn't true*. But there is something, I suppose, in the way that I frame shots, or put them together, that makes people think it *is* true.

He admitted to having an "episodic" rather than a "whole-sculpture" mind: "My whole metabolism is that I'm inclined to do the sum at the end and then realize I've left out one of the parts I'm adding up. *I'm not a perfectionist*, I am a poor chess player. I like a feeling of rough excitement in films. I like to shoot rehearsals rather than actual performances."

Not, then, an actors' director? "I certainly don't think so. I don't find actors more interesting than other parts of filmmaking; they're simply a part of the process, as opposed to the center of it. I like all the processes equally. I don't socialize with actors. My association is very strong with members of the camera department. Off duty I will play a record, watch television, pick up a book, or wander around the garden hoping it will all get better if I do nothing. I'm very involved in private life."

There was, it seemed, no goading Lester when one reporter suggested a distinct lack of warmth and humanity in him reflected in his interest in the mechanics of the filmmaking process rather than in the emotions of his characters. He responded in the manner of someone discussing a third, distinctly absent person. "That leaves you with two choices," he calmly suggested. "Either there *is* no inner humanity, or I am keeping it to myself. I leave it to you. I am conscious that I don't wish to give a lot away, so therefore I don't."

He continued to joust successfully when asked what, in his moments of self-reflection, he considered the major satisfaction he derived from filmmaking. "That there is enough satisfaction in it for me not to have moments of self-reflection," he immediately riposted.

Despite his stonewalling—for he has never been comfortable in the world of press relations—the Bionic Man had already sprinkled several clues for those discerning enough to pick them up. And for anyone even remotely familiar with his background, it was clear that he had inherited pragmatism and cynicism—of everything from "child genius" tags to clinical-psychology jargon—and an abhorrence of sentimentality (gushing warmth had never been a Lester home staple). When he declared that in *Petulia* the theme of non-communication had hit a personal nerve, he may have been harking back to the long silences between his parents that had left him feeling that this was the way the world worked. ("That's too facile," Lester suggests, while conceding that he may not be the best judge.)

His first year in Europe had removed any lingering doubts that he could make his way in any circumstances; while many young men talk about giving everything up and taking a year off, Lester had actually followed through. By enduring the experience with him, Deirdre had proved herself a worthy partner for life. Lester is the first to acknowledge his lack of emotional facility, especially to an intrusive press: "I'm guarded, certainly, and I'm not saying that I'm the most outgoing person you'll ever meet, far from it, but by the same token what you see is what you get."

It was as if Lester had intellectually, clinically, diagnosed the emotional stunting he had undergone at home and at school and chosen in Deirdre the "other half," with enough heart and warmth for both of them. "Opposites attract" had been taken to its logical conclusion—that opposites can go on to make the most effective life partners. "There's a wonderful balance between them," Rita Tushingham observes.

> In many ways Deirdre is the grownup, where with Richard there's always an element of the prankster. People that say he's remote don't know him at all. I know that some find Richard hard to approach, but it's exactly the same with me. I like to come back, say things in fun, and this is often misunderstood, especially in America, where the response is often a stiff, "Pardon me?" Richard's always one jump ahead, his mind is so quick, but you have to be on his wavelength to have a hope of keeping up with him.

A childhood that is emotionally crippling does not necessarily produce an emotional cripple, especially if corrective measures are taken. If several of his *Goon* colleagues—Sellers, Milligan and Bentine—can be seen as troubled individuals for whom humor provided at least a temporary release, Lester uses it more as a protective shield.

Deirdre is the first to admit that her husband is "no romantic," although he claims he is merely anti-sentimental. Charles Wood finds him

> *so* fastidious. His whole life is about exactness, always searching for the right phrase, the *bon mot*, the right image, that's

the clue to him, I think. He has impeccable taste, but he has a pretty rigid sense of what is correct. We're similar in a way, I do much the same thing, but it's not quite as bad—or as good—as Richard. Cold? No, I don't find him cold, I find him extremely warm and affectionate and superficially he's warm and outgoing. I mean I recognize there is a warmth, and I think he's got an enormous understanding of me but I don't have it of him. He's so incredibly private. We've grown up together in a sense, but I still don't know a great deal about him. One never really gets to know him properly. I feel that I don't know him any better now than when we first met. The clue is that I couldn't *write* him. Deirdre's protective of everybody, that's her nature, but she's *tremendously* protective of Richard.

Cold, clinical? "I guess that's probably entirely fair," says James Garrett (himself a fairly crisp and dry specimen):

There are people who fundamentally lack warmth. It's something I actually find quite easy to understand; it often means someone is intensely introspective and private. Richard is, his instincts are hermitlike, he always disappears into his house whenever he isn't shooting. One of the reasons he didn't like overtime was that he liked to go home at the end of the working day, and while he was perfectly capable of an extraordinary amount of hard work and application, he saw no reason to do anything his intellect told him was not required. And perhaps that kind of approach doesn't accommodate emotion. Or if you're incapable of expressing emotion and dealing with emotion—well, I don't know which comes first. I suspect he's genuinely quite a cold fish, and yet in no way insensitive. He's perceptive and not insensitive to other people and yet perhaps doesn't go out of his way to accommodate them. Yet he has passion, or he's capable of *being* passionate, although perhaps that's not the same thing as *having passion*. Let's say he's *intellectually* passionate, perhaps not *emotionally* passionate.

As a lapsed clinical psychologist, Lester was often amused to find the motivations behind his analytical style under attack. "Why the scathing tone?" Pauline Kael asked in a review of *Royal Flash*.

> Lester keeps showing us bawdiness, blood sport, lechery, and revels in trouncing it all. No one else has ever had such a brittle hauteur towards roustabout prankishness. Are the romantics who allow themselves dreams of courage and chivalry really such a serious enemy? His vision of the past is surely no more accurate. Lester is inventive all right, but a director with a quarter of his inventiveness and a little warmth would be more entertaining.

Andrew Sarris was another who took issue with the Lester "style" in the wake of *Royal Flash*:

> My problem as a critic with Lester, as with Kubrick, is that I sense a furious activity beneath the surface of the scenario, but I'm never quite sure what it means. Something in their psyches will always be hidden from view . . . A friend whose opinion I value highly has suggested to me that Lester's recent films are treasure troves of homosexual humor, and that, indeed, the elaborate gaps make absolutely no sense except as exorcisms of homosexual fear.

Lester's response to Sarris's proposition involves long and erudite theories that implicate the very wellsprings of human motivation, deep and fathomless, that lie, often unacknowledged, within us all. The single word that best summarizes his feelings, however, owes much to his training as a clinical psychologist and is a court-of-last-resort expression available to experts in the field whenever a more technical term seems inadequate. The word is "Bollocks!"

CHAPTER FIFTEEN

"Richard Lester? I'd certainly never work with him again."

—SEAN CONNERY, after *Cuba*

A visit in 1974 from Peter Guber, David Begelman's deputy from Columbia Pictures, began Lester's two-picture association with Sean Connery. Lester was shown seven cards by the energetic Guber. "On each of them is a story idea that Columbia owns," he explained, seated comfortably in Lester's Twickenham office, sipping coffee. "Pick the one you want and make it for us. I'm not going to leave this office until you agree."

Lester could hardly believe his ears. He was aware that *The Three Musketeers* had re-established him as a box-office director, but even so . . . After his years in the wilderness, and with the second *Musketeers* movie and *Juggernaut* already in the can, his rehabilitation seemed complete; he was once again a hot, "happening" director. Although the card he picked was the only one that held any appeal, it thoroughly gripped his imagination. "Robin Hood as an older man" was all it said, but that was enough. *"That's* what I'd like to do," said Lester. "You got it," Guber replied. The idea for the movie, it turned out, had come from writer James Goldman, who had written it as an original screenplay for Columbia in 1972. Since then it had ricocheted from one director to another, picked up again then abandoned. Now, it seemed, Lester had adopted Goldman's baby.

London's Berkley Hotel was the venue arranged for a meeting with Begelman, Lester, Judy Scott-Fox and assorted lesser luminaries. They agreed on a title, *The Death of Robin Hood*, discussed budget and casting and determined that Lester would both produce and direct. Begelman was in a rare mood, about to enjoy a European holiday with his wife Gladys; as soon as he was back at his desk in Burbank, contracts would be attended to.

Six months later there was no word from Begelman, Guber or Columbia Pictures; it was as if the project—and Lester—had suddenly ceased to exist. Guber's nickname of "Electric Jew," coined by his Columbia colleagues to describe his frenetic, wound-up enthusiasm that could just as quickly run out of juice, seemed all too appropriate. In a visit by Judy Scott-Fox to Columbia, Goldman's script was unearthed. It lay on producer Ray Stark's desk, labeled *The Death of Robin Hood: A Ray Stark Production for Columbia Pictures*. "How could you do this?" she asked a startled Begelman. "You shook hands with Dick Lester at the Berkley." Pausing only to deny that he had ever been at the Berkley in his life, Begelman terminated the discussion. It took Lester a year of constant pursuit to retrieve the project, with Stark still around as executive producer and with an associate, Richard Shepherd, also attached.

Although he first thought of Sean Connery as Little John to Albert Finney's Robin, Lester soon realized there was little chance Connery would be attracted to a supporting role, albeit a key one. He had first been introduced to Connery by Denis O'Dell in Twickenham Studios' canteen, when Connery and the producer were making *The Offense* with director Sidney Lumet. As his thoughts began to turn to him for Robin Hood, Lester became increasingly excited at the prospect.

In his efforts to break loose from his old James Bond image, Connery had already shown considerable mettle, if not commercial savvy, in choosing his roles. Lester had been particularly struck by his powerful performance in Lumet's *The Hill*, as well as in *The Offense*, together with Irwin Kershner's offbeat *A Fine Madness* and Martin Ritt's brooding *The Molly Maguires*. There was no doubt that Connery was at an extraordinarily difficult stage in his career; dramatically satisfying as many of these and other movies had been, they had done poorly at the box office. Dennis Selinger, Connery's man at the ICM agency, agreed to send Lester's Robin Hood script to Morocco, where Connery was filming *The Man Who Would Be King* for John Huston. The response from the star was positive: "Come and talk to me at my home in Marbella."

When Lester did, Connery's participation was confirmed. From this all subsequent blessings flowed, with Audrey Hepburn signed to play Maid Marian and a tremendous supporting cast lined up that included Nicol Williamson as Little John, Robert Shaw as the Sheriff of Nottingham, Richard Harris as King Richard the Lionhearted, Denholm Elliott as Will Scarlett, Kenneth Haigh as Sir Ranulf de Pudsey, Ronnie Barker as Friar Tuck and Ian Holm as King John (the King's twelve-year-old child bride was played by a slip of a girl named Victoria Abril, destined to become Spain's top female star).

Lester saw innocence and simplicity as the keynote of his hero. On Robin's return from the Crusades the world has turned, leaving him an overgrown adolescent, while Marian and the Sheriff have become sophisticated adults. Trapped in his own legend, Robin still believes that he can achieve whatever he wants simply by clattering across the fields and physically grabbing it. With Connery in real life a fairly elemental, uncomplicated man, Lester sensed the qualities he would be able to bring to the role: What he also loved was the concept of taking well-known figures familiar to the audience and making them twenty years *older*.

They are still recognizable, yet are totally different from the stereotyped images, behaving in political, physiological and emotional ways which are the reverse of which you might expect. They are no longer radicals, for one thing: their political thinking has shifted ninety degrees to the right, as happens to many radicals as they grow older. Added to that was the concept of Robin Hood as a small-time robber who had been inspired by a great emotional ideal that sent him off to the Crusades. Now he's back, disillusioned, trying to relive his past—trying to live up to an old image which was probably just a myth in any case.

He has come back to find that the world has passed him by. In fact the only person who has *become* anything since he left is the Sheriff of Nottingham. He has taught himself to read and write and become a liberal and an intellectual. He is even trying to look after the people. But Robin ends up making a general nuisance of himself: he keeps charging off dramatically through the fields of crops, destroying things for the sake of a quixotic attitude.

With filming under way in and around an oak forest near Navarre, in the Plain of Urbaza, Lester experienced some difficulty in gaining Audrey Hepburn's confidence. He wanted to aim for greater realism and cut down on the romance; she wanted every vestige of it retained. "With all these men I was the one who had to defend the romance in the picture," she recalled. "Somebody had to take care of Marian!" Lester admits that this was entirely correct. "I was intelligent enough in the end—just!—not to screw around with the key romantic moments. What helped was having Sean, who's no romantic himself. This enabled me to insert that little bit of lightness to leaven the romantic elements."

Hepburn was dismayed when, after driving a horse and cart alongside a river and being tipped into six feet of water,

"Will this movie ever end?"

Sean Connery in a reflective moment during the filming of *Robin and Marian*. (COURTESY OF RICHARD LESTER)

Lester insisted on including the scene in the movie, ad-libbing her rescue by the dashing Connery. When she lost her voice one day and was able only to croak out her words, Lester assured her it would be all right—she could post-synch the lines later. He changed his mind after deciding that her huskier tones suited the scene (in which Little John admits that he has always loved her). Down to the smallest detail, like having to make do with an aluminium chair from her trailer instead of the canvas variety normally provided, Hepburn let it be known, albeit in her supremely ladylike manner, that she was used to better things. Richard Shepherd, on the set every day as Ray Stark's eyes and ears, put it this way: "Audrey could get along with Hitler, but Lester is not in her scrapbook of unforgettable characters." In truth Hepburn had mixed emotions: "I've never made a film so fast," she confessed, "and yes, I'd like to have had more time. But he is very different, extraordinary and spontaneous. Everything has to be now, practically impromptu."

Lester recalls a romantic scene between Connery and Hepburn that was shot "night for night," in the middle of the forest. Normally a backlight would have been provided through a device like a distant campfire, but this was a sham Lester claims he wanted to avoid. The only light he remembers permitting was obtained by bouncing tiny lamps against sheets, the bare minimum to enable the actors' images to be seen. The word that came back from John Victor Smith in the editing department in Madrid was that the calculations had been slightly off; the actors were barely visible. The joke on the set was that if the scene were left as it was, cinematographer David Watkin would be next in line for the Oscar awarded to Walter Lassally for *Tom Jones*, which amounted to running blank film through a projector. Displaying a certain loss of nerve, Lester ordered the scenes reshot. Later, with

"Audrey, I don't care how rare that wildflower is, don't threaten me with it!"
(COURTESY OF RICHARD LESTER)

the editing process in full flow, it was decided to stick with the original material.

David Watkin remembers events quite differently. The scene was shot "day for night," he insists, with Hepburn particularly anxious over her first romantic scene in six years. Kodak had recently switched from their highly reliable standard stock film to something called "hot stock," which took less time to develop. There were several serious deficiencies, however; one of them was a red and green "crossover" that made it difficult to render the two colors accurately in one scene; if the red of an actor's face was reduced, green shadows would result. (Watkin had already exploited this deficiency, having discovered that toning down the ruddiness in Connery's face bestowed on the parched, arid fields of Spain a delightfully appropriate Sherwood green.) Unfortunately "hot stock" was out as far as interiors or "day for night" was concerned, and with Kodak claiming that there was no standard stock available, Watkin was forced, for the first time in his career, to turn to Fuji. The tried and tested "day for night" technique on standard Kodak involved underexposing the film by two camera stops. When applied to Fuji, with no time for tests, the results were the initial, dark scenes that Lester remembers as "night for night." At this point Kodak magically produced the old standard stock they had claimed was unavailable, and the scene was reshot.

"David's right, of course," says Lester, prompted by Watkin's recollection. "It *was* 'day for night.' It's a bit like the way I always picture my mother in a long white dress because that's what she's wearing in her photographs. I'm so used to seeing Sean and Audrey in that night scene that I'd superimposed memories of some other 'night for night' shooting." (Since "day for night" imposed many more restrictions than usual in shooting, including the inability to pan or include any skyline, Watkin sensed the increasing impatience of his director as the scene was painstakingly set up. As Lester continued to snap at his heels, Watkin turned on him and said, "The trouble with you is you're not emotionally equipped for 'day for night!' " Suppressing a smile, Lester asked, "David, can I have that as a epitaph on my tombstone?")

As Lester looked around at his cast of tax exiles—Connery, Shaw, Williamson and Harris—and realized that they were spending millions of dollars in Spain when they should have been in Nottinghamshire, he concluded that Britain's tax laws had been designed by a bunch of foreign spies hell-bent on depriving the country of revenue. There seemed to be no other logical explanation, for even Connery's post-synching had to be done in Paris.

Lester might have dispensed with a crowd marshall on the movie, since the formidable presence of his leading actor proved more than adequate in galvanizing any latecomers. Connery certainly had his work cut out coping with the variety of veteran drinkers who graced the cast of *Robin and Marian*, although working for the first time with Denholm Elliott held considerable compensation. While most of the unit was aware of his liking for a drink, few realized the lengths to which he was prepared to go to obtain it. With everyone else comfortably billeted in a first-class hotel, where Lester and Connery played frequent games of tennis in the cool of the evening, Elliott took himself off to a monastery several miles away where he had heard a rumor that the monks brewed a wicked liquor. There he asked for, and was given, a cell of his own, where he whiled away his off-duty hours. The thought of the bleary-eyed, RAF-blazered actor groping his way into the daylight each morning had several of his colleagues in paroxysms. When the laughter stopped, however, there invariably was Elliott, reasonably on time and totally letter-perfect.

That Lester was pushing the pace of shooting—too much so, in the opinion of several crew members—suited Connery, who had no intentions of even attending the cast party when filming was finished. The word back from John Victor Smith after he viewed the rushes of Connery's death scene, however, was not encouraging. "Sean doesn't look as if he's dying," he declared. "He's too bronzed and healthy-looking. Couldn't you pale him down a bit?" After a discussion with Connery, Lester reshot, but resisted stopping the scene at various stages to further "pale" his star. "With such an instinctive actor as Sean," he says, "I like to go for one continuous take. It's simply not fair on an actor to stop and start continuously and still expect a smooth performance." Goldman's last line for Robin as he shoots his final arrow, "Where it falls, John, leave me with my lady, put us close and leave us there," came out, in Connery's version, as "Where this falls, put us close and leave us there." The truncation was fine by Lester.

The overhead of the movie as "A Ray Stark/Richard Shepherd Production" escalated when Stark and his entourage visited the set, their wives and three reporters in tow, having jetted over from Los Angeles to Madrid and been met by a convoy of limos. After shaking hands with Connery, Hepburn, Lester and Shepherd and enjoying a bite of lunch, they were off to Biarritz for a week before undertaking the return trek, first by private plane to Madrid, then home by jet. "Sean has a reputation for insisting that he gets every penny of his money," says Lester, "and here we had a perfect example of how justified he is. His reputation is on the line, his career is up for grabs, yet he is forced to watch money being spent that will never appear on the screen. For a movie basically shot under a tree, *Robin and Marian* should have cost $1.5 to 2 million. Instead, with its enormous overhead and expenses, it ended up close to $5 million."

When it became clear that Stark, back in Burbank, seemed to know as much as Lester about daily events on the set, Richard Shepherd became the number-one suspect in the role of company spy. Sure enough, Nicol Williamson overheard him one day reviewing the day's gossip for Stark's edification. Marching into his hotel suite, Williamson grabbed the phone from the startled executive, ripped it out of its socket and stuffed it down the nearest toilet. "Tell *that* to Stark," he suggested.

Further cause for dismay was Stark's insistence on changing the movie's title from *The Death of Robin Hood* to *Robin and Marian* and subtitling the ad copy, "Love is the Greatest Adventure of All!" Worse was in store. Having worked so well with Michel Legrand on the score for *The Three Musketeers*, Lester looked forward to his reunion with the composer on *Robin and Marian*. A great fan of Sir Michael Tippett's early string compositions, Lester pointed Legrand in this direction. Although he saw that adaptation would be a daunting task, Legrand enthusiastically set out to compose a double concerto for violin, cello and string orchestra. Most of it, Lester felt, worked extremely well, but anticipating audiences' aural difficulty in unscrambling the score, dialogue and sound effects, he saw that confusion might result. Having worked wonders composing in the style of Tippett in just four weeks, Legrand reluctantly agreed to tone his piece down and redo three tracks. This meant that another recording session had to be paid for, which required Ray Stark's approval.

Having heard barely a word from his director up until that point—a fair-enough evaluation of how Lester's views a producer's function—Stark was unable to resist a somewhat sarcastic "Well, Richard, it's certainly not very often you phone *me*," before addressing the problem. "Let me hear what you've got first," he went on to suggest, a request even Lester felt was not unreasonable.

After listening to the tape that was promptly forwarded, Stark summoned Legrand and informed him that his score was "a piece of shit" that he intended to throw out completely. Furthermore, he would stage a competition among several other composers, excluding Legrand, and whoever came up with the best main theme would be assigned the task of rewriting the entire score. All of this was done without consulting Lester, who Stark was aware was up to his neck in his new movie, *The Ritz*, and firmly anchored at Twickenham Studios. Stark got around to calling Lester only when he had decided on John Barry as the "winner" of his competition; he then proceeded to play the triumphant track over the transatlantic phone for the benefit of his director.

Lester began a series of transatlantic calls of his own to Barry, asking him to at least listen to his ideas on a Tippett-like score. When Barry pointed out that this was not *film* music, Lester exasperatedly replied, *"Exactly. I don't want typical film music."* Since this was precisely what Stark had hired him to provide, Barry decided to disregard Lester's entreaties. There was one point on which Lester was insistent—it was vital, he explained, that Robin's triumphal return to Sherwood Forest from his years in the Crusades be accompanied by a rousing musical theme. Unable to attend Barry's recording sessions in Los Angeles, Lester sent Smith in his place.

Smith soon discovered he had an impossible task on his hands. As Lester's representative he was strictly monkey-in-the-middle. When he heard that Barry intended to place only a solitary horn over Robin's return, he found himself in direct confrontation with the composer as the session ended. "You'll have to do it again," he told Barry. "Richard will go crazy." Barry retorted, "Look, I've been hired to do this. I'm doing it my way and I won't fucking well do it again." Then he walked out. The implication was clear: "Dick Lester might have fucked up Legrand with his musical preferences, but he's not going to fuck *me* up."

Back at Twickenham, a decidedly apprehensive Smith played the tapes for his director. Rage turned to disbelief as the music unwound. "I *hate* it," said Lester. "It's *awful*. And badly played into the bargain." By the time the solo horn passage was relayed, he was apoplectic and began to direct his rage on Smith. "There was nothing I could do," his editor protested. "I was in an impossible position. John simply walked out on me." Lester continued to protest, all the way back to Stark, for whom he had a final compromise suggestion: If further re-recording was out of the question, how about combining the best of Barry's score with the best of Legrand's? It was Stark's turn to blow his top. "Richard," he snarled, "just deliver the goddamn film as per contract immediately."

In the often brutal battle of words Lester had lost two friends. The first was Legrand, who felt that Lester had lured him, however unintentionally, into an embarrassing debacle. Their association went back to the triumph of *The Three Musketeers*, and since then Lester had toyed with a musical version of Cyrano de Bergerac the composer had co-written with Johnny Mercer. Sad to say, the rift continues. Informed during a visit to Twickenham in the nineties that Lester was around, Legrand's response was, "Oh, *really?*" The second friend lost, albeit temporarily, was John Victor Smith, with whom Lester's relationship went back to 1964 and his first clip of the Beatles' "You Can't Do That." The two men buried the hatchet after meeting on a flight to Los Angeles two years after falling out over *Robin and Marian*; by this time Lester was working on the script of *Butch and Sundance: The Early Days*, and Smith was on his way to grade *Equus* for Sidney Lumet. After their second brandy Lester placed an arm around Smith's shoulder and murmured, "You know, John, it can be good for people to have a break from each other from time to time." The two resumed their partnership on *Cuba*.

Lester still knew he had a good movie in *Robin and Marian*, despite its score, but he loathed the misleading publicity Stark and Columbia had engineered. He had bitter previous experience of expectations being raised and not fulfilled, and was convinced that the picture should have been sold for what it was, perfectly encapsulated in its original title, *The Death of Robin Hood.*

Still, many of the reviews were ecstatic. "Of all the wonderful things about *Robin and Marian,*" Frank Rich wrote in the New York *Post,*

> the most wonderful of all is what the picture means in the context of the careers of its stars, Sean Connery and Audrey Hepburn, and its director, Richard Lester. The film has more to do with fresh beginnings than swan songs. While each of the three talents flared brightly in a single end-of-decade project—Hepburn in *Two for the Road,* Connery in *A Fine Madness,* Lester with *Petulia*—they were all at creative crossroads with no clear direction to take. With *Robin and Marian* all three return to the forefront of our movies . . . It's the work of people who have come to terms with themselves and their talents.

Andrew Sarris in the *Village Voice* was next in line, describing the movie as "one of the most affecting moviegoing experiences of recent years." In Time magazine the movie was judged "sentimental, flawed—and quite wonderful"; contrarily, the Washington *Post* found it "a keen disappointment." To the Cleveland *Plain Dealer* it was "fascinating," to the El Paso *Times* "an enchanting fairytale for adults," while John Simon in New York magazine had lavish praise for David Watkin's cinematography, and went on to celebrate the cast: "Can you ask for more than Hepburn and Connery? More than Williamson, Harris and Shaw? And each of them better than morning prayers or peace or food to eat?" The

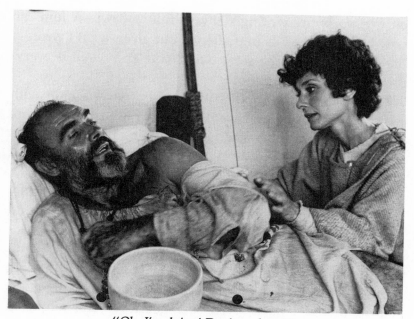

"Oh, I'm dying! Don't rush me!"
Sean Connery and Audrey Hepburn filming a scene from *Robin and Marian*.   (COURTESY OF COLUMBIA PICTURES)

New Statesman judged it "a tour de force, managed with magnificent dignity and conviction by actors and director alike"; to the Louisville *Defender* it was "a love story as touching as some of the best from earlier Hollywood"; to Rex Reed in the New York *Daily News* it was "A grand and enthralling saga . . . Everything about this film is mysterious, meaningful, straight from the heart, full of wisdom and beauty and magic. It represents the best work of Connery, Lester and Goldman."

As for Goldman himself, his feelings on the finished movie were spelled out in an introduction to the published screenplay: "Perfection, everybody knows, is unattainable," he wrote, "but this film comes close. That's not a judgment on my work; my writing's always full of flaws. A film can only be as good as its ingredients, but given what I wrote—the characters and the story detail—the end result is everything I dreamed. And more."

There was one piece of criticism from John Simon with which Lester may well have concurred: "John Barry's score is schizoid; inoffensive when just marching time, it becomes obviously sticky at the drop of a coif, maniacally bombastic at the toss of a javelin."

I have to admit to enjoying Barry's music, although it fully upholds his reputation for building an entire score around the minimum number of refrains. Either Lester or Goldman—or both—grabbed several opportunities to deromanticize the dialogue, but in a most beguiling fashion. "I haven't thought of her for years," says Robin of Marian on his return, then, "I never even said goodbye. She might be angry." When Marian accuses him of not writing, he replies, with that marvelous mix of innocence and honesty that Connery conjures up so well, "I don't know how." As romance is rekindled, the humor edges forward: "I've never kissed a member of the clergy . . . Would it be a sin?" For me the movie was lushly romantic yet uncloying, bittersweet and elegiac, the work of consummate craftsmen in every department.

■

A lot of water flowed under the bridge before Lester and Connery were reunited. Connery's stock was low following three flops in a row after *Robin and Marian*—the virtually unreleased *Next Man*, the soporific *Great Train Robbery* and the unintentionally disastrous disaster movie, *Meteor*. Since his return to Bond-age in *Diamonds Are Forever* in 1971, Connery had enjoyed only one moderate hit in John Huston's *The Man Who Would Be King,* apart from brief cameos in *Murder on the Orient Express* and *A Bridge Too Far; The Offense, Zardoz* and *The Terrorists* completed the roll call of flops.

Lester had had his own ups and downs since dallying in Sherwood Forest, first encountering a different brand of merry men in his gay bathhouse comedy, *The Ritz,* before returning to the land of myth, or Salkindworld, as a producer on *Superman—The Movie.* Then he undertook an ill-advised excursion to the Old West in *Butch and Sundance: The Early Days.*

Meantime, Charles Wood had turned out a steady stream of work, the finest of which, Lester felt, was for *Charge of the Light Brigade.* One of the funniest evenings he ever spent in a theater was watching *Veterans,* Wood's play based on the shooting of the movie, with John Gielgud playing himself and James Bolam as Tony Richardson. Unfortunately Gielgud experienced a crisis of confidence in the play during its out-of-town run in Brighton and handed in his statutory four weeks' notice. Faced with the prospect of replacing him, the Royal Court announced that *Veterans* would close after the month's run. Wood was devastated by the decision—it was, after all, his first chance for a stage hit, with seats sold out for every performance and lines for cancellations stretching around Chelsea's Sloane Square. Off Gielgud went to Hollywood to contribute his ancient seer to Ross Hunter's ill-judged *Lost Horizon* remake, in which all hands, including Gielgud, sank without trace in the Himalayas.

Another highlight of Wood's theatrical work was staged at the National Theater with *H,* a play depicting the horrors of the Indian Mutiny, in which the uprising was put down by strapping the mutineers over the barrels of cannons and setting them off. In Lester's recollection—which turns out, as in *Robin and Marian's* "day for night" episode, to have

273

been all in his mind's eye—Wood staged the event at the first curtain, with the lights blacked out just as the guns were about to roar and a suspension of sweet-smelling, fleshy-textured rose petals was fired simultaneously by compressed air, cascading into the audience. It was a truly marvelous *coup de theatre* typical of Wood's visual inventiveness—or at least it would have been, had it come off.

"That *was* my idea," Wood agrees, "and it's nice that Richard remembers it that way, except that it never happened!"

> He recommended a special effects expert to help me arrange the idea, but Lord Olivier refused to allow the compressed air on stage, deciding it was too dangerous. Then it was suggested throwing handfuls of petals from the gallery instead, but that seemed to me to be terribly weak and silly. Eventually the effects man dreamt up a basket suspended over the auditorium which would be upended by twisting a fishing line he would cast. Then we couldn't find enough petals and someone suggested bits of paper and confetti instead. That was it as far as I was concerned—we just abandoned the idea altogether.

Reunited with Lester on *Cuba* for the first time since the aborted *Flashman*, and with the aid of a book on the country by historian Hugh Thomas, the two men intended to portray the change from the Mafia-ridden fascist dictatorship of Batista to a socialist proving ground, all of it accomplished within the span of just three days. When Lester went on to declare, "I keep thinking about *Casablanca*," Wood decided to superimpose the character of a mercenary Robert Dapes, the first glimmering of a love story began to emerge. Character actors apart, ranging from Michael Hordern and Roy Kinnear to Peter Butterworth and John Bluthal, Lester had never before sought a repeat performance from any of his leading men. Since their first collaboration had gone so well and proved a high point in both their careers, it was perhaps inevitable that Connery sprang to mind for Dapes.

With the star provisionally on board, a deal was arranged by Judy Scott-Fox with producers Arlene Sellers and Alex Winitsky, who agreed to pay Wood's salary and otherwise finance development of the movie prior to a deal thrashed out with Steven Bach and David Field at United Artists. Even with Connery in the lead, the budget was modest; in addition to his salary the star agreed to take a net percentage position.

Diana Ross was an early choice for the role of Dapes's old flame, Alexandra Pulido, but declined the role after meeting Lester in her New York apartment. Ann-Margret expressed interest, but despite his admiration for her as an actress, Lester felt she was wrong for the part. His eventual choice of Brooke Adams sent him spinning off in a fascinating direction—that Pulido's original affair with Dapes had taken place when she was just fifteen years old. He had in mind the granddaughter of a Spanish-American friend of his, breathtaking and extremely sophisticated, and only twelve. "I loved the thought that this soldier had had an affair with a Latin American child-women," says Lester. "He has remembered it for years, building it up his mind, and yet this memory he has held on to for so long is just of a schoolgirl. And the girl has grown up, has her own life, has married and forgotten about Dapes. Ann-Margret is a wonderful actress and she might have made it into a very different film, but by the same token it might have become far more of a *love* story, and the basic reason I was interested in making *Cuba* would have disappeared. I was terrified of trivializing the revolution."

As Lester and Wood struggled to combine their separate threads of character development, love story and revolutionary conflict, Connery, in Lester's recollection, suddenly called to say he was available: "That meant we had to start immediately, otherwise we would have lost him." A first date set for shooting in Spain of September 1978, was postponed when the script proved a tougher nut to crack than either Lester or Wood had anticipated. Dapes was a man dumbstruck by the political machinations into which he had landed, and equally thrown by the unexpected cynicism of his former girlfriend. He had started out as a soldier during World War II, then drifted into counterinsurgency as a soldier of fortune in Malaya, then as a mercenary seeking out troublespots around the world. Now he was a pariah—yet he was still doing exactly the same job. "The role calls for that quality of innocence that Sean is wonderful at portraying on the screen," says Lester. "It's a marvelous skill, which is largely there because I think there's an element of truth in it."

From the beginning of their relationship on *Robin and Marian*, Lester had found Connery supremely easy to deal with, a straightforward person facing life straightforwardly. Unfortunately, Dapes's character was becoming obscured in *Cuba*'s background tapestry, as was his attempt to rekindle the flames of his affair with Pulido.

A script conference in Wood's Oxfordshire home was attended by Lester, Sellers and Winitsky. A large, loud, overbearing American lady entirely dressed in black, Sellers immediately took center stage with her concerns, leaving the subdued Winitsky stranded in the wings. "What kind of a love story is this, Charles?" she boomed, flicking at her script. "Why, I'm at page ten and they haven't even made it yet."

"It's *that* kind of love story," Wood replied, mentally battening down the hatches for the stormy discussion ahead.

Even the strong cast Lester assembled would prove a mixed blessing. It included Jack Weston, Hector Elizondo, Martin Balsam, Lonette McKee and Chris Sarandon (spotted by Lester in *Dog Day Afternoon*). And after his earlier stint with both Lester and Connery on *Robin and Marian*, Denholm Elliott was back, ready for another run at the character he portrayed so well on screen—ever so slightly seedy, constantly apologetic, very nicely turned out despite a fairly liberal sprinkling of dandruff on the navy club blazer, a soiled hanky stuffed up his sleeve.

When filming finally began on November 27—it was either that, or call the project off—the tug-of-war on the script was still unresolved. The situation rapidly descended into bedlam. Three days earlier, all army bases had been placed on full alert following the assassination of a Spanish general. Following this, Lester was informed that all the military hardware he had been promised was no longer available—and the entire *Cuba* unit was placed out of bounds. The boiler of the train they had hired locally blew up on the first day of shooting; a B–26 rented from Cornwall collided with a tree during rehearsals and was permanently grounded. No tanks, no train, no plane, and the freezing cold rendered it virtually impossible to portray the steamy heat of Havana with any great conviction.

"On big films when this happens," Lester admits, "you call up the place in Arizona where they keep all these old planes in mothballs and order a replacement, but I didn't have that kind of film or that kind of money.

The plane was supposed to have come in low over the train at the end and take Martin Balsam's head off with its propeller,

"Can I get you gentlemen something to drink?"
Martin Balsam, Richard Lester, Sean Connery and Hector Elizondo
(rear) on the set of *Cuba*.

but even the train didn't work. So I had to ad lib the whole
battle. It wasn't the way we intended it to be, it didn't have
the weight and structure. Originally there was to be a much
more detailed relationship between the two armies and how
they fought, as well as the unexpectedness of one side's
capitulation. All that had been carefully worked out, but we
had nothing to do it with, just a few extras and a cane field.
Anybody with any sense would have shut the production
down for six weeks, or tried to get an insurance claim, and
start all over. That's what a grownup would have done, but
I'm simply not capable of doing that.

By the end of the ten-week shoot, filming at several dozen
locations from Seville to Jerez to Cadiz, Lester's nerves were

completely shot. He had improvised the crucial evacuation scene as best he could, using mock-up tanks that were fashioned out of hardboard mounted on Land Rovers, and had as utilized the ground B–26 and stationary train. It proved a battle against impossible odds. A little of O'Dell's earlier ingenuity in obtaining a landing craft for *How I Won the War* would have gone a long way, but on this occasion nothing fell into place.

Worse, the script still stubbornly refused to gel. "You can never foresee these things," Lester contends. "I mean, going in, I always expect each movie to be as good as anything before, because you just continue hoping and intending that each draft will be an improvement on the last. And nothing ever comes out exactly as you want anyway. Anybody in life will tell you that."

John Victor Smith felt moved to question several points in the movie. One was a romantic scene between Connery and Adams. "Sean doesn't seem comfortable," he suggested. Lester looked thoughtful for a moment, then replied, "Maybe you're right. The music'll have to do it." During another episode Smith queried the stiff tweed jacket, cavalry twill trousers and hat Connery wore in a jeep. "Surely he's a bit overdressed? And who gave him that hat??" "Mmm," Lester replied, burying his head in his hands.

After viewing the rough cut of the movie, Connery expressed his view that the love story had become lost in the mix. Lester and Smith had another try, folding in black and white dupes to produce a second, more romantic assemblage. It did nothing to help. Although aware that in *Cuba* he had failed to produce a world-beater, the vehemence of the reviews still shook Lester.

"The picture begins by *telling* you it's going to be bad," Stanley Kauffman maintained in New Republic, "and in the

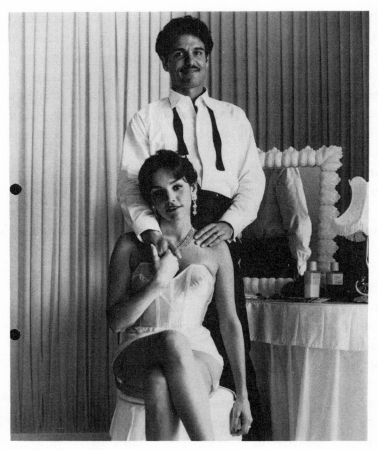

"Smile, Brooke!"
"Can't. I've seen the dailies!"
Brooke Adams and Chris Sarandon in *Cuba*.
(COURTESY OF UNITED ARTISTS)

perspective of Lester's accomplishments and talent, it is a bitter reminder of filmmaking realities." Pauline Kael in the New Yorker found "a plot that is so unconvincingly presented and so imperfectly worked out that we are not simply bored and disappointed but almost affronted at the misuse of so much promising stuff." Variety found "uniformly unsympathetic characters enacting a vague plot." The Boston *Phoenix* didn't know "how so much eyewash could exist in one screenplay."

The isolated voices of support that have appeared for the movie over the years do nothing to disguise the blot that *Cuba* represents on Lester's artistic record. Withering criticism from Connery, who described the movie as "a fatal error . . . a case of patchwork," and adding that "Lester hadn't done his homework" was relayed secondhand. "I haven't made too many mistakes," the star declared publicly at a press conference, "but I made one with *Cuba*."

Connery, to put it bluntly, had been made to look ridiculous for the first and only time in his career, whether dressed inappropriately (as he was throughout), constantly seen arriving *after* the action has taken place, or simply in his portrayal of a lummox yearning to recapture an old romance and seething at his lover's response: "There's nothing that makes the old days memorable—*and I include you, Robert.*" With Dapes at the center surrounded by a plethora of half-sketched characters, *Cuba* is a disaster for which Lester must take total blame—first, for starting the movie prematurely, without a satisfactory script; second, for not calling a halt when the promised infrastructure in Spain dematerialized; and third, for framing his leading man so ineptly. Connery had never looked better in his career than in Lester's *Robin and Marian*; with the possible exception of *Zardoz*, he had never looked worse than in *Cuba*. The overall effect was as if a bunch of aliens from outer space had tried to analyze and replicate the glory that was *Casablanca*.

Lester himself harbors few illusions:

I think we got overinterested in Sean's character and his love affair and shunted the revolution into the background. Then we tried to balance it with the strength of Sean's personality. Maybe there would have been more chemistry with Ann-Margret, but I really felt she had the wrong look for someone who should be Cuban. Brooke looked right, was the right age and spoke fluent Spanish, but maybe we got too interested in that aspect of things. And, in all fairness, her part was underwritten. So was Chris Sarandon's, for that matter. For all the terrific cast, I suspect it would have been better to take out two or three and build up those remaining. It was just too complex and kept shifting back and forth, a hopeless, total mess-up.

Apart from one very brief encounter with Connery in a golf club, where minimal pleasantries were exchanged, Lester hasn't heard from the actor to this day. Considering the superb reviews the same team received for *Robin and Marian*—among the most glowing of their respective careers—the impasse is all the sadder, and, it seems, irrevocable.

"Sean is a very strong character and things come out in a very black and white way," says Lester, regret etched on his features. "I don't expect to hear from him until one of us dies. It's as simple as that."

CHAPTER SIXTEEN

With Butch and Sundance *he may simply
have been deciding that it was a fairly harm-
less way of finding out if he could work in the
States. It's the only rational explanation I've
ever been able to come up with.*

—JAMES GARRETT

After *Robin and Marian* and its extravagant costs, Lester
looked for a project that could be achieved inexpensively,
and certainly one where all of the budget would be up on
the screen. When *The Ritz* arrived from Judy Scott-Fox it
struck him, financial considerations apart, as an extremely
funny, affectionate piece of work written by an author who
seemed to *like* his characters, reversing the trend then prevailing in comedy. Originally staged off-Broadway, Terrence
McNally's play centered on a straight man's attempt to
escape his Mafia pursuers by hiding out in one of New York's
gay bathhouses.

With most of the original cast available, he set about
securing his leading players from their ranks, reversing the
normal Hollywood trend. Although *The Ritz* had been written for Jimmy Coco, Jack Weston had gone on to star in the
New York production. He was promptly signed to repeat his

role of the hapless, on-the-run Gaetano Proclo. The role of bathhouse chanteuse Googie Gomez, vaguely reminiscent of Bette Midler in her early career at the Continental Baths, went to Rita Moreno. Treat Williams's mastery of a startling falsetto secured him the role of Michael Brick, the young detective posing as a bathhouse regular. The supporting cast included Jerry Stiller, Paul Price, Kaye Ballard and George Coulouris. Look closely and you'll recognize F. Murray Abraham playing Chris, an outrageous drag queen, a far cry from his later Salieri in *Amadeus*. Then there was silent movie star Bessie Love in a rare cameo. Only the familiar faces of Dave King and Lester regular Peter Butterworth betray the fact that the movie was shot in Britain.

Production designer Philip Harrison rose to the occasion by producing a large set at Twickenham that showed the multitiered levels of the establishment, complete with adjustable pillars that could be swung around to show either a plastered, mirrored or translucent side. Since the set also had its own built-in lighting, all that remained to be done each morning was to adjust the pillars, switch on the required lights and shoot a hectic average of up to eight minutes per day in a frantic twenty-five-day schedule. After his sterling work on seven Lester movies, beginning with *A Hard Day's Night*, Paul Wilson was finally promoted to cinematographer.

Lester found filming *The Ritz* a total delight. That he and his cast laughed their butts off for the three weeks of shooting might have been taken as a bad sign, bearing in mind the legend that the more laughter on set, the less in the auditorium. Rita Moreno endeared herself to everyone with her raunchy brand of humor, as well as her regular habit of taking the crew out to a pub in Islington and getting them smashed. "Take this woman away," the publican repeatedly

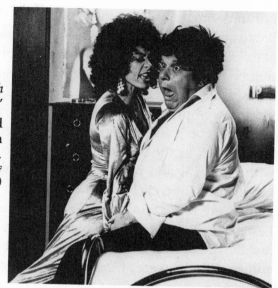

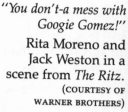

"You don't-a mess with Googie Gomez!"
Rita Moreno and Jack Weston in a scene from *The Ritz*.
(COURTESY OF WARNER BROTHERS)

pleaded. "We can't have this language in an English pub!" In line with the role he was playing, Treat Williams became known as "Mr. Straight Arrow" by the crew. Jack Weston was a wonderfully funny man in the Zero Mostel mold, if a little more controlled in between his giggling fits.

The Ritz was made as a negative pick-up for Warners in one of the five three-picture deals Lester was offered over the years; that he made just two movies out of them all says a lot about movie contracts. Apart from accepting development cash as a contribution to his overheads, his policy has been never to take personal fees in advance, lest he appear to be incurring a debt. Warners' were more than a little surprised when Lester handed over the final print in record time. "We didn't even know you'd started shooting!" their production head declared.

From the beginning it was clear that *The Ritz* was not destined to be one of Lester's great critical successes. "An unfunny thing has happened to *The Ritz* on its way from the Broadway stage to the screen—the life has been kicked out of it," Frank Rich of the New York *Times* pronounced, adding that "what was light and benignly funny on stage comes out abrasive, flat and nasty on film." Joseph Gelmis of Newsday: "It is incomprehensible why Lester, who was already a master of comic invention and flair a decade ago with *A Hard Day's Night*, or the sophisticated sexual comedy of manners with *Petulia*, would want to waste his time on something so utterly bland and clichéd as *The Ritz*." According to Rex Reed in the New York *Daily News*, the movie was "noisy and inept. Lester has bludgeoned the play to death and what remains just lies there in a comatose condition. I have no idea what audience the makers of this film think they are appealing to. Gay audiences will throw up. Straight audiences will want to have everyone arrested!"

In Britain the picture was judged "stubbornly unfilmic" in the columns of Films and Filming by Gordon Gow, with the farce "often breaking down." For every crumb of comfort—After Dark which praised not only Lester's "frantically paced direction" and "McNally's knowing and zany script," but "the performances of dizzying skill," the best of which was judged to radiate from Rita Moreno—there was a John Simon, who headed his column in New York magazine "Flattening the Ritz" and complained that the film had been transposed rather than translated to the cinema.

Lester admits it was a project that raised several difficulties, among them the portrayal of gays in a way that might be considered offensive, which is the last thing he had wanted to do:

> When you make a film about the gay community, do you cast gays? One wants to be evenhanded and sensitive, yet you

don't want to go overboard in either direction. Ostensibly you're "making fun" out of people being gay, yet trying to keep a balance. I kept saying to myself. "This is a straight farce. One review said I was a man who was not gay and had no idea what it was like. Well, that's certainly true—and I'd never been to a bathhouse, but I was working from Terry's material. Since he knows whereof he speaks, I felt I was working from a fairly authentic source."

Quite apart from the sexual politics, there was the underlying difficulty of making farce work on screen, a point conceded by several critics. Although circumstances were quite different to those prevailing on *A Funny Thing Happened on the Way to the Forum*, Lester's last, less than ecstatic, excursion into the genre, the basic problem remained. While he loved good farce, he was well aware of the risks involved in its transference to film, where the mechanical elements that activated the form on stage simply did not exist.

Lester had been careful to avoid seeing the stage version of *The Ritz*; he did not want to be hampered by preconceived notions. In hindsight, he considers that if he had seen the play in its original habitat, he might have realized just how much it depended on theatrical "business" to stay afloat. Purity of vision can carry a fairly hefty price tag.

Even so, the movie is studded with hilarious moments, starting with its opening scene. Here even the family dog is in mourning as the godfather (Papa Vespucci, in a nifty cameo from veteran George Coulouris) expires. The sounds of lamentation that follow are broken only by the indiscreet "whoosh" of Proclo's breath freshener. Rita Moreno's "Everything's Coming Up Roses" has to be heard to be believed; Paul Price is a standout as the "chubby chaser" forlornly proffering a Zabar's bag of goodies.

Although *The Ritz* has its coterie of admirers, this author included, Lester had turned out another movie that failed, following its critical drubbing, to find a mainstream audience. The only comfort lay in the relative ease with which the film's miniscule $1 million budget would be recouped via television and home video.

■

Way back in the early sixties, immediately following *Mouse on the Moon*, Lester had sworn off the idea of undertaking any further sequels, especially to other directors' work. As the second half of a two-part epic he filmed himself, *The Four Musketeers* had neatly avoided such categorization. Bearing in mind his complete lack of interest in Westerns, it seems all the more surprising that he would choose to make a follow-up to George Roy Hill's smash hit, *Butch Cassidy and the Sundance Kid*, even though it was, strictly speaking, a "prequel."

Western or no western, Lester had enjoyed the movie enormously, as did millions around the world. And he was taken with the script Judy Scott-Fox forwarded for what became *Butch and Sundance: The Early Days*. He decided to ignore the advice of several friends who expressed concern about the project—no matter how well it turned out, it would be compared unfavorably with its predecessor. And the charismatic specters of Paul Newman and Robert Redford would invariably look over the shoulders of whomever was chosen to portray them as younger men.

Lester's casting choices eased any doubts he may have entertained on that score. Tom Berenger struck him as an extraordinarily straightforward, no-nonsense young actor, and William Katt had starred in a successful TV series. Both seemed to have enough youthful charm to complement their seasoned counterparts. And Lester went to painstaking

Close your eyes and think of Redford and Newman.
William Katt and Tom Berenger in *Butch and Sundance: The Early Days*.   (COURTESY OF TWENTIETH CENTURY-FOX)

lengths to surround them with a top-notch supporting cast, all of whom would break through on their own: Peter Weller (in his first role, years before *Robocop* and *Naked Lunch*), Brian Dennehy, Christopher Lloyd, Vincent Ciavelli and Jill Eikenberry (with *L.A. Law* still in the distant future). Of Hill's original cast, only Jeff Corey made a return appearance. The versatile Judy Scott-Fox found herself playing the role of the madam in the brothel sequence.

Although the movie was "A William Goldman Production" ostensibly written by Allan Burns, Lester soon found Goldman, as author of the original movie, displaying a proprietary interest in the writing process. It was to Goldman that he had to turn whenever he wanted any changes made.

During his usual research, on the lookout for elements of authenticity that would distance the movie from a "traditional" Western, Lester discovered from old mail-order catalogues how much it had cost back in the 1880s to buy small arms. A gun was as expensive as a washing machine; homesteaders had the choice of a new outfit for their wives or a handful of bullets. The discovery that ammunition was so expensive led to a scene where Berenger holds back and buys only a dozen bullets.

The locations chosen for the movie were beautiful, exotic and often strange. A helicopter flew Lester over the sacred Indian burial grounds in New Mexico, near his film location. On the first day they arrived there was a brilliant, early spring blue sky. The clay that covered the ground was a bauxite-like bright red, studded with bright green bushes. The clear, pure air, the intensity of the sunlight on the landscape and the beating of the bright colors against each other produced an eerie, hallucinatory sense that the entire vista was on the move. The unique background to another scene involved a virtual forest of cone-shaped rock formations, each with what looked like a small rock perched on top laid there by some giant hand; the effect was of small hats sitting on top of cones. The "hats" were in fact the top layers of rock, eroded by wind and rain and attached to their limestone cone bases. An authentically Mormon main street constructed nearby for the movie was flooded for a shootout that had the participants up to their knees in water.

The town of Telluride, Colorado, where the unit moved next, was the original location where the real Butch Cassidy had held up his first bank. It was also the first town in the Old West to install electricity for street lighting and electrify the silver mines by running a cable down the main street.

After a morning spent shooting at 11,500 feet, Lester was snowblind for a day.

Since this was his first "real" American film, as opposed to the "Brits-on-location" jaunt on *Petulia,* Lester was obliged to join the American Directors' Guild and was allowed to bring over only his production designer, Brian Eatwell, and editor Anthony Gibbs. The American cameraman he chose was Laszlo Kovacs.

Lester eventually felt hemmed in by the first film's giant shadow, unable to repeat what the characters had already done, unable to move a muscle without reference to the original in case it made a hash of subsequent developments. "I came to realize that I had painted myself into a corner," Lester admits.

> When you are filming a subject you get an instinct, and it happens over and over again, that between certain pages there's going to be a dead patch where you need to insert something—you need to write a scene, maybe just thirty seconds long, but something that will give you an explosion of energy. You wake up at four in the morning—well, I always do!—and realize that you're in trouble. So you've got to invent something, or suddenly you feel that a character has been left out of the film too long and you haven't noticed, so you've got to try and get him back in at some point. This kept proving impossible. What it comes down to is that Goldman has a great ability to seduce with his scripts. They read so beguilingly that it's difficult to imagine what might go wrong. I guess I'm not good at prejudging to that extent.

Judy Scott-Fox was present during much of the filming and saw at first hand the legendary Lester boredom threshold threatening to burst its banks. "Richard is the most intelligent and best-read director I know," she acknowledges, "but

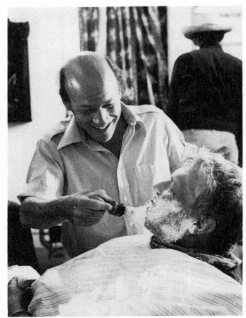

Richard Lester doubling as unit barber for Brian Dennehy while filming *Butch and Sundance: The Early Days*.
(COURTESY OF TWENTIETH CENTURY-FOX/RICHARD LESTER)

he's also *incredibly* impatient. If something doesn't come together instantly or is delayed for any reason, he gets bored with it. On *Butch and Sundance*, which was a more leisurely shoot than most of his, I still had to tell him not to rush it, that nobody would either appreciate or remember that he'd brought it in on time."

In post-production Patrick Williams's score successfully melded a combination of Irish music with steel fiddles, spoons and Jews' harps to reproduce the immigrant music of the period. Perhaps because he felt the movie wasn't funny enough on its own, Lester admits to overloading his usual quota of soundtrack jokes before sending the finished print to Gareth Wigan, head of Twentieth Century-Fox. He was in for a shock. "We're going to redub the movie," Wigan informed him. "What we've got sounds too much like a

Lester dub." After Lester retorted, "Are you saying you want a *Wigan* dub?" relations began to sour.

In despair, Lester sought out Goldman and his co-producers, Steven Bach and Gabriel Katzka, and was surprised and disappointed at their lack of support. While they never claimed to agree with Wigan, the general feeling was that they would be around Twentieth Century-Fox a lot longer than Lester would.

Bach was fact negotiating to join United Artists as their head of production, on the way to authorship of *Final Cut,* his account of the ultimate Western debacle, *Heaven's Gate.* "Should I take their offer?" he agonized to Lester. "I suggest you make out a list of all the heads of production in Los Angeles over the years," came the reply. "And if you want to add your name to that list, and be associated with that lot, go ahead." Bach signed. Back at Fox, meanwhile, the redubbing was duly performed, sideline jokiness was removed, and conventional Western sound effects substituted for the authenticity Lester had tried to reproduce.

Variety previewed the *Butch and Sundance* "prequel" unpromisingly, going straight to what many felt was the heart of the matter: "There's no star chemistry, nor any marquee value. Berenger and Katt acquit themselves admirably, but they simply can't compete with the ghosts of two superstars." The "patented Lester highjinks" they detected in the first half-hour that "peter our surprisingly soon" led to their verdict that the movie faced "a long, hard box-office trail." Richard Schickel in Time magazine dammed the movie with faint praise as "an amiable entertainment . . . not really a success," although he found Berenger and Katt "persuasive." David Ansen in Newsweek sketched an alarmingly avuncular portrait of Lester, describing him as relating the youthful adventures of *Butch and Sundance* "with the wistful chuckles of a kindly uncle recollecting his naughty nephews' antics. Here, he says, holding up a photo of a famous escapade, remember this one?" Then Ansen turned stern: "The viewer may feel like a stranger at a family reunion . . . if their names had been Fritz and Moonrise, would anyone have bothered to tell this story?"

Kathleen Carroll in the New York *Daily News* found the movie "oddly ingratiating," despite "Lester's lackadaisical direction." Kevin Thomas in the Los Angeles *Times* found Berenger and Katt "attractive and ingratiating," with the "very deft Lester . . . proceeding from one vignette to the next without building up much steam." In the Miami *Herald*, Bill Cosford offered the opinion that "the real problem with the movie is in the script, which doesn't really have much to say." He still discerned "wonderful moments, despite all the flaws."

In Britain, one timorous soul in the *Sun*, advanced the opinion that the movie was "Every bit as good as, if not better than, the original," while the Guardian found it "pretty, impressionistic, but essentially vacant." To Alexander Walker in London's Evening Standard it was "surprisingly enjoyable," to the Sunday *Telegraph*, "The movie meanders hither and thither . . . but it still holds the interest." Variety's prediction of the level of box-office business would prove all too accurate. Pleasant though the movie was, it played more like a pilot for a television series than a theatrical release. In the opinion of Judy Scott-Fox, her client had become too engrossed in the minutiae of the period to the detriment of plot.

"It wasn't hellishly good," says Lester, candid as always, "but I think I succeeded in my own mind in making it look more like a Victorian film than a Western. Or maybe that's *another* piece of self-delusion!"

CHAPTER SEVENTEEN

Rightly or wrongly, I regard Richard as having done Superman II *and* Superman III *for his "fuck you" money, the biggest compromise of his life.*

—JAMES GARRETT

In 1975 the Salkinds and Pierre Spengler obliquely handed Lester his first real opportunity to collect his *Musketeers* percentage. It was an offer to direct their new project, Ilya's latest brainstorm: *Superman—The Movie.* Lester turned it down, explaining that he didn't like fantasy films in general. He was also totally unfamiliar with the material, comics having been banned in the Lester household. And the best gags in *Musketeers* had been those of social observation, based on situations in real life. His main problem with Superman, therefore, centered on how Metropolis ran. He had no idea how much Lois Lane paid for her apartment, what it cost to buy a new pair of shoes, or what the unemployment rates were. With nothing, in other words, to grab hold of—as well as a "gut aversion" to the whole idea—he indicated that the producers would be better seeking someone else. The one piece of advice he did offer was that they make the movie as a period piece, which at the time they had no intentions of doing.

The Salkinds turned to director Guy Hamilton to shoot the movies (since they intended to pull a *Musketeers* and film *Superman I* and *II* simultaneously) in Rome's Cinecitta Studios. When costs began to escalate, a switch to England was arranged, where it looked as if it would be much cheaper. ("Little did we know!" says Spengler.) This meant losing Hamilton, who had just begun his UK tax exile, and handing over the reins to Richard Donner. Two weeks after shooting commenced the Salkinds and Spengler were looking at huge problems and enormous overages, for to them Donner was proceeding by a process of elimination, unwilling or unable to spell out in advance exactly what it was he wanted. "We must consider replacing him," Spengler informed his partners. Alex Salkind's feeling that this might be a problem with Warners', their distributors, proved all too correct. The company had already been sent a four-minute promo reel Donner had put together, mainly consisting of Marlon Brando as Jor-El on Krypton, and were thrilled with the material. (So, for that matter, were the Salkinds and Spengler; it was the unconscionable *cost* of the four minutes that had them agitated, together with the fact that communications with their director consisted of shouting matches.) When Warners', as Alex had predicted, refused to countenance Donner's dismissal, Spengler came up with another suggestion: "Let's do it another way. Let's hire Richard Lester as producer to move things along."

Lester's invitation from Alex Salkind was nothing if not intriguing: Had he ever considered *producing* a film he wasn't directing? Replying that it had never occurred to him, Lester gathered that the team was in deep trouble, and that they wanted him to act as a peacekeeping intermediary. He was curious—and, he admits, opportunistic—enough to fly to Paris to meet them, astutely accompanied by his lawyer. The

Salkinds then found their characteristic language routine used against them, and neither Lester, nor his attorney were able to understand a single word of the *Superman* proposition until the question of his *Musketeers* percentage was satisfactorily sorted out. Alex reluctantly ended the impasse by signing a hastily penned but totally binding agreement on a napkin, suitably witnessed and speedily pocketed by Lester's lawyer.

While adamant that he would in no way usurp Donner's authority, Lester agreed to act as third-credited producer and attempt to steward *Superman*'s progress, serving as liaison between the Salkinds and their director. There was one other significant stipulation: his salary would be paid every Thursday.

On his return to Britain, Lester immediately set up a meeting with Donner, where he stressed that he had not the remotest ambition to take over the picture. He would make no suggestions on his own; he would not speak to any members of the cast or crew unless sanctioned by Donner. He would give opinions and be delighted to help, but only if asked. The bottom line of his message was simple: "You have to know you're not threatened by me. I'm here for reasons that don't have much to do with this picture."

He still had the nagging feeling that Donner felt it was all a plot from the beginning that he take over—and in retrospect Lester feels that the Salkinds' ploy was indeed to force Donner's resignation. "When [Lester] first came in I thought he was going to direct," Donner later confirmed. "But he said, 'Look, these people have owed me money for a long time. This is my way of getting it back . . . There is no way I would ever direct this, I don't want to.' From then on it was just a pleasure. The guy was a big help and I really liked him."

The production was so far behind, even in the early stages, and in such serious trouble financially that Lester immediately suggested abandoning the idea of shooting *Superman I* and *II* simultaneously; they should cut their losses and concentrate on the first movie's overwhelming technical problems. If they couldn't overcome those, he pointed out, footage for *II* would be worthless in any case—nobody would want a sequel. (An exception was made for the scenes with Gene Hackman, all of which were planned for *II*.) Another idea that proved valuable was to create a second model unit, since that work had been proceeding at an agonizing snail's pace; to this end Lester teamed cameraman Paul Wilson, a stalwart from previous outings, with model specialist Derek Meddings, who had been unavailable when the project began. Apart from this and a few minor script suggestions, Lester's main function on the set every day for six arduous months was to keep the peace between Donner and the Salkinds, and coordinate a second live unit under John Glen.

He watched as Spengler, the team's nuts-and-bolts man on location, took daily phone calls from Alex that lasted an average of three hours each. Unable to travel to locations by airplane, due to claustrophobia, old man Salkind still liked to keep in touch. Multilinguist though he was, Lester was aware that the elder statesman hardly read in English at all. The story was that after having a revised script of *Superman* flown to him in Geneva and asking that it be read to him, Alex promptly fell asleep as the second page was reached, snoozed through to the end, then woke up and pronounced it "terrific."

Lester had never encouraged any other director to visit his set while he was working and had never strolled, in a spare moment, over to anyone else's; it was something he would have considered the height of bad manners. On the series he had shared with Joe Losey there had been no time, let alone inclination, for any cross-pollination.

Looking back, Lester could see that he had developed a technique that came straight from working in other media and within stringent budgetary limits. And film directors' personalities, he is the first to admit, emerge in the way they work. He maintains that it is nonsense for producers and completion bond executives to say, "Don't worry. He's learned his lesson. He's going to be economical now." It would be like saying to John Schlesinger, or Michael Cimino, or David Lean (to name but three highly disparate examples) "Do this picture, knock it off in five weeks." The inevitable reply would be, "I can't do it. It's not in my nature." Lester knew by the same token that it was in *his* nature to do just that.

What he stumbled on during his first day on the *Superman* set, therefore, was nightmarishly foreign to him. It was a scene between Ned Beatty and Valerie Perrine halfway up a mountain road. As they rehearsed over and over—for an episode destined to occupy forty seconds of screentime—with a huge crew standing by and spare cameras on hand, Lester could see a mass of black clouds gathering in the distance. In between rehearsals Donner and his people were served coffee, sat around, told jokes, and by the time they got around to a take the first of the clouds had drifted over. Unwilling to shoot until the light was perfect, Donner decided to wait until the cloud had passed. Instead, a ferocious storm broke out that lasted for three solid days, during which nothing was shot.

Lester was stunned. He knew he would have had five takes in the can before the first cloud had reached them, and if for any reason he was still unhappy he would have shot a couple in cloud. Telling the story today, Lester stresses:

This is *not* a Dick Donner vendetta; it would have been the same if I'd walked on to a David Lean set. Dick's not alone, people do it all the time in the film industry and I'm sure he had his reasons. I knew then, though, that if I started to think that this is the way it should be done, because this is the way other people work, I'd be finished. I'm at the opposite extreme—all for *getting away with it*. I'm not saying that in any way to be superior; other people do terrific films with their different ideas.

At weekends, while filming was proceeding on location in Calgary, Lester commuted to Colorado and New Mexico to prepare his own film, *Butch and Sundance: The Early Days*, due to start in the spring of 1978. By the time the *Superman* unit moved to New York in the summer of 1977, natural disasters gave way to urban breakdown. The idea was to shoot the *Daily Planet* building outside the *Daily News* headquarters, where Clark Kent is glimpsed for the first time as an adult, bumping into Lois Lane. To capture New York's magnificent CinemaScope skyline, cameraman Geoffrey Unsworth set up three generators and floodlit the building. Just as they were ready to shoot, the rest of the city suddenly vanished. It was the beginning of the infamous 1977 blackout; all that was left, picked out in stark relief by Unsworth's generators, was the *Daily News* building. From the way it looked, it could have been a model.

In the day and a half it took to resume normality to the city, with shooting suspended, Lester watched as the fabric of society in a substantial portion of the U.S. was torn asunder. There was no power in hotels, toilets failed to flush, tempers flared in the heat, food was cheese sandwiches and lukewarm drinks. Near Central Park, Lester watched in horror as one limousine driver killed another with a baseball bat, fighting over a fare.

Even with services back to normal he still felt like a stranger in his own land, a refugee from abroad. When the hotel lobby failed to come up with a U.S. adaptor for his English razor, he made his way to Fifth Avenue and the electronics stores. "This isn't going to be one of the greatest sales of all time. All I need is a little white plug for my razor," he lightheartedly advised the toothpick-chewing individual behind the counter. "Why don't you grow a beard?" the asisstant asked, turning away.

When a clutch of reporters turned up on the set one day, Lester, out of respect for Donner having requested no personal publicity, found himself buttonholed by one sharp-eyed scribe who had spotted a chair with his name on it. "That's your chair," he was accused. "What are you doing here?" Spengler overheard Lester's reply—"I'm not sitting in my chair"—before he abruptly walked away.

Back in Britain, as filming drew to a close, Lester, flanked by Spengler and Donner, pointed out what he saw as a major defect in the movie's finale: "There's no jeopardy for any of the principals. It's something we've got to resolve." What he came up with was the revival of an early idea in Mario Puzo's first draft—to kill Lois Lane. How to bring her back to life? By stealing the planned ending of the second movie where Superman turns back time, thereby undoing the deed. "Not bad for someone with no interest in comic books or their heroes," Spengler suggests. "Richard provided us with the perfect climax."

Despite a final cut of *Superman—The Movie*'s positive reception, warfare between Donner and his producers continued unabated. The Salkinds contended that Donner had gone way over budget, citing an astronomical $130 million; Donner countered that since he had never laid eyes on a budget in the first place, how could he possibly have exceeded it?

And his assignment, originally scheduled for nine months, had gone on for two years and four months, including pre- and post-production, with no additional salary forthcoming.

Lester's feeling was that despite everyone else's efforts, it was Christopher Reeve who had held *Superman* together. When things were going badly and no one could figure out how *Superman* should look in flight, Reeve came up with the answers; he could be on a wire and give the illusion of flight far better than any stuntman. He had the necessary feel, patience and determination to do it, and his loyalty to the project endured throughout the series.

When the credit titles were prepared, Spengler recalls a meeting with Lester.

> I said to him, "Richard, how shall we put your name?" He replied, "You shouldn't." When I asked him why not and pointed out that I was happy to share the credit with him, he said, "No, Pierre. I think the film is going to be sensational, a huge success, but I think it would be unfair to you because you really did produce the movie, and although I helped all I could I wouldn't dream of taking a producer's credit. Also it would be a puzzling thing for the world to see my name up there, since I'm obviously known as a director and it might start raising questions in people's minds about Donner. And this is Donner's film."

One month before Warners' scheduled U.S. première in November 1978 with President Jimmy Carter in attendance, Alex Salkind demanded a $15 million payment from the company before he would release the negative. Although the cash was ostensibly earmarked for additional foreign rights for Warners', the transaction was openly referred to as ransom money. Since the company had already spent $7 million promoting the movie's Christmas opening, with 750 American theaters depending on it—and ready to sue if the company failed to deliver—they were left with no alternative but to pay up. "The end was inevitable," a Warners' representative admitted. "From the moment Alex said, 'I've got the negatives; if you want a print for the opening you're gonna have to give me something,' we were resigned to pay. We would have sent in the marines to get it."

According to the Salkinds, the timing was purely coincidental, although they concede that their bankers were breathing down their necks because they had undersold *Superman's* foreign distribution rights and badly needed the extra money to pay off their creditors. In the end Warners' was happy as the money poured in from all around the world, including the additional territories they had been pressured into purchasing.

Just to add to the merry-go-round, Salkind père found himself under arrest in Switzerland as the première approached. According to several news reports, he was accused of stealing $20 million from a German concern owned by William Foreman, a Los Angeles magnate. A spell in jail was averted only when he cited his diplomatic status in Costa Rica, whereupon he was flown to Mexico, despite his terror of flying, under sedation. When witnesses retracted their earlier testimony, Foreman and Salkind reached a civil settlement. Although all criminal charges were dropped, Foreman still claimed that $20 million of his German company's money had been "misappropriated" by Salkind for investment in movies. Salkind paid $23.4 million to buy out Foreman's interest in *Superman*. As for the claim—possibly made with an eye to minimizing future profits for participants—that the final cost of *Superman* was $130 million, Warners' wryly summed up the situation to one investigative reporter: "You will *never* know what Alex Salkind spent on that film."

With a special showing of *Superman* taking place at the White House to benefit the Special Olympics, Alex fleetingly revealed a glimpse of his paternal persona, an aspect not fully appreciated up to that point. In a telephone call to Gordon Arnell, Warners' head of publicity, Alex requested that a picture be taken of his son shaking hands with the President of the United States. Presented with the photograph, Alex promptly cut out Ilya's head from the shot and replaced it with his own!

■

Donner claims to have felt betrayed when he heard that Lester had agreed to direct *Superman II*. "The circumstances were completely different when I came to do the sequel," says Lester. "I'd made two films, *Butch and Sundance: The Early Days*, and *Cuba*, and I'd been nowhere near the Salkinds or *Superman*. Dick was out long before I got involved in *II* and an intermediate director, Guy Hamilton, came on the scene for a while. Moreover, a lawsuit had started between Donner and the Salkinds and it would have been most unwise for me to get involved in any way."

From his insider's vantage point, Spengler vividly recalls the scenario. Soon after the opening of the first movie and its enormous success, he called Donner in a fence-mending attempt: "Let's enjoy a break, then let's get together to discuss the sequel." Later he attended director Richard Fleischer's regular New Year party with guests invited to bring along their least-favorite Christmas presents for redistribution. There he bumped into *Variety* columnist Army Archerd, who said, "I understand you and Donner had horrible fights."

"True," Spengler admitted, "but as far as I'm concerned

it's all forgotten. The main thing is our new movie and I'm looking forward to working with him on that."

Archerd promptly called Donner and was told, "If Pierre's doing it, I'm not." Faithfully reporting this in his column, Archerd signed off with, "Sounds like a job for Superman!" After consultations with the Salkinds, Spengler still tried to resume contact with Donner, who remained belligerent and uncooperative. "Why are we breaking our heads over this guy? He's not cooperating and he's going to be even worse to deal with than before," said Alex. "Let's see if we can persuade Lester to direct this time." Contacted by the team, Lester considered their extremely generous offer and decided to pass. Disappointed, the Salkinds turned to their original choice of director and presented Guy Hamilton as a *fait accompli* to the powers at Warners. "Sorry," they were told, "we want Donner."

"He's made that absolutely impossible."

"Well, if you can't get him, Lester's the only other choice as far as we're concerned."

"We've already talked to Richard. He turned our offer down."

"Double it. Warners' will pay the difference."

Faced with the Salkinds' and Warners' joint fee, the highest ever for a director at that time, Lester proved his humanity to any lingering doubters and agreed to take over. "If you want me that much," he told Spengler, "fine, I'll do it."

His decision wasn't all to do with money, Lester maintains:

Frankly, I liked the idea of what was going on, I sussed out that it was going to be dead easy. It was a different way of working from what I was used to, with all the sequences storyboarded and no ad-libbing required. I went on to learn more on *Superman II* technically than on all my previous films combined, and enjoyed working with up to four units at a time; if a major problem developed at one unit it was, "Sorry lads, they're desperate for me elsewhere, let me know when you're at the next stage!" As for those who thought I took on the assignment for the "fuck you" money, they're wrong. If you need a lot of money to do something on your own, or to maintain your independence, it has that "fuck you" value, but that wasn't the case with us. Our children were through school, the house was paid for and a week's work each year on commercials would have met all our needs. So that was simply not a factor.

Superman's Lois Lane, Margot Kidder, was withering in her criticism of the Salkinds' behavior towards both Donner and herself—and made them pay dearly for that treatment. "They tried to screw me out of $40,000," she said, "a huge amount of money to me and very little to them. I was in the middle of a divorce and badly in debt and I had my child to look after. But I was recommended to a lawyer who had helped all the people on *Musketeers* and as a result I renegotiated my deal and made a fortune on *Superman II*. They were behaving totally illegally and it ended up costing them a million." Donner, she maintained, had made both her career and Christopher Reeve's, as well as earning the Salkinds "billions"; then the Salkinds turned around and stabbed him in the back: "I have nothing but contempt for them." (For the record, the Salkinds maintained that it took *Superman III* before the costs of the first movie were recouped and they began to make a profit.)

Reeve agreed with Kidder, maintaining that Donner had been "fired" without his knowledge before Guy Hamilton was briefly appointed. He fumed that he had been powerless to act, since all the contracts had been signed before he was informed. The Salkinds were summed up as "untrustwor-thy, devious and unfortunate as people." (Donner, still awaiting his profit percentage from the first movie as *Super-man II's* première neared, reflected: "The sickness of these people is that they think everybody is out to kill them. Eventually I guess everybody is.")

Reeve and Kidder were also in agreement about Lester, having come to know and trust him in his role as producer. "Lester was under tremendous pressure arriving on the set and did a good job," said Kidder. "When I met Lester I really liked and respected him and I didn't blame him for what had happened at all," Reeve added. Part of the reason why *Superman II* was "such a good movie," he would main-tain, was due to "Lester's enormous skill as a director. If it hadn't been for that and the major legacy left by Donner"— footage estimated by Reeve to be around 25 percent of *Superman II*, including all the scenes with Gene Hackman— "it would have been a joke. Because in my view the way *Superman II* was produced is the lowest you can go without actually cheating." Reeve stressed that he was talking about the production, not the finished movie, which he termed "different from *Superman I*, but not in quality, a simpler film, a lighter film, and neither better nor worse."

In his footage estimate Reeve was overlooking several points. In the scramble to get the first movie finished, at least half a dozen directors were called in for certain se-quences, including Peter Duffel, production designer John Barry and veteran director Andre De Toth. And although all of Hackman's scenes were indeed directed by Donner, most of them had to be rescripted, re-edited and revoiced by Lester, with additional scenes shot using doubles.

Much of this was done to accommodate the new storyline necessitated by the departure of Marlon Brando, yet another

"Yes, I direct as well as produce!"
Richard Lester, Jackie Cougan and Margot Kidder on the set of
Superman II.   (COURTESY OF RICHARD LESTER)

in the long list of litigants suing the Salkinds. The choice
was either to cut Brando out of *II* or risk a court injunction
against the sequel. Ultimately, Donner's "legacy" can be
more accurately placed at 10 percent of *Superman II.*

■

While Lester dickered with the Salkinds' offer to direct
Superman III, he tried in vain to get Warners' behind several
of his personal projects. "You're into blockbusters," was
their message. "Stick with them for now. Once *Superman III*
is finished, we'll talk again." Despite the enormous amount
of money the Salkinds and Warners' were prepared to pay—
another industry record—Lester hung up on their offer,
relayed personally by Warners' Bob Shapiro, and strolled
through the house to find Deirdre. Well aware of the sums

being bandied about, she was busily sponging away at the windows in a pair of rubber gloves. "I've definitely turned it down," he told her, shrugging morosely. Deirdre stared at him for a moment in disbelief, then drew back her arm and flung her soapy blue sponge straight at him. As it bounced off his right ear she said, "Don't be so *stupid*. Bloody well phone them back and tell them you'll do it." Impressed by the force of his good woman's argument, Lester proceeded to do just that.

Given a relatively free hand, Lester decided to move the emphasis of *III* towards social realism, setting the first scene in an unemployment office and hiring the most naturalistic actor he could find—Richard Pryor—for a key role, all in an attempt to anchor the subject to a base of reality and reduce the mythic element he felt had already been thoroughly explored. "If you were trying to make a genuine political point in *Superman*, that would be absurd," he agrees. "But I certainly wanted to approach it from a fresh, oblique viewpoint."

Lester found Pryor a delight to work with, the only slight initial tension arising from everyone's assiduous avoidance of any mention of his color, in case it caused offense. Lester's first sight of Robin Williams, a longtime friend of Pryor's, came when Williams landed on the set unexpectedly one day, loudly demanding, "All right, where's the fucking nigger?" Once everyone got over that particular shock, they were able to relax.

"Richard was wonderful," Lester recalled. "He never said the same line the same way twice, or even the same words twice. It would have driven some directors nuts, but it didn't bother me at all. I think he does it to keep himself fresh. He's the sort of person who inspires absolute devotion on minimal acquaintance. He reminded me a lot of John Lennon

"OK, I'm sorry I sat in your chair, Richie. To make up for it you can sit in mine."
(COURTESY OF RICHARD LESTER)

in that way. They're both people you find yourself caring desperately about as soon as you meet them. They also shared the ability to cut very simply to the heart of an idea."

Lester saw another side of Pryor's personality when he returned from a short break in Hawaii in an outrageously bad mood. It was as if someone had thrown a Jeykll and Hyde switch. The camera operator to whom he was extremely rude had to be physically restrained from hitting Pryor. Next day, it was all over. "He's like a bird with a broken wing, not physically strong at all," says Lester. "I couldn't help feeling I'd seen the syndrome before twice in my life, first with Spike, then with John."

Much as he admired Pryor's work, he ended up concerned that perhaps he had given him too much leeway and devoted too much footage to him. Lester went back to the scenes that showcased Pryor and cut a minute or so from each of them. It turned out that Warners' had different ideas, convinced that every Pryor moment was box-office gold. As soon as they discovered that Lester had snipped certain scenes, they were on their collective knees begging for the footage to be reinstated. Against his better judgment, Lester obliged.

A later development that struck him as ironic emerged when the Salkinds' sale of the movies to television turned out to hinge, with a dollar escalator, on each of the series running for three hours with commercials. Instead of producers and studios cutting out footage, there was a trawling of the cutting room floor to find any discarded bits they could put back in. Lester had distinctly mixed feelings about the nineteen minutes of his "rejects" that were reinstated for television airing—if only, he agonized, he had had the sense to burn the negatives!

Overall, Lester's instincts in accepting the projects were justified—he regards *Superman II* and *III* as two of the smoothest-running productions he has ever made, with less of the constant pressure he had always felt to get five minutes in the can each day. "And no matter how short, long, cheap or expensive," he points out, "I invariably wake up at five in the morning when I'm in a movie and ask myself three questions. First: 'Am I going to be found out today?' Then: 'Have I thought of everything?' Finally: 'Have I thought of *anything*?' " On the technical side there were challenges he particularly enjoyed—the leap into the river in *II* and Superman's fight with his alter ego in *III*. Most of all, perhaps, he had relished the iconoclastic aspect of his work on them. And Pryor was not the only one supplying laughs on the filming of *III*.

After shooting a sequence for the movie in the morning, Lester asked Reeve not to change for lunch, since they would be continuing the same scene in the afternoon with just a change of lens. Reeve agreed, and with Lester behind him, duly lined up in the canteen, replete in his unmistakable outfit with the big *S*, the boots, the works. A moment later Lester spotted Sir John Gielgud at a nearby table having lunch. After saying hello, he introduced Reeve. "Hello, dear boy," Gielgud greeted him, eyeing the actor. "And what are you up to these days?"

Comparing the merits and demerits of the three *Superman* movies very much depends on how seriously you take your superheroes. Donner's *Superman—The Movie* held greatest appeal to those who prefer their legends unsullied, their myths unchallenged. "Long, lugubrious and only patchily entertaining . . . with far too many irrelevant preliminaries and a misguided sense of its own importance," Leslie Halliwell complained in his *Guide*. The New Yorker found it "cheesy-looking," its plotting "so hit or miss that the story never seems to get started." Pauline Kael may have been on target in maintaining that the movie gave the impression "of having been made in panic—in fear that style or too much imagination might endanger its approach to the literal-minded." The "literal-minded," as well as millions of perfectly happy kids, forked over a bountiful $82 million in American and Canadian net rentals (in terms of tickets sold, *Superman—The Movie* outstripped Warner's supposedly record-breaking *Batman*).

Lester's first sequel, able to dispense with all the material that arguably had weighed down Donner's movie, enjoyed "the luxury of getting down to action almost immediately,"

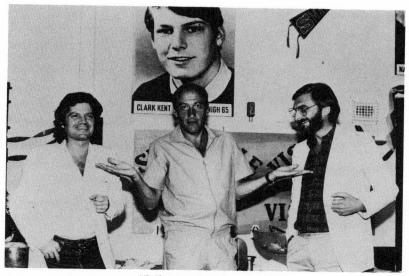

"Who are these people?"
Ilya Salkind, Richard Lester and Pierre Spengler on the set of *Superman III.* (COURTESY OF WARNER BROTHERS/RICHARD LESTER)

as *Variety* pointed out, summing it up as "a solid, classy, cannily constructed piece of entertainment." To *Rolling Stone's* Michael Sragow it was "one of the zippiest comic strip movies yet," beginning with the opening reprise of *Superman* highlights that had "far more flair than the sum total of that dead-head epic." David Ansen in *Newsweek* pronounced the movie "a success, a stirring sequel," while noting the wholesale junking of Donner's "epic lyricism"; Lester's vision was "harder-edged, fleeter on its feet, less reverential."

Hollywood Reporter claimed to detect a new, caring element in Lester's work, "an emotional warmth absent from the first movie." Andrew Sarris in the *Village Voice* seemed to approve the switch from Donner's "rollicking adventurousness" to a comparatively gray and somber version, which

313

he attributed to "Lester's dark, uneasy, fragmented view of human existence a well as Superman's understandable need to evolve on screen." In Time magazine Richard Schickel enthused over "that rarity of rarities, a sequel that readily surpasses the original"—not, he hastened to point out, a task requiring lofty wit given the "crudeness" of the original. "Since the major change on the credits is the substitution of Richard Lester for Richard Donner as director," Schickel continued, "it seems logical to single him out as the one responsible for making Superman soar." Janet Maslin in the New York *Times* saw *Superman II* as "a marvelous toy. It's funny, full of tricks, and manages to be royally entertaining."

"*Superman II* isn't just as good as *Superman*, it's significantly better. I mean, head and shoulders above," declared Merrill Shindler in Los Angeles magazine. Howard Kissel agreed in the columns of *Women's Wear Daily*: "*Superman II* is a much more entertaining and intriguing film than its predecessor." David Denby in New York magazine had seen the original *Superman* as "one of the most disjointed, stylistically mixed-up movies ever made. But now all is well. When Lester took over, he brought unity and a high style to the material . . . Few movies have made the confrontation of man and supernatural powers so astonishing and so funny. *Superman II* is easily the best spectacle movie of this season." Even Pauline Kael in The New Yorker, normally no great Lester champion, was enthusiastic, detecting "old-fashioned virtue, charm, and a lot of entertaining kinkiness too . . . Lester is in his element in *Superman II*. It's more sheer fun to see than anything else around."

Having been virtually written off at the end of the sixties, Lester had bounced back spectacularly in the seventies with the *Musketeers* saga, *Juggernaut* and *Robin and Marian* before hitting another fallow patch with *The Ritz, Butch and Sundance* and the disaster that was *Cuba*. Now, with the marvelously exhilarating *Superman II* in the eighties, an unprecedented third act had begun. His ups and downs were rapidly becoming the stuff of legend, yet even while the movie was flying high at the box office—in its opening three days in the U.S. *Superman II* grossed a record $14 million and ended up netting a staggering $65 million—Lester kept his feet firmly planted on the ground. "You've thrilled to the T-shirt," he remarked during an exhaustive European publicity tour for the movie, "now see the movie!"

Although less ecstatically received, *Superman III* has its supporters, myself included. Returning to Donner's mythological well would have been one trip too many. Lester's refreshingly irreverent approach in *II* was carried to its dark yet hilarious extreme in *III*. Jack Kroll in Newsweek found it "cute and clever," while Rolling Stone's Michael Sragow again enthused over "the funniest, liveliest and most original Superman movie yet." To Garry Arnold in the Washington *Post*, however, it was a "not-so-super sequel . . . even Pryor can't save it." Arthur Knight in Hollywood Reporter disagreed. He saw the movie as "big in every way, with spectacular stunts" and "great fun," as well as "surprising warmth." In Britain Charles Shaar Murray in the New Musical Express described *Superman III* as "the wittiest, most energetic and the most insistent" of the series and had a novel suggestion for the Salkinds. Why not take Richard Pryor's character and make *Gus Gorman II*?

The telegram that was dispatched from Warners' to Lester listed a slightly reduced first-weekend take of $13.3 million for *Superman III*, still the second-highest figure at that point in the company's history. YOU HOLD BOTH RECORDS, Bob Shapiro's message ended. This time net receipts ended up at a profitable but decidedly shrunken $37 million. Either hardcore Superman fans preferred their hero straight, or the diminishing returns of sequelitis had set in.

Offered *Superman IV* by the Golan/Globus team at Cannon (the Salkinds having sold the rights for an undisclosed sum), Lester wisely decided it was time to bow out, convinced that the possibilities had been exhausted in three movies. The public seemed to agree. Although the equation had worked perfectly well for almost fifty years in countless episodes of comic strips, transferring them into endless full-length movies was a different proposition. *Superman IV*'s plunge to just $8 million in net receipts still came as a major shock, and halted the series—temporarily, at least—in its tracks.

CHAPTER EIGHTEEN

Even if I'd had an Academy Award screenplay between Superman II *and* III, *Warners' wouldn't have financed me. It was simply in their best interests to make sure I was starved of other work so that I was available to do what they wanted me to do.*

—RICHARD LESTER

One of the fairly modest movies Lester wanted to make "between *Supermen*" was a comedy scripted by Charles Wood that would have starred Robin Williams as a small-time Russian Shakespearean actor whose neat sideline in Stalin impersonations gets him into all kinds of trouble in the Soviet Union. Williams's nightclub act featured a routine in which he played a Russian comic doing jokes nobody understood. Expressing great enthusiasm, Williams offered to hold off on other projects for a year while Lester tried to set the project up. Dan Rissner's first question at Warners' was, "Couldn't you set the movie in America?" At Universal, Lew Wasserman's response was, "We don't want to make another goddamn picture about a bunch of goddamn commies."

Turning closer to home, Lester sent the package to HandMade Films, set up by George Harrison and his partner Denis O'Brien. More specifically, he sent the package to O'Brien himself, not wishing to presume on past friendships. He was still surprised at the shortest of short shrifts O'Brien gave the project, returning the treatment with an extremely businesslike if not curt letter turning it down. The Robin Williams Russian project was dead on the vine.

An adaptation of Joseph Conrad's *Victory* was next on and off the agenda. Writer Christopher Hampton was approached first, before a switch to Harold Pinter, for whom a considerable sum of money was raised. The biggest problem with Pinter's script, although brilliant, was in its typically uncompromising spareness. Pinter certainly made little effort to beguile his readers William Goldman–style. "There were several problems with *Victory*," Lester concedes. "Almost all of Conrad's heroes are negative people. It would have been a film of reacting rather than acting, with a lot implied rather than stated, a lot of holding back and a lot of torment, and certainly no happy ending. Absolutely everybody turned it down, although I think several would have backed it had the leading characters been alive at the end and heading off into the sunset. There was never any question of Harold or myself doing that."

Then there was "Doonesbury" cartoonist Garry Trudeau's *Zoo Plane*, describing his exploits in the press entourage covering Jimmy Carter's whistle-stop world tour in Air Force One to spread his human rights message. Lester and Trudeau agreed to take no money and develop independently their movie adaptation of the trip, where everything conceivable had gone hilariously wrong at each stop. Landing late in Egypt, Carter had caught the entire honor guard at their prayers on the tarmac and assumed they had been praying for his safe arrival. The locations that were scouted and the cast plans that were drawn up all came to nothing as yet another project withered for lack of studio interest.

Contacted by Steve Martin to consider directing *Three Amigos*, Lester was at first undeterred by the switch from social reality to singing crows in Martin's draft script ("fixable??") and visited a museum in Oxford where he found some extraordinary photographs of Mexico at the turn of the century. Off he went to a meeting at Orion in Los Angeles with Mike Medavoy, Martin and his team, where he spread out his archival photos. The reception was decidedly glacial, and Martin finally spelled it out: "The trouble is you don't seem to realize we just want to make a big dumb movie."

"I'm sorry, I'm not smart enough for that," Lester replied.

One glance at a Sunday *Times* color supplement photograph showing the Municipal Swimming Baths in downtown Tokyo packed with several thousand bathers gave Lester an idea for a project that came to be known as *Made in Japan*. He kept envisioning Walter Matthau having gone off to buy ice cream, trying in vain to find the friend he came in with. He was put in touch with ex-actor Ed Clinton, the blond, handsome thirty-something scriptwriter of *Honky Tonk Freeway*. ("Perfect for you," Judy Scott-Fox decreed before waltzing off to join Ray Stark at Rastar, whereupon Lester signed with Creative Artists Agency.) Back home in England, Charles Wood was brought in on the project before it was abandoned altogether.

Wood's stream of work, besides his unproduced screenplays for Lester, had continued throughout the seventies and into the eighties and included *Don't Forget to Write*, an autobiographical television series with George Cole and Gwen Watford based on his "adventures in the screentrade"; *Hadrian VII* for John Schlesinger (unproduced), *Wagner* for

Tony Palmer; a television series based on Gerald Durrell's books, *My Family and Other Animals*; and Richard Eyre's BBC-TV production of the Falklands saga, *Tumbledown*.

After he had waxed enthusiastic over Donald Barthelme's *The King*, a novel depicting the court of King Arthur during World War II—"This is the film we were both born to make," Wood declared—he hurried off to produce a script. "I don't think Richard really liked the book as much as I did," he reflected. "I *loved* it. It's sheer poetry, all about honor and concepts of heroism, about royalty and their power. To be truthful, I don't think it will ever make a film. I turned in my draft and Richard announced that he didn't like it—and that was that, we haven't spoken since. Before *The King* came up, we'd more or less decided not to work together again in any case, just to be mates instead. We should have left it at that." (The two are now reunited as "mates.")

From the very beginning of his career Lester and the powers-that-be in the movie industry have been at odds, the moguls unwilling to finance what he has wanted to do, while he in turn has refused to compromise and accept work purely for the money—despite some surprising choices. Over the years the list of turn-downs has grown and grown. Here are just a few, together with Lester's off-the-cuff commentary.

First, the sixties:

• FIGURES ON A LANDSCAPE: "I knew John Cohn and Stanley Mann; they were two of the American community here and would submit almost all their material to me. I didn't care for this one."

• A CLOCKWORK ORANGE: "This was the Terry Southern version, when he owned the rights before Kubrick. Burgess and I were on the same wavelength. I only met him once but liked him enormously. It appealed, but I am almost squeamish when it comes to violence and practically incapable of putting it on the screen."

• THE MASTER AND MARGARITA: "Clive Nicholas introduced me to the book and I was tempted, but I thought it was rather arrogant for an Anglo-Saxon to have a go at it."

• MYRA BRECKENRIDGE: "I didn't fancy it. I'd known Vidal and enjoyed his company, but I'm no better at sex than I am at violence."

• CATCH–22: "Zero had asked me if I could get this together, with him playing Milo Minderbinder. This was at the time of *How I Won the War* and I told Zero I was going to attempt the English version instead."

Into the seventies:

• THE SEVEN PERCENT SOLUTION: "I was tempted."

• THE EBONY TOWER: "I didn't think it would work as a film."

• PLAZA SUITE: "I considered it too theatrical."

• THE WIZ: "I loved the soundtrack and we started talking, but I thought it was unfilmable and haven't changed my opinion after seeing Sidney's movie."

• DICK TRACY: "I hate comic strips and comic strip heroes. I think it was that thing about *Help!* being a pop art musical that I was submitted every cartoon character for years to come—unlike Alain Resnais, who loves the stuff and was never offered."

• POPEYE: "Ditto."

• A FAREWELL TO ARMS: "That came up twice. I'm not a Hemingway fan, but I think George C. Scott was attached at some point and I actually toyed, then thought better of it."

• SOMEONE IS KILLING THE GREAT CHEFS OF EUROPE: "Just silly."

- GRAY LADY DOWN: "Submarines? Not for me, not even with Charlton on board."
- METEOR: "A piece of rubbish."
- THE SEDUCTION OF JOE TYNAN: "This was submitted as *The Senator*, with Alan Alda attached. I quite liked the material but was in the middle of other things."
- PLAY IT AGAIN, SAM: "Woody wasn't attached at the time."
- RIDDLE OF THE SANDS: "Not for me."
- SERGEANT PEPPER'S LONELY HEARTS CLUB BAND: "I said no way is that going to be a film."
- THE CLERK: "This was Oliver Stone; he came to Twickenham before *Midnight Express* and we talked. Both Judy and I were impressed by him and she helped him afterwards."
- RAGING MOON: "I thought the subject matter was mawkish and I disliked it. It was submitted to Bryan Forbes when he was busy saving the British film industry. He turned it down, then suddenly took it on as a director later."
- AMERICAN HOT WAX: "This was good fun, a good script, but by this time anything with pop music was really not on for me. Enough was enough."
- SILVER BEARS: "I liked the idea, but there were too many vague areas."
- NOMADS: "I met with John McTiernan, who had written the script and had originally wanted to direct it himself. I told him not to give up, even if it took years. He didn't and it did."
- STING II: "A very bad script. Don't you think following one George Roy Hill smash was stupid enough?"
- DOG DAY AFTERNOON: "It came with a seven-page treatment. I knew this was a terrific idea for a film, but I didn't know how these people would have behaved. I'm not street-conscious, and it needed someone who could shape the

material. Also someone who knew New York like the back of his hand. They got both in Sidney."

- TOMMY: "Didn't like it and didn't like Ken's version either. Tina was great, then there was Olly rolling around in all those baked beans."
- DON'T LOOK NOW: "One of the best films Nic made and he did a far better job of it than I would have."
- THE SAILOR WHO FELL FROM GRACE WITH THE SEA: "I liked Mishima's story but didn't think transferring it to a Western setting would work."
- THE ROSE: "I suppose I was offered this—as *Pearl*, three times—because I'd known Janis from *Petulia*. I turned it down because, like most of these things about troubled stars, all we're seeing is the downside, life's hell, and you never get any sense of joy or exuberance. The reason people loved John Lennon or Janis Joplin, the really endearing qualities which they had, without which they wouldn't have been able to touch people so many times, was never examined."
- THE ADVENTURES OF BARON MUNCHAUSEN: "I felt it wouldn't work. There's a great difficulty in sustaining audience interest when you've got a madman as a hero not responding to plot conditions."
- MAN OF LA MANCHA: "Ditto."
- PRIVATE BENJAMIN: "I like Goldie Hawn and I thought about it and it was nice to be asked. It made a lot of money, but I thought it was an awful film."

Now for the eighties and beyond:

- OUT OF AFRICA: "Nic and I both had a go at it, and we all knew there was a film in there somewhere, but I don't have any sort of passion for Africa."
- THE PRINCE OF TIDES: "Psychobabble."

- AN OFFICER AND A GENTLEMAN: "Okay, but I had no feel for it."
- RETURN TO OZ: "I didn't care to."
- NOT A PENNY MORE, NOT A PENNY LESS: "Didn't appeal to me at all."
- BORN YESTERDAY: "I could picture every character from the original film and knew I could never make it better."
- LADYHAWKE: "I'm not a sword 'n' sorcery person."
- FATAL ATTRACTION: "Too much sex and violence for me."
- ROMANCING THE STONE: "I turned this down three times. I knew it was going to work, but at that time I was trying to set up the Robin Williams movie. Bob Zemekis did a marvelous job; it turned out better than the script and I don't think I could have done it as well."
- BEST FRIENDS: "Just not interested."
- LITTLE DORRIT: "I liked *reading* Dickens."
- AUTHOR! AUTHOR!: "Al Pacino was sullen and unresponsive to ideas when we met. I didn't think it would work. Israel I liked, but I didn't think he produced a good screenplay."
- SCANDAL: "Deirdre and I had known the Astors socially and had been to Cliveden, where we shot *Help!* We had a wonderful time there. I had lived through it and felt it was not quite right."
- AT PLAY IN THE FIELDS OF THE LORD: "I think it's a book a hundred people thought would make a good film. I'd have been very surprised if it had worked."
- TAIPAN: "I liked *Shogun*, didn't like this. It should have been a mini-series; it wasn't right to condense it."
- DESPERATELY SEEKING SUSAN: "I think it was a better film than a script, but it was fun. I wouldn't have thought of Madonna. I didn't even know who she was at that time."
- INTO THE NIGHT: "No interest."

- HAND-CARVED COFFINS: "Very interesting, very disturbing, but not for me."
- LEVIATHAN: "Sea monsters? Definitely not me."
- THE MOSQUITO COAST: "I liked Paul Theroux book, but thought the third part of it needed to be changed, I didn't like the ending."
- FLASHDANCE: "Not me."
- COCOON: "Ditto."
- CLUE: "I thought it would work and told Debra and Lynda it should be set in one of these great 1930s palaces on the coast, like the Coronado. They kept it modern."
- THE PRINCESS BRIDE: "I agreed to do this and I don't know what happened!"
- THE DIAMOND AS BIG AS THE RITZ: "I had a feeling about it, nothing was what it seemed. I still think something could be done."
- GORKY PARK: "I liked the book, but I was working with Harold at the time on *Victory*."
- 20,000 LEAGUES UNDER THE SEA: "Dino thought it would be a good idea to remake it. I said it would not. Simple as that."
- SCARAMOUCHE: "Dustin Hoffman submitted it; we met in a restaurant in Beverly Hills (we'd first met in Britain when he was doing *Agatha* and shared a driver). We talked a lot and I like Dustin. I said, 'Everything I know about your working and everything you know about my working means we should never work together—you're obsessive and I'm sloppy,' and he said, 'No, I'm not really like that. I do careful preparation but once we start I'll play around as much as you like.' Maybe he has given up on the idea; I certainly have."
- GOOD MORNING, VIETNAM: "Another one I agreed to, then heard no more."

- SOMETHING WICKED THIS WAY COMES: "I didn't like the story."
- HIGHLANDER: "Didn't like the idea."
- A VERY PRIVATE LIFE: "I knew Michael Frayn slightly, but didn't think this was good material for a film. I bid $15,000 instead for an option on his *Noises Off*, then was just pipped at the post by a mere $985,000 by Steven Spielberg."
- EVITA: "I've had this through my hands three times. I love one or two of the songs and one of my happiest memories is of watching the 1978 World Cup on television, when Ally McLeod was the Manager of the Scottish Team and they went to Argentina and the fans had saved up to support them—"Ally's Tartan Army"—and they lost every game, it was a total disaster. The BBC covered it all and put together footage with 'Don't Cry for Me, Argentina' on top, showing the despair of the team. It was funny and sad.

"I always felt that the whole Evita/Peron/Argentina story was fascinating. She was an amazing character, but what I felt was wrong was you'd have to address yourself to the problem of her meeting Che Guevara as the author's theatrical device, because of course it never happened, they never actually met. And most of the operatic stuff was extremely badly written, and Peron was just a cipher in it. I read a script Ken Russell wrote, but I didn't think he had solved any of the problems. I also read a version by Glen Caron, which was very good, but it was going to cost $40 million. So they had to get it down to below $25 million. When I asked how much was already on board, how much we could really spend, I was told $17 million before Madonna was paid. So there was no way unless you got rid of all but three or four musical numbers and wrote interesting dramatic scenes; otherwise there was nothing going for it. If you made the film politically interesting you would alienate the people who wanted to hear the music, and if you made it a musical it would seem full of holes and artificial. So there it rests."

Over the years Lester had also received fairly regular submissions of projects from U.S.-based Italian entrepreneur Dino De Laurentiis, to all of which he had courteously replied, after due consideration, that he wasn't the right director for the subject. Dino's decision to open his own distribution set-up meant shouldering the risk of the American market on his own and becoming totally dependent on territorial pre-selling around the world to raise finance. Since Paramount, Universal and MGM—repeatedly stung with the likes of *Flash Gordon, Ragtime* and *Dune*—were not exactly beating a path to his door, he was arguably left with little alternative. And he could still rely on the backing of Credit Lyonnais' *eminence grise* of film finance, Frans Afman.

Dino's enthusiasm for distribution, matched only by a concomitant desire for studio ownership—in Wilmington, North Carolina, no less—knew no bounds. Overnight he acquired extensive and lavish offices on Wilshire Boulevard and surrounded himself with a staff of close to three hundred personnel, many of whom were seen either as expensively hired malcontents or second-raters from other companies. (Who, the argument ran, would give up the security of a job at Warners' or Fox to join Dino on his mighty adventure unless he or she was being offered a significant premium on their old salaries?) Now the tail began to wag the dog, with Dino, his daughter Rafaella, and their distribution pundits in regular board meetings deciding what movies should be made.

It was at this stage that Lester was asked to contribute, and a deal was worked out whereby he could make one film in the course of a year; providing it was kept within a $5 million budget, Dino had no right of veto. In addition, Lester was to seek out other material that needed a distribution deal or production money. In exchange for all this, Dino would pay Lester's overheads at Twickenham.

Lester knew of films that had been completed and were on the lookout for American distribution, and wasted no time in passing the word around. For two years he had been working with British Screen and the National Film Development Fund (part of the Department of Trade and Industry) on a panel that met once a month, talking to individuals seeking money to develop a script. (The government grants available enabled up to £18,000 to be allocated for a draft screenplay.)

At Lester's initial meeting with Dino, the mogul announced that he had just returned from Australia, where he had set up yet another studio. During the visit he had seen a newspaper clipping of a book he described as "Fattalshore"—did anyone know it? Lester replied that he had indeed read *The Fatal Shore* by art critic Robert Hughes, and yes, it was a marvelous book that would make a wonderful film or TV series; Dino should buy it right away. Although he had only Lester's word for it, Dino bought the book without bothering to read it himself and allocated $350,000 for Hughes to write his own screenplay. Lester flew back to his home base convinced, despite the committee structure of Dino's set-up, that DDLF (Dino De Laurentiis Films) was going to be a terrific company to work with.

The first project Lester found that really excited him was a movie already arranged at MGM before the deal foundered over the fine print. Suddenly it was free—for one week only. If Dino showed any enthusiasm, he had a window of opportunity in which to match or exceed MGM's offer. The script was duly dispatched by courier to Dino with Lester's highest recommendation, further expressed in personal phone calls to the great man himself, as well as to Rafaella. It was set up and ready to roll, it was stressed, with the cast signed and ready, and at a total cost of $7 million, it simply could not lose. Since neither Dino, Rafaella, nor the dreaded distribution committee expressed any enthusiasm, unanimously pronouncing the comedy "not funny," Cleese, Kline, Curtis, Palin and *A Fish Called Wanda* reverted to MGM.

Lester went on to recommend a further eight projects, all of which Dino chose to turn down. Among them were *Sour Sweet*, based on the book by Timothy Mo, ultimately made elsewhere ("No Chinese films make money"); a children's movie shot in Czechoslovakia; and *The Book of Daniel*, eventually directed by Sidney Lumet. For a while Dino had the rights to *Dead Ringers*, later made for Fox by David Cronenberg. Considering that it was about a serial killer gynecologist, Lester thought it was odd that the bulk of the enthusiasm expressed within DDLF came from the women in the company.

While turning down everything Lester submitted, Dino offered him movies to direct. Apparently undaunted by the original having bombed, he put forward *Dune II* and then *Total Recall*, then set for production in Australia, which he described as "a psychological thriller with very few special effects—not expensive to do." Lester declined them both, beginning to feel distinctly sour. Given his proven track record and experience in the world of filmmaking, why were his projects dismissed so readily?

One of their last meetings was in Cannes during the festival, where Dino was staying at the Hotel du Cap with Frans Afman. As usual, the mogul was charming, and Lester was flattered to hear from Afman that he was his "favorite director," but on the business side there was nothing doing. Not long afterwards, following one of the most disastrous production slates in recent movie history, Dino's company went bankrupt, leaving Lester to pay his own overheads for the last month of their deal.

Within months Rafaella called to ask if Lester would care to direct her own first film, a children's movie about a reindeer entitled *Prancer*. Soon the irrespressible Dino himself was back in business under a new banner, and, like his daughter, contacted Lester. He was about to remake an old project of his, *Once Upon a Crime*; would Lester care to direct? Lester declined both offers—not out of sour grapes, but because neither held the least appeal.

It never was a marriage made in heaven, but how few of Dino's were? Charles Wood recalls being commissioned by director Michael Winner to update *The Merry Widow* under Dino's aegis. The result—The Merry Widow from Hell?—we have fortunately been spared.

■

Finders Keepers emerged as a Richard Lester movie almost by default. It had first been sent to him in 1975 as a novel by Charles Dennis, *The Next to Last Train Ride*, with a draft script attached. After turning it down, he heard that Terence Marsh, his friend and production designer on *Juggernaut* and *Royal Flash*, had acquired the rights and had begun to rewrite it, hoping to make his directorial debut with the piece. Sensing Warners' jitters about dealing with a first-timer, Lester offered them a safety net over any technical problems that might arise by acting as executive producer. Soon Marsh felt that he was being given the runaround by the studio. If only he could get this or that star interested; if only he could

Louis Gosset, Jr., Beverly D'Angelo and Michael O'Keefe filming *Finders Keepers*. (COURTESY OF CBS/RICHARD LESTER)

change one or two plot points; if only the budget could be pruned; one more rewrite might just do it . . .

In the end Warner Brothers did the merciful thing and put *Finders Keepers* into turnaround, where it was snapped up by CBS Theatrical Films, eager to add to their first slate of movies. That was the good news; the bad was that the company would only go with a name director. Giving in, Marsh asked Lester to consider directing the movie, enabling him to at least produce the screenplay he had co-written with Ronny Graham. To save the project from slipping away from Marsh completely and possible oblivion Lester agreed.

As one reviewer later put it, the screenwriters had supplied him with enough plot material for several movies in the frantic tale of a stolen $5 million hidden in a coffin in a railway baggage car, pursued by a cast of characters who would have done Preston Sturges proud. Standing in for Eddie Bracken, Betty Hutton, William Demarest, *et al.* were Michael O'Keefe as an inept con man, Louis Gossett, Jr. as his guardian angel, Beverly D'Angelo as the tart with a heart (or, as O'Keefe's character describes her, "the mind of a maniac and the mouth of a longshoreman") and Ed Lauter and Pamela Stephenson as a couple of careless crooks. Also on hand: Brian Dennehy as a small-town sheriff and David Wayne as the world's most ancient train conductor. Lester had originally considered Jamie Lee Curtis for the female lead—until D'Angelo called him at 4:00 A.M., insisting that she had to be in the movie, that she'd even do it for nothing. "I thought that was either gross stupidity or amazing instinct," Lester recalls with a smile. "It really pissed me off that she'd destroyed my sleep. Then I thought, 'Wait a minute, that's exactly what the character I'm looking for would have done.' "

With Alberta, Canada (Smallville in *Superman III*) standing in for Nebraska, and a train hired for the occasion that was supposedly shuttling between Oakland and Nebraska (shades of *A Hard Day's Night*), Lester pondered between scenes on the wisdom of venturing yet again into farce. "It's the hardest form of comedy to film," he suggests. "It's tragedy played at double speed. Characters are earnestly trying to sort out situations they don't understand or wish they weren't in. Watching a farce on the stage, the audience has no difficulty, because the bed under which someone is hiding remains in view. The audience knows what door leads to whose bedroom. But a film is close up and varied points of view can confuse the geography."

By the time *Finders Keepers* was released in the U.S., in May 1984, there were already several strikes against it. The production company, CBS Theatrical Films, had gone bust.

Having rejected it in the first place, Warners' were now entrusted with its distribution. Lester remained cautiously optimistic. He had had a wonderful time making the movie (shades of *Help!*), the editing process had been great fun, and composer Ken Thorne had enthused that it was the funniest comedy he had ever scored. The film opened to several stunning reviews. "Will have you weeping with laughter," Archer Winsten raved in the New York *Post*. Vincent Canby in the New York *Times* pronounced it "unexpectedly satisfying." Playboy saw it as a "happy surprise . . . these madcaps prove that screwball comedy is amazingly alive and well." The New Yorker found it a "far-out, entertaining movie." Hollywood Reporter discovered "A real treasure for filmgoers."

Then there was the very considerable downside. Variety found it "maddening," its "interesting cast wasted"; Lester's touch wasn't "necessarily heavy, merely frantic." The Atlanta *Journal* described it as "really awful stuff and the cast can't be blamed. Miss Stephenson plays a blonde bimbo better than anybody since Barbara Nichols, but she doesn't get a single laugh. Neither does anybody else." "Makes *Silver Streak* seem like a masterpiece," Kevin Thomas wrote in the Los Angeles *Times*.

In Britain the same extremes of opinion were recorded. Against was Time Out: "While Lester's variable output has been a lot more variable than most, nothing in his assorted canon quite prepares us for the full ghastliness here . . . a doomed exercise"; City Limits: "Lame excuse for a comedy"; the Evening Standard: "It is a pity to see only slim vestiges of [Lester's] talent in an obvious, ponderous comedy"; New Statesmen: "Like a failed Preston Sturges."

In favor were the *Financial Times*: "Lester has so many good gags up his sleeve he doesn't care if we miss a few while we blink"; Sunday *Times*: "A gem of a comedy"; Sunday *Telegraph*: "Wisely, Lester barely pauses for breath . . . there's lightness, brevity and pace"; London *Times*: "Old-fashioned, farcical cinema, highly derivative, but neat and tidy"; the *Daily Telegraph*: "A remarkable return to form that assays, with complete success, that difficult and dangerous genre, the crazy comedy."

Critical notices are one thing, audience response quite another. In the case of *Finders Keepers*, it is not too difficult to see what turned viewers off. There were several pluses: a fresh, outstanding comedy performance from the talented Michael O'Keefe, a delightful 'turn' by veteran David Wayne, a deft appearance by the wonderfully funny, ridiculously underrated Pamela Stephenson. Then there were the minuses: sloppily cued Beach Boys accompaniment to an early scene; Beverly D'Angelo too foulmouthed to be funny; a vastly overcomplicated, overpopulated plot, and a setting in 1973, mainly to allow O'Keefe to impersonate a returning Vietnam vet accompanying a dead buddy, supposedly the occupant of the coffin. Britain's Time Out offered its own pithily accurate exclamation for the period setting: "I could only imagine that the script has been hanging around for the last eleven years and in the panic of disinterment no one bothered to update it."

"I didn't think it was that bad," Lester says today. "It made some money, under the title *Cash-Cash*, for a small distributor in France who picked it up and dubbed it, but everybody else just seemed either to hate it or simply to ignore it."

Many felt that this was precisely what Lester should have done. Although one can see the attraction of an apparently lightweight caper movie after the *Superman* blockbusters, *Finders Keepers* was a retrograde step, a movie out of its time.

CHAPTER NINETEEN

"I know nobody goes out of a cinema saying, 'That was a great film, they were bang on budget.' "

—RICHARD LESTER

Lester's nickname, The Bionic Man, was retired in October 1987 with the onset of a particularly nasty bout of hepatitis A traced to oysters eaten six weeks earlier in the south of Spain. When he failed to respond to treatment, cancer of the liver was feared. After tests ruled out this dread possibility, hepatitis C, a much more serious strain than hepatitis A, was considered. Two weeks on steroids—which Lester realized would forever taint his amateur status, and his tennis backhand is still regarded as suspect—fortunately confirmed the diagnosis of the less dangerous A strain. Three months of acute discomfort, with Lester lying flat on his back in an agonized fever of itching, had still to be endured before the worst of the symptoms began to fade; only after six months did real recovery begin. During this period Creative Artists Agency's Rick Nicita earned Lester's undying gratitude and respect. One of the world's busiest and most successful agents, Nicita still unfailingly phoned him every single week and kept him up to date with what was happening in the world of movies from which he otherwise felt excluded.

■

After splitting with the Salkinds, Pierre Spengler was casting around for his first independent project. He realized that any question of a return to Dumas and the *Musketeers* hinged on reassembling the original cast, with Michael York's D'Artagnan as the lynchpin. Over dinner in Los Angeles the actor was asked if he would consider coming back. "Absolutely, yes," York assured him. Although Spengler had automatically submitted every other project he had considered to Lester, all of which had been turned down, Lester's reaction to the suggested "class reunion" was an unhesitating, *"There* you've hit it. I'd *like* to do that." George MacDonald Fraser was promptly contacted to adapt Dumas's *Twenty Years After* as *Return of the Musketeers*, with the other musketeers standing by to repeat their roles.

After encountering what he considered surprising difficulty in raising development money, Spengler sent the script to his ex-lawyer Tom Pollock at Universal, who agreed to accept the movie for the U.S. in a negative pick-up arrangement. Locations in Hungary and Czechoslovakia were ruled out once again in favor of Spain, where Lester assured Spengler he could trim two weeks from the schedule to compensate for the higher cost of shooting. C. Thomas Howell was cast as the son of Athos; Kim Cattrall as Milady's daughter (a son in Dumas's version, but a young female lead opposite Howell was required); Philippe Noiret was Cardinal Mazzaras; Roy Kinnear was back as Planchet; Geraldine Chaplin as Anne of Austria; Jean-Pierre Cassel as Louis XIII and Christopher Lee as Rochefort. (Spengler: "Unfortunately, you were killed in the last one." Lee: "Wait a minute, maybe I didn't die!")

One of the advantages of having three and a half hours for the original movies was that most of Dumas's numerous plot strands were able to be incorporated. Since *Twenty Years After* was almost as long as the first book, and the plot almost as complex, it was much more difficult to condense into a film scheduled to last under two hours. Then there were the bits that had to be added to give Richard Chamberlain's Aramis some kind of continuity, since he had agreed to give just one week of his time. "Basically, Richard didn't want to do it," says Lester. "I think he thought that that part of his life was over. We should all have thought that."

Set up by Spengler as a British/French/Spanish co-production, with an extremely modest $10 million budget, what was needed to remind audiences of past glories was a two-minute introductory clip from the original movies. Unfortunately the Salkinds' demand for something approaching a million dollars rendered this impossible; although Spengler's split with the team was portrayed as amiable, it obviously wasn't *that* amiable.

In Michael York's version of events, the keynote of the movie was struck on the first day of filming when Chamberlain fell from his horse. Although he came to no harm, York himself was next to join the accident list when a stuntman inadvertently pulled him from his mount. Four weeks into the eight-week schedule came a scene in Toledo in which young Howell and his three companions—York, Oliver Reed and Kinnear—were to ride across the Alcantara Bridge that spans the Tagos River. Due to be shot in the morning, it was postponed when stuntmen insisted on additional sand and peat covering for the road to cushion any bumps. All of the personnel were the same as on the original *Musketeers* shoot, with the same stunt double for Kinnear testing whatever he did in advance to ensure Kinnear's safety. After one rehearsal, with Lester asking if the group could go just a little bit faster, the lead rider—Howell—took off. Kinnear's horse tried to catch up with the others and, having reached the end of the run, stumbled on an incline and threw him.

With an ambulance standing by, Kinnear was helped on to an air cushion immediately, and within a few minutes was rushed off to a clinic in Toledo, where a decision was taken to have him moved to Madrid. Spengler was there when the actor was wheeled in and found him in good spirits despite his obvious discomfort. "Seemed like a good idea at the time to get on that horse!" he cracked. Spengler left, aware that Carmel, Kinnear's wife, was flying out to be with her husband. The news that the 238–pound actor had suffered a dislocated and fractured pelvis caused enough concern, although he was reported next morning to be responding to traction treatment. Later that day, when news of his death as a result of shock and hemorrhage came through, it was greeted with stunned disbelief. Lester was in his apartment in Madrid when the message was relayed by Spengler. A maid found him crying uncontrollably.

For the first time in his life Lester wanted to abandon a film halfway through. "Pierre, I cannot do this," Spengler was told. "I cannot carry on with this film."

"Richard, I beg of you, *don't quit*," Spengler pleaded. "In memory of Roy, let's finish the picture together." At a subsequent meeting with Frank Finlay, York and Reed, this was agreed upon.

Because of what York perceived as Lester's callousness towards Kinnear's wife, the actor has since publicly criticized him. "People take it upon themselves to judge Richard," says Spengler, anxious to set the record straight.

The day after Roy died I tried to call Carmel, but she'd flown back to break the news to her three children. I tried to call her again at home the next day, and so did Richard, but the phone was constantly busy, we couldn't get through. The day after that two of her lawyers came on the set and began their interrogations. Everyone immediately shut up; I certainly did. Richard said it wasn't so much the lawyers as far as he was concerned—it was for me, I was the producer and had to take a more cautious legal position, he didn't have to—but there was an undertone of "Should I have put Roy on that horse?" He also told me he has a problem dealing with death, one of the very personal things that go into the man's character. It took him a while, then finally, four or five days later, when Carmel came back to Madrid, he did go and see her at her hotel and spent some time with her.

Spengler, it turned out, already had first-hand experience of Lester's "problem":

My girlfriend died in an accident during *Superman II*, and I attended her funeral in Paris. On the day I returned I went along to the studio where the music for the movie was being recorded. And Richard just said, "Hi," and not another word. I could see from his expression that things were going on inside, but he couldn't talk to me about it. He can't discuss the subject, he has a block. No one can judge someone else's feelings in circumstances such as these, and I resent the fact that some people presume to. The biggest irony, of course, is that *Return of the Musketeers* would never have gone ahead without the initial agreement of Michael York.

Every night Lester locked himself in his quarters and would talk to no one until he was back on set next morning. Because he was still recovering from hepatitis, he was unable even to have a drink.

It is impossible to overstate the pall that was cast over the unit by the tragedy. It took a scene fully a week later, in which Milady's daughter beheads her mother's executioner, to temporarily lift the gloom. After Lester had indicated that he wanted a flight of crows to take off as the axe fell, the local ornithological expert turned up with half a dozen pigeons he had enterprisingly dyed black. *"They're* not crows," Spengler protested. "It's not possible to train crows," he was huffily informed. "If you want birds to fly on cue, these are the nearest you're going to get." Spengler and several of the crew began to roar with laughter as they imagined the pigeons' reaction to the charade: "Fucking show business!" "How did you get in on this gig?" "Maybe we should join a union!" "How long were you in makeup?" Lester was the only one who declined to join in the temporary respite. For him the nightmare continued in post-production when he was faced constantly with images of his old friend.

Universal tried for a while to get out of their pick-up commitment following a disastrous preview at their Cineplex Odeon center in Universal City. Lester attended the first showing with John Victor Smith, following which a few adjustments were made. At the second "sneak," which Lester declined to attend, the results were scarcely better. The key element in Universal's argument against ultimately granting the movie a theatrical release was the $8 to $10 million they would need to splash out in prints and ads, which they made clear would be good money thrown after bad; it was better to go for guaranteed recoupment of their advance by selling the movie direct to cable, followed by video. When a theater release in Britain exposed *Return of the Musketeers* for the first time to the critical light of day, the reaction was devastating—"confused," "boring" and "incomprehensible" among the most common epithets pressed into service. Far too much plot had undoubtedly been crammed in, which no amount of voice-over or titles could explain away. Leonard Maltin's *Movie and Video Guide* still provided a notice that left honor reasonably intact: "Lester's follow-up to his two classics of the seventies is only partially successful, sometimes straining for a jaunty charm that just isn't there, but actually gets better as it goes along. And the director hasn't lost his flair for inventive slapstick action sequences."

For Lester the movie's fate was of no importance compared to the death of Kinnear. "How do you go on after that?" he asks today. "Roy was a wonderful man, the best, someone I'd spent more than twenty years making films with. For me the light has gone out of being a filmmaker. It's gone. There hasn't been a day in the years since that I haven't thought about it. The idea of doing anything again involving action, anything that carries an element of risk— and all comedy has that element—is something I'm not yet able to face."

■

Get Back began with a phone call from Paul McCartney in March 1987. He requested a short film to be screened as a prelude to his new band's appearance on stage. "First there were The Beatles, then Wings, now is now!" was the message to be conveyed in about ten minutes. With Paul off on vacation, Lester set to work and came up with the idea of three linked projectors and working with a single sound-track, giving the possibility of three different movies shown side by side.

Six songs were chosen to bridge the gap from 1964. For documentary footage to accompany them, Lester conducted polls at dinner parties to learn what images lingered most vividly from those years; they had to be strong enough to work on their own while reflecting their year of origin. Moments from the war in Vietnam were cited, the 1969 moon landing, the flower power era, all the way to Tiananmen Square. Names like Andy Warhol, Muhammad Ali and Jacqueline Kennedy Onassis were mentioned most often. Most of the images selected were strong stuff—war casualties, napalmed children and Lester decided to keep them in. They were the visual testimony of the times, and if the footage was to have the necessary resonance, Lester felt that these graphic images could not be edited out. He also had home movie material of Paul with Michael Jackson, together with footage of Paul and his family at their farm in Scotland.

In the end the specified ten minutes stretched to seventeen, with Paul's band filmed at Elstree in their playing positions so that when the end of the film was reached the pictures would fade and the band would emerge live on stage. (Paul eventually opined that this was decidedly arch and decreed that the band stroll on casually and pick up the song where the soundtrack left off.) At this point Lester had carried out the entire exercise for fun, and for very little money. The same conditions largely applied to the full-length concert version Paul now envisaged, which would emerge as *Get Back*, a movie souvenir of his "final" world tour. After the nightmare of *Return of the Musketeers*, the suggestion came at just the right time for Lester. This was something he *could* tackle. "You can see what was attractive about taking on *Get Back*," he says. "It was hardly one's idea of a career move, just purely a case of pointing the camera here and there, a lovely, simple thing to do. It was the great old-age-pension film directing job, shooting for a day and having a month off."

He had no wish to emulate pop movies of the past he had found deeply embarrassing—pop stars trawling their psyches, exposing themselves, engaged in backstage hilarity—yet when all that was removed, what was left? At the beginning Paul had wanted to be seen wandering in a rain forest talking about ecology and conservation, the quintessence of what Lester did *not* want.

From a sales point of view there was an understandable eagerness to have something other than twenty songs performed in concert. The movie was presold by its backers, Allied Filmmakers, as containing loads of Beatles archive material, which Lester knew either not to exist or to be owned by Apple, who intended to use it itself at some point. Paul was less than anxious to unearth a lot of Beatles memorabilia—the tour was, after all, a year of his life. The attraction for Lester remained the recording, the fixing in time of what was in theory the last time these songs, many of them original Beatles hits as well as Paul's later work, would be sung on a world tour by the man who had written them.

Rather than simply hire the audience, point twenty-five cameras at everyone and pin all their hopes on an unlikely "definitive" concert, Lester decided to shoot in a variety of venues in an attempt to show what it was like to tour for over a year, in different cities and countries, whether it was a football stadium in Rio de Janeiro with 184,000 in the audience, or a 6,000- to 12,000-seater, which was how the tour actually started. Only when demand ludicrously exceeded supply was the decision taken to do one big stadium each week rather than five in the smaller venues; apart from anything else, the strain on Paul's voice was telling. (With insufficient material shot in North America, extra shooting was later carried out in Philadelphia, Boston and Chicago.) Lester also set out to capture the rapport that Paul had with the rest of the band, the marvelous warmth he sensed. The band members actually liked each other as well, and got along, for the most part, without friction.

He was given a unique opportunity to watch Paul at rehearsals:

He never says, "I hate that." Whenever anyone makes a suggestion, whether it be to do with a musical chord, the stage lighting or the running order of the show, he'll say, "That's pretty good, let's see where we can take that. Listen, this is why we get paid the extra," or "Come on, we're sounding just like an ordinary rock band," the subtext of all that being, "Offer me choices." I've watched hours of film of Paul taking the band through their paces, working day and night, listening to stuff that sounded absolutely terrific to me—but not to him. He's a perfectionist.

He's musical through and through, always involved with it, always close to an instrument, always tapping a rhythm with his hands if he's not playing, always with a little song on the go. He's enormously enthusiastic. He had a long period when he was trying hard not to be a Beatle, just to be himself. He was as much responsible for the breakup as anyone but was aggrieved that the other three were against him whether he was right or not. Yoko and the other two, for that matter, are still against him. Ringo and George ask, "How's the boy?" I don't get that from Paul about them, in fact I've never heard Paul badmouthing the others.

He's probably tried too hard in the early days to divorce himself from a wonderful body of work, but now he has come to terms with the fact that he'll always be a Beatle. Paul is a shrewd businessman, very careful with his money, and he's tried hard to bring up his children in state schools with no privileges. He would rather have a rock band than an Rolls-Royce. He has a wonderful gift of producing an unexpected wrong turning in his musical phrases; suddenly a bar is missing, a chord is different. In the middle of one there are a couple of bars in 5/4 time. One song has a phrase which I think alternates 4–4–3–2 time. It's odd, but it's instinctive and it feels right. He doesn't notate, but he has a shorthand system of his own.

For a young group of people, the Beatles had an extraordinary instinct of whom to entrust themselves to. Out of nowhere they chose Brian, George Martin and me, and all of us did the best we could by them.

I don't think we should worry about Paul. He mucks in on his farm; he has real mud on his wellies, unlike David Hicks who told his tenant farmer he could do what he liked as long as the cows were black and white. Linda will be helping with the lambing and they look after their own horses. They have rugs made of wool from their favorite sheep. They lead a simple but idyllic life.

Lester's technique, filming twenty songs on many different nights, with a constantly changing audience—from Japanese to Italian to Spanish—posed enormous technical problems when it came time to synchronize the footage. Since Paul and the band never counted themselves in on a metronome, the tempos were never exactly the same. One soundtrack had to be chosen, with Paul's lips matched to the track until it looked exactly right.

The tour, and Paul's decision to dedicate a song to the memory of John, helped him lay to rest the ghost of being a Beatle once and for all; his decision to proceed in the first place, rearranging the original Beatles material, already demonstrated the extent to which he had come to terms with himself.

As for the remaining ex-members, Lester last met Ringo and his wife Barbara when they were in Fiji together for Billy Connolly and Pamela Stephenson's wedding. Although Ringo had generally reacted least well to pressures, he had given up drinking at that point and seemed settled and happy.

George still has a connection with Eastern mysticism; he sponsors a group of Hari Krishnas in a large house deep in the heart of Hertfordshire, and supported the deeply dippy Natural Law Party in Britain's 1992 general election. Lester keeps bumping into him at parties, where George invariably offers the latest of his constantly changing telephone numbers. Lester finds it hard to accept his invitations to visit. "Does he really mean it?" always runs through his mind.

"Do you remember me?" George asked him a couple of years ago at one party. "What are you talking about?" Lester replied. "Of *course* I do."

"Well, you see, I'm trying to become *un*famous and finding it much more difficult than being famous," George explained.

Get Back's highlights for me, besides the feast of music and memories, were Paul introducing "Put It There" with charming anachronism ("from our latest LP") and dedicating "Let It Be" to George, Ringo and John, "my buddies." As Monthly Film Bulletin put it, "McCartney and his band are excellent, and *Get Back* does what one assumes was its primary job, to produce a music video." On that level Lester certainly succeeded, and although it hardly constituted a return to mainstream filmmaking, *Get Back* provided at least a series of snapshots of an unforgettable time.

CHAPTER TWENTY

"I hated those Musketeers films. You know what we need? The guy who directed those Beatles movies!"

—Paramount Pictures executive

Richard Lester's extraordinary body of work contains at least four masterpieces in *Petulia*, *Robin and Marian*, *How I Won the War* and *The Bed Sitting Room*, together with the hugely successful Beatles, Musketeers and Superman duos. And it's easy enough (especially for me) to overlook *The Knack*, still regarded by many as the seminal sixties movie, or enormously entertaining items like *Juggernaut* and *The Ritz*. Even if he never made another movie, his position as one of the most skillful and innovative filmmakers of our time is secure.

Lester is an intensely private man, a cross, in marine terms, between a hermit crab and a clam. In his personal life, as he portrays it, there have been few diversions or blind alleys, in marked contrast to his professional fortunes: happily married for over thirty-five years to the same woman; two grownup children; two grandchildren. "Oh, there's a lot about me you still don't know," he gleefully informed me at one of our last meetings. That he wasn't entirely joking was

347

certified by Charles Wood's admission: "I know as little about him now after thirty years as I did at the beginning."

It is perfectly true that Lester could never be portrayed as Captain Ahab obsessively pursuing the Great White Whale, nor is he Conrad's tragic Lord Jim, perpetually seeking atonement. He's not a man of towering highs and plummeting lows with the odd car chase flung in—what he *is* is a creature of considerable modesty and charm, with a complete lack of flamboyance and an underlying, intriguing complexity beneath his buttoned-up exterior. Asked on one occasion to hold forth on his innermost thoughts, Lester produced the first completely silent stretch of tape in almost forty hours of recording. Finally, his features contorted almost in pain, he offered an apologetic, "I don't think I can," followed by another long patch of agonized silence.

I began my final interview by asking him to clarify his feelings on something that struck me as astonishing, an issue that he himself had never chosen to raise. Did he find it an irony to have based himself in Britain for most of his working life and never to have received British money for his movies?

"I chose to live here, educate my children here, base my movies here—yet in thirty years it's true that I've never been given a penny of British money for my films. Oh, I tell a lie, I stand corrected, we're both forgetting that £70 for *The Running, Jumping and Standing Still Film*. Yes, there is an irony in that, as well as in the corollary that I've been working here with money from a country I can't stand."

Did he consider himself a driven man?

"I'm not driven, I've never felt that. I do worry a lot about religion and the harm it does, I'm so against it. I care enormously about personal privacy, the relationship between the press and the public and the damage it does."

Deirdre and Richard
Lester today.
(COURTESY OF
RICHARD LESTER)

Had he attempted to deliver messages in his movies?

"Not really, except perhaps for *How I Won the War*. In *The Bed Sitting Room* the environment wasn't the *reason* we made the movie, it was a by-product; the reason was the play that existed by Spike and John Antrobus. There are threads, if you like—the laughing nuns in the Porsche in *Petulia* was all about the cynicism of organized religion."

Could he sum up the Richard Lester Film Directing Technique?

"There's the Stanley Kubrick method, maybe the Warren Beatty *Reds* method of shooting eighty, ninety, a hundred takes of something quite simple over and over again so it becomes boring for everybody until they go through the boredom threshold and come out the other side and possibly something quite wonderful is captured. *Possibly!* For me the concept of producing freshness through boredom is totally foreign. My ideal would be to have the crew and actors come to a take and produce spontaneity, theatrical surprise, a sense of raggedness, almost like observing a firecracker going off in a small room. A director to me is a highly paid dustman. You've got all these good performers and you've hired them to be terrific—you don't expect them to be terrible—and me, who can't act—I've never told an actor how to act in my life and never will. I might ask him to offer me something different, a few choices, then decide which one of them to throw away and which to keep. It's simply a question of choosing what to discard."

Is he content with the way Britain has developed while he's been there?

"Well, things have definitely changed. In the fifties and even into the sixties people had the ability to be idiosyncratic and to be left alone to get on with their lives without being asked to conform to certain rituals—do what you like within reason, just don't frighten the horses! That's no longer the case. We're becoming more and more influenced by America, where everything is forever hyper; if you like something it has to be the greatest, the we're-number-one-syndrome; your dog's been killed, you cry on television, all that stuff about the prayers of middle America. That's simply not me, and now we're coming round to that here. The problem with most people as they grow older is that things aren't the same as they remember them to be. And by that time there's a fear of going to search for a new place to live which you hope will be the same as what you remember it was like here. It's Aesop's fable of the dog with a bone in its mouth looking at its reflection in the water and dropping the bone to grab the bigger one it sees reflected—life would be better in Paris, etc. I don't think I've got the courage to throw everything over and start all over again. Deirdre and I talk about it a lot, as I'm sure a lot of people do, then think, 'Are we going to lose more than we gain?' "

Has he ever made a film purely for the money?

"I can say, hand on heart—or at least, hand on crotch—that I've never taken a film unless I thought I was equipped to do it and could do a good job. *Not* for money, *never* a gun for hire, I only did what I wanted to do—except maybe *Finders Keepers*. The rest were my choices. I have tended to rush into projects, but one shouldn't underestimate the sense of responsibility to co-workers, many of whom naturally ask 'What are we going to do next?' I'm talking about operators, continuity girls, editors, who may have turned something else down to make themselves available. So eventually—and sooner rather than later—you have to say 'What are the risks, what are the odds that the material will come together?' and 'Is it good enough to turn into a polished film?' And this leaves the producer or director unable to pull out despite subsequent developments—maybe the script hasn't worked out, or a crucial leading player has become unavailable—and means that his heart is no longer in it. That's why I always try to avoid making decisions on a purely financial basis. Charles Wood would turn over in his grave, but I've never found it easy to say 'I'm going to take your script to another writer.' I generally don't do it, except in a very few cases, and yes—some of the films might have benefited from the studio system of being passed from writer to writer until everything works in them."

He has never been a big filmgoer?

"No. The 'shared experience in the dark' people talk about has meant less to me than in most cases. I am interested in films and other people's work and what makes them work—like why do 100 million people think *Robin Hood—Prince of*

Thieves is the best film of the year to see? I have *that* curiosity.

He is constantly accused of being anti-romantic.

"I know, and it's wrong. I'm certainly not a romantic, but I'm not *anti*-romantic. What I am is desperately anti-*sentimental*, anti-*nostalgic* for the past, for one's childhood, for anything. I'm talking about that *false* nostalgia which dictates that everything was wonderful in the past. If someone talks to me about the good old days, I positively rush to find out what was horrible—kids with no shoes, working down the pits, all of that, in an attempt to find a balance. Then there's the *patronizing* nostalgia, typified in the movie *Genevieve*, where it's easy to get your laughs at people driving around in funny old cars that were actually the cutting edge of their day.

Has he at any point in his life had his heart broken?

"No."

Never suffered from unrequited love?

"No."

A love affair that went badly wrong?

"No."

How about his occasionally fractious relationships with the press?

"Look, we all play games. *We're* both playing games now. There are games and games. There are some games where both sides try to allow the other to retain some dignity, and that's a game, that's *today's* game. I don't see any reason to switch on false bonhomie to suit the occasion."

After his long stretch since the success of *Superman III*, does he have a fear of failure about going ahead with another project?

"In the past I've always felt I could be successful at whatever I wanted to achieve. Now, in my sixties, I'm *totally* less confident. When you're young it's only natural to as-

assume immortality. Now, yes, maybe it is the fear of failure that I take things to a certain stage before the enthusiasm wanes. The more one looks at material the more the imponderables begin to loom larger and push the good bits to the side until they fall over the edge. It's a chance to fail again, so you start to find reasons why the film will go wrong and begin to dwell on the negative aspects, unlike at the start of your career where you looked for the bits that would come off and told yourself you could finesse the rest."

What will break the deadlock?

"Pure chance, I believe. My trouble is that I've never been bored. I'm happy to read a couple of books a week. I love the preparation and cooking of a meal, pushing a mower in the garden, watching hours of sport on television, listening to the World News in the morning. Most people I know get bored on holiday by the third day, or are unable to switch off. Not me. Direct me to wherever we're going and I'm gone, out of it, loving it. I'm really very happy with my life. It's been as untroubled a life of success leading to material and emotional comfort as I could possibly have wished. I feel privileged to have had a marvelous life meeting marvelous people. I've got a body of work I can leave behind me and I've accomplished an enormous amount that I've wanted to and there's nothing that eats into me now. In a way I'm not interested in opening up the box again, because I'm happy with the way I am—why fuck it up? Except, of course, it would be great at this stage to turn out a wonderful movie."

The variance of receptions greeting Lester's remarkable range of work, both at the time and retrospectively, may best be understood in the context of playwright Elmer Rice's summation: "A good play is more likely to succeed than a bad one. However, good plays often fail and bad ones often

"What do I do next?"   (COURTESY OF RICHARD LESTER)

succeed. It is therefore impossible to establish any clear correspondence between artistic excellence and commercial success. Nevertheless, it must be recognized that success is often equated with excellence, and failure with the lack of it."

For all the undisputed artistic excellence and commercial success Lester has achieved, he accepts with amused equanimity, after a three-act career and twenty-two movies, that if he tumbled several hundred feet off a cliff tomorrow, BEATLES DIRECTOR IN DEATH DRAMA would be the inevitable headline. "And why not?" he asks. "If it hadn't been for them, I doubt if we'd be sitting here now. And don't forget, only Shakespeare has more than three acts!"

True enough—up until now, that is.

FILMOGRAPHY

THE RUNNING, JUMPING AND STANDING STILL FILM
(Columbia, 1959)

DIRECTOR: *Dick Lester*
SCREENPLAY: *Peter Sellers, Spike Milligan, Dick Lester*
PRODUCER: *Peter Sellers*
CINEMATOGRAPHY: *Dick Lester*
EDITORS: *Dick Lester, Peter Sellers*
MUSIC: *Dick Lester*
RUNNING TIME: *11 mins.*
CAST: *Peter Sellers, Spike Milligan, Leo McKern, David Lodge, Graham Stark, Bruce Lacey, Mario Fabrizi*

IT'S TRAD, DAD
(Columbia, 1962)

DIRECTOR: *Richard Lester*
SCREENPLAY: *Milton Subotsky*
PRODUCER: *Milton Subotsky*
CINEMATOGRAPHY: *Gilbert Taylor*
ART DIRECTOR: *Maurice Carter*
EDITOR: *Bill Lenny*
MUSIC: *Various Artists*
RUNNING TIME: *73 mins.*
CAST: *Helen Shapiro, Craig Douglas, Timothy Bateson, Felix Felton, Frank Thornton, Bruce Lacey, Hugh Lloyd, Arnold Diamond, Ronnie Stevens, Arthur Mullard, Derek Nimmo, Mario Fabrizi, Derek Guyler, David Jacobs, Pete Murray, Alan Freeman*

MOUSE ON THE MOON
(United Artists, 1963)

DIRECTOR: *Richard Lester*
SCREENPLAY: *Michael Pertwee, based on the novel by*
Leonard Wibberley
PRODUCER: *Walter Shenson*
CINEMATOGRAPHY: *Wilkie Cooper (Eastmancolor)*
PRODUCTION DESIGNER: *John Howell*
ART DIRECTOR: *Bill Alexander*
EDITOR: *Bill Lenny*
MUSIC: *Ron Grainer*
RUNNING TIME: *85 mins.*
CAST: *Margaret Rutherford, Bernard Cribbins, Ron Moody,*
David Kossoff, Terry-Thomas, June Ritchie, Roddy McMillan, John
Le Mesurier, Michael Trubshawe, John Phillips, Tom Aldredge,
Peter Sallis, Jan Conrad, Hugh Lloyd, Mario Fabrizi, Archie
Duncan, Richard Marner, John Bluthal, Frankie Howerd

A HARD DAY'S NIGHT
(United Artists, 1964)

DIRECTOR: *Richard Lester*
SCREENPLAY: *Alun Owen*
PRODUCER: *Walter Shenson (Proscenium Films)*
CINEMATOGRAPHY: *Gilbert Taylor*
ART DIRECTOR: *Ray Simm*
EDITOR: *John Jympson*
MUSIC: *The Beatles, George Martin*
RUNNING TIME: *85 mins.*
CAST: *John Lennon, Paul McCartney, George Harrison, Ringo*
Starr, Wilfred Brambell, Norman Rossington, Victor Spinetti,
John Junkin, Anna Quayle, Derek Guyler, Michael Trubshawe,
Kenneth Haigh, Richard Vernon, Eddie Malin, Robin Ray,
Lionel Blair

THE KNACK—And How to Get It
(United Artists, 1965)

DIRECTOR: *Richard Lester*
SCREENPLAY: *Charles Wood, from the play by Ann Jellicoe*
PRODUCER: *Oscar Lewenstein (Woodfall)*
CINEMATOGRAPHY: *David Watkin*
ART DIRECTOR: *Assheton Gorton*
EDITOR: *Anthony Gibbs*
MUSIC: *John Barry, Alan Haven (solo jazz organ)*
RUNNING TIME: *84 mins.*
CAST: *Rita Tushingham, Ray Brooks, Michael Crawford, Donal Donnelly, John Bluthal, Wensley Pithney, William Dexter, Peter Copley, Dandy Nichols, Charles Dyer, Helen Lennox, Edgar Wreford, George Chisholm, Frank Sieman, Bruce Lacey*

HELP!
(United Artists, 1965)

DIRECTOR: *Richard Lester*
SCREENPLAY: *Charles Wood, based on a story by Marc Behm*
PRODUCER: *Walter Shenson (Subafilms)*
CINEMATOGRAPHY: *David Watkin (Eastmancolor)*
ART DIRECTOR: *Ray Simm*
EDITOR: *John Victor Smith*
MUSIC: *The Beatles, Ken Thorne*
RUNNING TIME: *92 mins.*
CAST: *John Lennon, Paul McCartney, George Harrison, Ringo Starr, Leo McKern, Eleanor Bron, Victor Spinetti, Roy Kinnear, Patrick Cargill, John Bluthal, Alfie Bass, Warren Mitchell, Peter Copley, Bruce Lacey*

A FUNNY THING HAPPENED ON THE WAY TO THE FORUM
(United Artists, 1966)

DIRECTOR: *Richard Lester*
SCREENPLAY: *Melvyn Frank and Michael Pertwee, based on the musical comedy by Burt Shevelove and Larry Gelbart, with music and lyrics by Stephen Sondheim*
PRODUCER: *Melvyn Frank*
CINEMATOGRAPHY: *Nicolas Roeg (Eastmancolor)*
PRODUCTION DESIGNER: *Tony Walton*
EDITOR: *John Victor Smith*
MUSIC SCORE: *Ken Thorne (Irwin Kostal M.D.; music and lyrics, Stephen Sondheim)*
RUNNING TIME: *98 mins.*
CAST: *Zero Mostel, Phil Silvers, Jack Gilford, Buster Keaton, Michael Crawford, Annette Andre, Patricia Jessel, Michael Hordern, Leon Greene, Inga Nielson, Myrna White, Lucienne Bridou, Helen Funai, Jennifer and Susan Baker, Janet Webb, Pamela Brown, Beatrix Lehmann, Alfie Bass, Roy Kinnear*

HOW I WON THE WAR
(United Artists, 1967)

DIRECTOR: *Richard Lester*
SCREENPLAY: *Charles Wood, based on the novel by Patrick Ryan*
PRODUCER: *Richard Lester (Petersham Films)*
CINEMATOGRAPHY: *David Watkin (Eastmancolor)*
ART DIRECTORS: *Philip Harrison, John Stoll*
EDITOR: *John Victor Smith*
MUSIC: *Ken Thorne*
RUNNING TIME: *110 mins.*
CAST: *Michael Crawford, John Lennon, Roy Kinnear, Lee Montague, Jack MacGowran, Michael Hordern, Jack Hedley, Karl Michael Vogler, Ronald Lacey, James Cossins, Ewan Hooper,*

Alexander Knox, Robert Hardy, Sheila Hancock, Charles Dyer,
Bill Dysart, Paul Daneman, Peter Graves, Jack May, Richard
Pearson, Pauline Taylor, John Ronane, Norman Chappell, Bryan
Pringle, Fanny Carby, Dandy Nichols, Gretchen Franklin,
John Junkin

PETULIA
(Warner/Seven Arts, 1968)

DIRECTOR: *Richard Lester*
SCREENPLAY: *Lawrence B. Marcus; adapted by Barbara Turner*
from the novel, Me and the Arch-Kook Petulia, *by John Haase*
PRODUCER: *Raymond Wagner (Petersham Films)*
CINEMATOGRAPHY: *Nicolas Roeg (Technicolor)*
PRODUCTION DESIGNER: *Tony Walton*
EDITOR: *Anthony Gibbs*
MUSIC: *John Barry*
RUNNING TIME: *105 mins.*
CAST: *Julie Christie, George C. Scott, Richard Chamberlain,*
Arthur Hill, Shirley Knight, Pippa Scott, Joseph Cotten, Kathleen
Widdoes, Roger Bowen, Richard Dysart, Ruth Kobart, Ellen Geer,
Lou Gilbert, Nat Esformes, Maria Val, Vincent Arias, Eric Weiss,
Kevin Cooper, Austin Pendleton, Barbara Colby, Rene
Auberjonois, Josephine Nichols, De Ann Mears, The Grateful
Dead, Big Brother and the Holding Company, Members of the
Committee, Members of the American Conservatory Theater

THE BED SITTING ROOM
(United Artists, 1969)

DIRECTOR: *Richard Lester*
SCREENPLAY: *John Antrobus, adapted by Charles Wood from the*
play by Spike Milligan and John Antrobus
PRODUCERS: *Richard Lester, Oscar Lewenstein*

CINEMATOGRAPHY: *David Watkin (Eastmancolor)*
PRODUCTION DESIGNER: *Assheton Gorton*
EDITOR: *John Victor Smith*
MUSIC: *Ken Thorne*
RUNNING TIME: *91 mins.*
CAST: *Rita Tushingham, Dudley Moore, Harry Secombe, Arthur Lowe, Roy Kinnear, Spike Milligan, Ronald Fraser, Jimmy Edwards, Michael Hordern, Peter Cook, Ralph Richardson, Mona Washbourne, Richard Warwick, Frank Thornton, Dandy Nichols, Jack Shepherd, Marty Feldman*

THE THREE MUSKETEERS
(The Queen's Diamonds) (Twentieth Century-Fox, 1974)

DIRECTOR: *Richard Lester*
SCREENPLAY: *George MacDonald Fraser, based on the novel by Alexandre Dumas,* père
PRODUCER: *Alexander Salkind*
CINEMATOGRAPHY: *David Watkin (Technicolor)*
PRODUCTION DESIGNER: *Brian Eatwell*
EDITOR: *John Victor Smith*
MUSIC: *Michel Legrand*
RUNNING TIME: *107 mins.*
CAST: *Michael York, Oliver Reed, Raquel Welch, Richard Chamberlain, Frank Finlay, Charlton Heston, Faye Dunaway, Christopher Lee, Geraldine Chaplin, Jean-Pierre Cassel, Roy Kinnear, Michael Gothard, Sybil Danning, Gity Djamal, Simon Ward, Nicole Calfan, Georges Wilson, Angel Del Pozo, Rodney Bewes, Ben Aris, Joss Ackland, Gretchen Franklin*

JUGGERNAUT
(United Artists, 1974)

DIRECTOR: *Richard Lester*
SCREENPLAY: *Richard de Koker, with additional dialogue
by Alan Plater*
PRODUCER: *Richard de Koker*
CINEMATOGRAPHY: *Gerry Fisher (Panavision, DeLuxe color)*
PRODUCTION DESIGNER: *Terence Marsh*
EDITOR: *Anthony Gibbs*
MUSIC: *Ken Thorne*
RUNNING TIME: *110 mins.*
CAST: *Richard Harris, Omar Sharif, David Hemmings, Anthony
Hopkins, Ian Holm, Shirley Knight, Roy Kinnear, Roshan Seth,
Cyril Cusack, Freddie Jones, Kristine Howarth, Clifton James,
Mark Burns, Gareth Thomas, Andrew Bradford, Richard Moore,
Jack Watson, Bob Sessions, Liza Ross, Michael Egan, Ben Aris,
Paul Antrim, Colin Thatcher, Terence Hillyer, John Stride,
Michael Hordern, Norman Warwick, Freddie Fletcher, John
Bindon, Caroline Mortimer, Adam Bridge, Rebecca Bridge, Julian
Glover, Kenneth Colley, Tom Chadbon, Kenneth Cope, Barnaby
Holm, Victor Lewis, Paul Luty, Simon MacCorkindale*

THE FOUR MUSKETEERS (The Revenge of Milady)
(Twentieth Century-Fox, 1975)

DIRECTOR: *Richard Lester*
SCREENPLAY: *George MacDonald Fraser, from the novel* The
Three Musketeers *by Alexandre Dumas* père
PRODUCER: *Alexander and Michel Salkind*
CINEMATOGRAPHY: *David Watkin (Technicolor)*
PRODUCTION DESIGNER: *Brian Eatwell*
EDITOR: *John Victor Smith*
MUSIC: *Lalo Schifrin*

RUNNING TIME: *103 mins.*
CAST: *Oliver Reed, Raquel Welch, Richard Chamberlain, Michael York, Frank Finlay, Simon Ward, Christopher Lee, Faye Dunaway, Charlton Heston, Geraldine Chaplin, Jean-Pierre Cassel, Roy Kinnear, Nicole Calfan, Eduardo Fajardo, Michael Gothard*

ROYAL FLASH
(Twentieth Century-Fox, 1975)

DIRECTOR: *Richard Lester*
SCREENPLAY: *George MacDonald Fraser, from his own novel*
PRODUCER: *David V. Picker and Denis O'Dell (Two Roads Productions)*
CINEMATOGRAPHY: *Geoffrey Unsworth (Technicolor)*
PRODUCTION DESIGNER: *Terence Marsh*
EDITOR: *John Victor Smith*
MUSIC: *Ken Thorne*
RUNNING TIME: *118 mins.*
CAST: *Malcolm McDowell, Alan Bates, Florinda Bolkan, Britt Ekland, Oliver Reed, Lionel Jeffries, Tom Bell, Christopher Cazenove, Joss Ackland, Leon Greene, Richard Hurndall, Alastair Sim, Michael Hordern, Roy Kinnear, David Stern, Richard Pearson, Rula Lenska, Margaret Courtenay, Noel Johnson, Elizabeth Larner, Henry Cooper, Stuart Rayner, Ben Aris, Bob Peck, John Stuart, Frank Grimes, Paul Burton, Tessa Dahl, Claire Russell, Kubi Choza, Meg Davies, Roger Hammond, David Jason, Alan Howard, Bob Hoskins, Arthur Brough*

ROBIN AND MARIAN
(Columbia, 1976)

DIRECTOR: *Richard Lester*
SCREENPLAY: *James Goldman*
PRODUCER: *Richard Shepherd and Denis O'Dell (Rastar)*

CINEMATOGRAPHY: *David Watkin (Technicolor)*
PRODUCTION DESIGNER: *Michael Stringer*
EDITOR: *John Victor Smith*
MUSIC: *John Barry*
RUNNING TIME: *107 mins.*
CAST: *Sean Connery, Audrey Hepburn, Robert Shaw, Richard Harris, Nicol Williamson, Denholm Elliott, Kenneth Haigh, Ronnie Barker, Ian Holm, Bill Maynard, Esmond Knight, Veronica Quilligan, Peter Butterworth, John Barrett, Kenneth Cranham, Victoria Merida Roja, Montserrat Julio, Victoria Hernandez Sanquino, Marguerita Manguillon*

THE RITZ
(Warner Brothers, 1976)

DIRECTOR: *Richard Lester*　·
SCREENPLAY: *Terrence McNally, from his play*
PRODUCER: *Denis O'Dell (Courtyard Films)*
CINEMATOGRAPHY: *Paul Wilson (Technicolor)*
PRODUCTION DESIGNER: *Philip Harrison*
EDITOR: *John Bloom*
MUSIC: *Ken Thorne*
RUNNING TIME: *91 mins.*
CAST: *Jack Weston, Rita Moreno, Jerry Stiller, Kaye Ballard, Treat Williams, F. Murray Abraham, George Coulouris, Paul B. Price, John Everson, Christopher J. Brown, Dave King, Bessie Love, Tony de Santis, Ben Aris, Peter Butterworth, Ronnie Brody*

BUTCH AND SUNDANCE: THE EARLY DAYS
(Twentieth Century-Fox, 1979)

DIRECTOR: *Richard Lester*
SCREENPLAY: *Allan Burns*
PRODUCERS: *Gabriel Katzka, Steven Bach*

363

CINEMATOGRAPHY: *Laszlo Kovacs (DeLuxe color)*
PRODUCTION DESIGNER: *Brian Eatwell*
EDITOR: *Anthony Gibbs*
MUSIC: *Patrick Williams*
RUNNING TIME: *112 mins.*
CAST: *Tom Berenger, William Katt, Jeff Corey, John Schuck, Michael C. Gwynne, Brian Dennehy, Peter Weller, Jill Eikenberry, Judy Scott-Fox, Christopher Lloyd, Vincent Ciavelli*

CUBA
(United Artists, 1979)

DIRECTOR: *Richard Lester*
SCREENPLAY: *Charles Wood*
PRODUCERS: *Alex Winitsky, Arlene Sellers*
CINEMATOGRAPHY: *David Watkin (Technicolor)*
PRODUCTION DESIGNER: *Gil Parrondo, Philip Harrison*
EDITOR: *John Victor Smith*
MUSIC: *Patrick Williams*
RUNNING TIME: *122 mins.*
CAST: *Sean Connery, Brooke Adams, Jack Weston, Hector Elizondo, Denholm Elliott, Martin Balsam, Chris Sarandon, Lonette McKee, Danny de la Paz, Walter Gotell*

SUPERMAN II
(Warner Brothers, 1980)

DIRECTOR: *Richard Lester*
SCREENPLAY: *Mario Puzo, David Newman, Leslie Newman*
PRODUCERS: *Alexander Salkind, Pierre Spengler*
CINEMATOGRAPHY: *Geoffrey Unsworth, Robert Paynter*
(Panavision/Technicolor)
PRODUCTION DESIGNERS: *John Barry, Peter Murton*

EDITOR: *John Victor Smith*
MUSIC: *Ken Thorne*
RUNNING TIME: *127 mins.*
CAST: *Christopher Reeve, Gene Hackman, Ned Beatty, Jackie Cooper, Sarah Douglas, Margot Kidder, Valerie Perrine, Susannah York, Terence Stamp, Jack O'Halloran, E. G. Marshall, Marc McClure*

SUPERMAN III
(Warner Brothers, 1983)

DIRECTOR: *Richard Lester*
SCREENPLAY: *David Newman, Leslie Newman*
PRODUCER: *Pierre Spengler*
CINEMATOGRAPHY: *Robert Paynter (Panavision/Color)*
PRODUCTION DESIGNER: *Peter Murton*
EDITOR: *John Victor Smith*
MUSIC: *Ken Thorne*
RUNNING TIME: *125 mins.*
CAST: *Christopher Reeve, Richard Pryor, Jackie Cooper, Marc McClure, Annette O'Toole, Annie Ross, Pamela Stephenson, Robert Vaughn, Margot Kidder*

FINDERS KEEPERS
(CBS/Warner Brothers, 1984)

DIRECTOR: *Richard Lester*
SCREENPLAY: *Ronny Graham, Charles Dennis, and Terence Marsh, from Dennis's novel,* The Next to Last Train Ride
PRODUCERS: *Sandra Marsh, Terence Marsh*
CINEMATOGRAPHY: *Brian West*
EDITOR: *John Victor Smith*
MUSIC: *Ken Thorne*
RUNNING TIME: *96 mins.*

CAST: *Michael O'Keefe, Beverly D'Angelo, Lou Gossett, Jr., Pamela Stephenson, Ed Lauter, David Wayne, Brian Dennehy, John Schuck, Timothy Blake, Jim Carrey, Jack Riley*

RETURN OF THE MUSKETEERS
(Universal, 1989)

DIRECTOR: *Richard Lester*
SCREENPLAY: *George MacDonald Fraser*
PRODUCER: *Pierre Spengler*
CINEMATOGRAPHY: *Bernard Lutic*
EDITOR: *John Victor Smith*
MUSIC: *Jean-Claude Petit*
RUNNING TIME: *101 mins.*
CAST: *Michael York, Oliver Reed, Frank Finlay, C. Thomas Howell, Kim Cattrall, Richard Chamberlain, Philipe Noiret, Roy Kinnear, Geraldine Chaplin, Christopher Lee, Eusebio Lazaro, Jean-Pierre Cassel*
(Dedicated to Roy Kinnear)

GET BACK
(Buena Vista, 1990)
(a.k.a. Paul McCartney's GET BACK)

DIRECTOR: *Richard Lester*
PRODUCERS: *Henry Thomas, Philip Knatchbull (Front Page Films/ Allied Filmmakers in association with MPL)*
CINEMATOGRAPHY: *Robert Paynter, Jordan Cronenweth*
EDITOR: *John Victor Smith*
MUSIC: *Performed by Paul McCartney, Linda McCartney, Hamish Stuart, Robbie McIntosh, Paul "Wix" Wickens, Chris Whitten*
RUNNING TIME: *89 mins.*

DELETED SCENE FROM A HARD DAY'S NIGHT

57 EXT. STREET

PAUL comes down the street looking about him for RINGO. In the street is an old building, the sort of place that is highly favored for TV rehearsals. There is a sign on the door saying "TV Rehearsal Room." As PAUL draws near, a load of actors and extras, etc. are leaving, they are in costume, they are the ones who earlier had been going to a word rehearsal. When PAUL gets near the entrance he decides to go inside.

58 INT. HALL

PAUL enters and wanders about. He reaches a door, pushes it open and looks in. He sees a girl clad in period costume. She is moving around the room and obviously acting. PAUL watches her for a moment and then decides to go in.

59 INT. REHEARSAL ROOM

PAUL goes into the room. The girl is in mid-flight. She is very young and lovely and completely engrossed in what she is doing. The room is absolutely empty except for PAUL and herself. She is acting in the manner of an eighteenth-century coquette, or, to be precise, the voice English actresses use when they think they are being true to the costume period . . . her youth, however, makes it all very charming.

367

GIRL If I believed you sir, I might do those things and walk those ways only to find myself on Problem's Path. But I cannot believe you, and all those urgings serve only as a proof that you will lie and lie again to gain your purpose with me.

She dances lightly away from an imaginary lover and as she turns she sees PAUL, who is as engrossed in the scene as she was.

GIRL (*surprised*) Oh!

PAUL (*enthusiastically*) Well . . . go 'head, do the next bit.

GIRL Go away! You've spoilt it.

PAUL Oh! Sorry I spoke.

He makes an attempt to go. He simply continues to look steadily at the girl, then he smiles at her. She is undecided what to do next.

GIRL Are you supposed to be here?

PAUL I've got you worried, haven't I?

GIRL Of course not. I asked who you are, that's all.

PAUL No you didn't, you asked me, "Was I supposed to be here?"

GIRL I'm warning you, they'll be back in a minute.

PAUL D'you know something, "They" don't worry me at all. Any road, I only fancy listening to you . . . that's all but if it worries you . . . well . . .

GIRL Of course it doesn't worry me, I can . . . (*she interrupts herself*) . . . Who are you?

PAUL (*smiling cheekily*) Another worrier.

GIRL (*accusingly*) You're from Liverpool, aren't you?

PAUL (*ironically*) How'd you guess?

GIRL (*seriously*) Oh, it's the way you talk.

PAUL (*innocently*) Is it . . . is it, really?

GIRL (*suspiciously*) Are you pulling my leg?

PAUL (*looking her straight in the eye*) Something like that.

GIRL (*unsure*) I see. (*airily*) Do you like the play?

PAUL Yeah . . . I mean, sure, well, I took it at school but I only heard boys and masters saying those lines, like, sounds different on a girl. (*smiles to himself*) Yeah, it's gear on a girl.

GIRL Gear?

PAUL Aye, the big hammer, smashing!

GIRL Thank you.

PAUL Don't mench . . . well, why don't you give us a few more lines, like?

GIRL (*pouts*)

PAUL You don't half slam the door in people's faces, don't you? I mean, what about when you're playing the part, like, hundreds of people'll see you and . . .

GIRL (*cutting in*) I'm not . . .

PAUL Oh, you're the understudy sort of thing?

GIRL No. (*aggressively*) I'm a walk-on in a fancy dress scene. I just felt like doing those lines.

PAUL Oh, I see. You are an actress though, aren't you?

GIRL Yes.

PAUL Aye. I knew you were.

GIRL What's that mean?

PAUL Well, the way you were spouting, like . . . (*he imitates her*) "I don't believe you, sir . . ." and all that. Yeah, it was gear.

GIRL (*dryly*) The big hammer?

PAUL (*smiling*) Oh aye, a sledge.

GIRL But the way you did it then sounded so phoney.

PAUL No, I wouldn't say that . . . just like an actress . . . you know . . .

He moves and stands about like an actress

GIRL But that's not like a real person at all.

PAUL Aye, well, actresses aren't like real people, are they?

GIRL They ought to be.

PAUL Oh, I don't know, any road up, they never are, are they?

GIRL What are you?

PAUL I'm in a group . . . well . . . there are four of us, we play and sing.

GIRL I bet you don't sound like real people.

PAUL We do, you know. We sound like us having a ball. It's fab.

GIRL Is it really fab or are you just saying that to convince yourself?

PAUL What of? Look, I wouldn't do it unless I was. I'm dead lucky, cos I get paid for doing something I love doing. *(he laughs and with a gesture takes in the whole studio)* . . . all this and a jam butty too!

GIRL I only enjoy acting for myself. I hate it when other people are let in.

PAUL Why? I mean, which are you, scared or selfish?

GIRL Why selfish?

PAUL Well, you've got to have people to taste your treacle toffee.

She looks at him in surprise.

PAUL No, hang on, I've not gone daft. You see, when I was little me mother let me make some treacle toffee one time in our back scullery. When I'd done it she said to me, "Go and give some to the other kids." So I said I would but I thought to meself, "She must think I'm soft." Any road, I was eating away there but I wanted somebody else to know how good it was so in the end I wound up giving it all away . . . but I didn't mind, mind, cos *I'd* made the stuff in the first place. Well . . . that's why you need other people . . . an audience . . . to taste your treacle toffee, like. Eh . . . does that sound as thick-headed to you as it does to me?

GIRL Not really, but I'm probably not a toffee maker. How would you do those lines of mine?

PAUL Well, look at it this way, I mean, when you come right down to it, that girl, she's a bit of a scrubber, isn't she?

GIRL Is she?

PAUL Of course . . . Look, if she was a Liverpool scrubber . . .

(PAUL *starts acting a Liverpool girl, he mimes about then turns, extending his leg*)
Eh, fella, you want to try pulling the other one, it's got a full set of bells hanging off it . . . Y' what? . . . I know your sort, two cokes and a packet of cheese and onion crisps and suddenly it's love and we're stopping in an empty shop doorway. You're just after me body and y' can't have it . . . so there!

GIRL (*shattered*) And you honestly think that's what she meant?

PAUL Oh, definitely, it sticks out a mile, she's trying to get him to marry her but he doesn't want . . . well . . . I don't reckon any fella's ever wanted to get married. But girls are like that, clever and cunning. You've got to laugh. (*He laughs*)

GIRL Well it's nice to know you think you're clever.

PAUL (*grinning*) And cunning.

GIRL And what do you do about it?

PAUL Me? Oh, I don't have the time, I'm always running about with the lads . . . no, we don't have the time.

GIRL Pity.

PAUL (*not noticing the invitation*) Aye, it is, but as long as you get by, it's allright, you know . . . bash on, happy valley's when they let you stop. Any road, I'd better get back.

GIRL Yes.

PAUL (*going*) See you.

GIRL Of course.

PAUL stands at the doorway, shrugs, then goes out. After a moment the GIRL starts to act her speech. She is still using her actress voice.

GIRL If I believed you sir. I might do (*she breaks off and smiles*) . . . clever and cunning (*she starts again but this time she delivers the lines in a saucy, teasing manner*)

PAUL pops his head back round the door.

PAUL Treacle toffee . . . wowee!

He disappears and the GIRL laughs delightedly.

END SCENE

INDEX

377